Ronsard, Petrarch, and the *Amours*

Ronsard, Petrarch, and the *Amours*

Sara Sturm-Maddox

University Press of Florida

Gainesville · Tallahassee · Tampa · Boca Raton
Pensacola · Orlando · Miami · Jacksonville

Excerpts from Sara Sturm-Maddox, "Ronsard's Metamorphosis: Petrarchan Play in the Amours of 1552," *Comparative Literature Studies*, vol. 23, no. 2, pp. 103–18, copyright 1986 by The Pennsylvania State University. Reprinted by permission of The Pennsylvania State University Press.

Printed in the United States of America on acid-free paper

04 03 02 01 00 99 6 5 4 3 2 1

Library of Congress Cataloging-in-Publication Data
Sturm-Maddox, Sara.
Ronsard, Petrarch, and the Amours / Sara Sturm-Maddox.
p. cm.
Includes bibliographical references and index.
ISBN 0-8130-1721-1 (alk. paper)
1. Ronsard, Pierre de, 1524–1585. Amours. 2. Petrarca, Francesco,
1304–1374—Influence. I. Title.
PQ1676.A63S78   1999
841'.3—dc21   99-34227

The University Press of Florida is the scholarly publishing agency for the State University System of Florida, comprising Florida A&M University, Florida Atlantic University, Florida International University, Florida State University, University of Central Florida, University of Florida, University of North Florida, University of South Florida, and University of West Florida.

University Press of Florida
15 Northwest 15th Street
Gainesville, FL 32611-2079
http://www.upf.com

For Mark,

freest and brightest of spirits,

from his ma.

CONTENTS

PREFACE

In 1554, two years following the appearance of Pierre de Ronsard's first collection of his *Amours,* Olivier de Magny bestowed upon his fellow poet the title of "[le] Pétrarque Vandomois." Other titles were soon to follow, frequent among them that of the "French Petrarch." In this book I argue that the coveted accolade has a special status because the French poet's engagement with Petrarch contributes, in differing but always substantial proportion, to the shaping of each of the three major lyric collections routinely associated with his indebtedness to the Italian master: the *Amours* of 1552 to 1553, the *Sonets pour Helene* of 1578, and, added to the *Second livre des Amours* in the fifth collective edition of his *Oeuvres* in that same year, the small sequence "Sur la mort de Marie." His strategy in these *recueils,* we will find, gives singular prominence to the relation between the textual Ronsard and the textual Petrarch as protagonists of their respective collections. In each the adoption of a Petrarchan posture, which Ronsard shared with many poets both contemporary and in generations past and to come, is recuperated within a poetic "story" in a manner that in turn gives special meaning to his claim to the title of the "French Petrarch." It is perhaps paradoxical that what ultimately emerges from his appropriation of the Petrarchan persona is Ronsard's own poetic "I," his unique and uniquely resonant poetic voice.

This book took shape over a period of some ten years. A segment of Chapter 2, now revised, appeared in "Ronsard's Metamorphoses: Petrarchan Play in the *Amours* of 1552," *Comparative Literature Studies* 23.2 (1986): pp. 103–18; copyright 1986 by The Pennsylvania State University and used by permission of The Pennsylvania State University Press. The rest of the material appears here in print for the first time, but many of my arguments have been shared with students and colleagues, in seminars and in conference sessions, and I am grateful for the questions raised on those occasions, which have repeatedly challenged me to formulate more questions of my own. I am also grateful to the two readers of this book in manuscript for their sensitive and insightful comments and to the Camargo Foundation in Cassis, France, for affording the extraordinary collegial environment in which some of these pages achieved final form.

In addition to the ever-renewed encouragement and occasional prodding through these many years of my husband, Don, I have benefited greatly through the best and the worst of times from the warm and generous support of friends, to whom my gratitude is offered *di cuore*. This book is dedicated to one of the very best of them.

Introduction

In bestowing the title of "Pétrarque Vandomois" on Ronsard,[1] Olivier de Magny's gesture was of course not particularly novel or new. Well over two centuries earlier, for example, Giovanni del Virgilio, initiating his verse correspondence with Dante, had styled his friend as another Virgil, or indeed—"Alter . . . aut idem"—as Virgil reborn.[2] In sixteenth-century France the bestowal of such titles was prevalent to the point of banality, often with the promise of a literary immortality that posterity has subsequently denied.[3] Had not admirers acclaimed the neo-Latin poet Macrin as the "French Horace" and welcomed Clément Marot, playing on the poet's own name, as the new "Maro," the "Virgile françois"—a title Ronsard was soon to wrest from him?[4] The title of "Pétrarque Vandomois" was not the first of those avidly collected by Ronsard in the course of his long poetic career, nor was it to be the last or even the most grand: many years later, alluding to the success of the poet's lyrics, Hélène de Surgères would nominate him "l'Apollon de ce temps, l'Homere de la France" [the Apollo of our age, the Homer of France].[5] A portrait inscription identified him as "Pierre de Ronsard, Gentilhomme Vendosmois, l'Homere ou le Virgile de France et le Pere des Poëtes françois" [Pierre de Ronsard, Gentleman of the Vendôme, the Homer or the Virgil of France and the Father of French Poets].[6] And at the end of the century, Etienne Pasquier was to inscribe him into a tradition-hallowed sequence of illustrious precursors: in the French language, he declared, Ronsard had represented "un Homère, Pindare, Théocrite, Virgile, Catulle, Horace, Pétrarque."[7]

The fashion, however, should not blind us to the fact that the case of Ronsard and Petrarch is singular. Petrarch's own status was of course singular: the Italian's acknowledged primacy as the reigning prince of poets was confirmed by Thomas Sébillet, for example, in his *Art poëtique françois* of 1548, which identifies Petrarch as "le prince des Poëtes italiens, duquel l'archetype des sonnets a été tiré" [the prince of Italian Poets, from whom the archetype of the sonnet has been derived].[8] It was perhaps only an interesting coincidence that Ronsard's editor Gabriel

Buon brought out in the same year—1565—both the *Coronement de Messire François Petrarque poète Florentin faict à Rome* that marked the apogee of the French cult for the Italian poet and Ronsard's own poetic treatise, the *Abrégé de l'art poétique*.[9] In any case, the status of poetic royalty had been awarded to the French poet in turn as early as 1553, when Maclou de la Haye proclaimed him, not the "Poète des Princes," but the "Prince des Poètes."[10]

Ronsard, of course, shared the ambition to write "like Petrarch" with numerous other poets intent on exploiting the intermittent favor of the Petrarchan mode; the enterprise was both avowed and disavowed by most of the poets of the latter half of the sixteenth century. It is obvious, and we have often been reminded, that the Italian poet's celebrated *Canzoniere* afforded the aspiring young French poet a sort of handbook, a repertory of amorous motifs to which he constantly recurred "pour s'entraîner en quelque sorte et prendre le ton."[11] Like his contemporaries, we know, Ronsard found in the Petrarchan tradition a "flexible convention which expresses itself in an arsenal of commonplaces, images, or topoi";[12] his Petrarchism, it has been suggested, lies "above all in the motifs and the diction which he employs."[13] A handbook, an arsenal, a *répertoire*—and not only a rhetoric but an attitude: those notions of Love, lover, and lady—"une attitude amoureuse"—which rapidly became the staples of Renaissance love lyric.[14] In this collective imitative practice of the French poets, moreover, Joseph Vianey insisted in an emphatic and widely repeated *mise au point* that Petrarch and his text were often largely occulted by what we have come to term "Petrarchism." The common judgment that these poets imitated Petrarch, he declared, was only a half-truth at best, and at worst "presque une erreur."[15]

Yet Ronsard, for one, did indeed imitate Petrarch, consistently and directly, and much evidence amassed in recent decades—evidence to which the present study contributes in its identification of a number of hitherto unnoted resonances—confirms that he was indebted less to a Petrarchan tradition vaguely defined than to the Italian master himself. The notes to Henri and Catherine Weber's edition of the *Amours*, cited throughout this study because of the richness of its documentation of Petrarchan sources, afford ample evidence of the priority accorded to Petrarch; statistical method, Charles Dédéyan points out, confirms that Ronsard turns to him directly perhaps nine times out of ten.[16]

To estimate the weight of this textual borrowing is not the object of this book, which instead builds on the ample testimony to Ronsard's close reading of Petrarch as the foundation for a new exploration of its significance. Critical opinion has long been as divided concerning that signifi-

cance as concerning its extent: thus the poet's own occasional pronounce-
ments have been often cited to assure us that Ronsard's Petrarchism was
never more that a Petrarchism *de commande*, a pretense, an artifice.[17] Or the
collection of *Rime sparse* is framed as the text to which Ronsard turns for
themes, images, and movements only when he is devoid of personal in-
spiration.[18] Precisely the contrary is argued here, that for Ronsard himself,
to write "like Petrarch" did not mean merely to translate or imitate locally,
to master the master's idiom so as to produce a "petit sonnet petrarquizé"
like those whose favor in courtly circles he appraised with undisguised
condescension.[19] Readers need not expect to find here discussion of a
number of the poems most prominent in critical assessments of Ronsard's
imitation of Petrarch, notably many of the sonnets that have a static qual-
ity as moments, as set pieces easily anthologized.[20] While his imitative
practice is often similar to that of other Petrarchan poets in its distinctly
mosaic quality, its juxtaposition of fragments from multiple source-
poems—a phrase here and there, an image, a topos—that are subjected,
more or less successfully, to a synthetic blending,[21] this book instead di-
rects attention to that practice as it emerges at the level of the collection as
a whole.

Each of the three collections of love lyrics examined here takes as its
point of departure what we may term poetic impersonation. In this sense
as in others, of course, they afford a particular, and particularly sugges-
tive, case of a more generalized phenomenon central to the European love
lyric, one in which "the experience of *being* Petrarch has been confronted
again and again in the six centuries since his death."[22] And such a relation
was deeply rooted in the poetic practice of its age; as Richard Griffiths
points out, rhetorical training afforded sixteenth-century poets experi-
ence in the adoption of the first-person lyric voice, in what amounted to
"writing on behalf of other people,"[23] and textual self-portraiture is char-
acteristic of imitative practice in the period. "Rewriting," as Terence Cave
acutely observes, "betrays its own anxiety by personifying itself as the
product of an author; it imprints on itself—one might even say *forges*—an
identity. Hence the lack of any radically 'new' discourse is supplemented
or compensated for by the grammar and topics of personal identity."[24]

When, with Ronsard, the rhetorical "habit of impersonation" funda-
mental in the practice of many of his contemporaries is adopted by a poet
intent on playing out a compelling role in the highly theatrical culture of
mid-sixteenth-century France, we find a new emphasis on the importance
of the poetic persona, one that frequently achieves priority over the poetic
style. The works explored here are Ronsard's earliest and his last major
lyric collections, separated by a wide span of years during which he

moved away from the Petrarchan inspiration. And in each of them, reexamination of the Petrarchan presence challenges us to reevaluate Ronsard's self-positioning with regard to the Petrarch of the *Rime sparse*.

This strategy of self-representation informs what will be termed in Chapter 1 "lyric self-fashioning." It indicates here something quite different from Ronsard's own use of the term "se façonner," by which he intends the poet's modeling of his art in close imitation of an admired model.[25] I use the term instead to indicate the fashioning by the poet of the first-person lyric persona within his works, as a specific and highly suggestive instance of that act of "poetic self-creation" for which, as John Freccero remarks, Petrarch remained for centuries the model "even for poets who, in matters of form, thought of themselves as anti-Petrarchan."[26] In Ronsard's case in particular, there are not negligible points in common with the phenomenon described by Stephen Greenblatt as "Renaissance self-fashioning." Writing of sixteenth-century England, Greenblatt observes "an increased self-consciousness about the fashioning of human identity as a manipulable, artful process"; such fashioning, he points out, "may suggest the achievement of . . . a distinctive personality, a characteristic address to the world, a consistent mode of perceiving and behaving."[27] Such, we might say, aptly describes the *collective* poet-amator recognizable in the works of numerous aspiring Petrarchan poets—a young Ronsard and his contemporaries—as they attempted to define their relation to the Italian master in mid-sixteenth-century France.

What marks Ronsard's adaptation as dissimilar, at least in part, from that of these other "imitators" is his response to the *Rime* at the level of the collection as a whole: a strategy, not of "writing *like* Petrarch," but rather of a form of lyric impersonation that in effect resolves itself as "writing *as* Petrarch." Here Greenblatt's observations are particularly pertinent. With the "representation of one's nature or intention in speech or actions," he suggests, "we may grasp that self-fashioning derives its interest precisely from the fact that it functions without regard for a sharp distinction between literature and social life. It invariably crosses the boundaries of the creation of literary character, the shaping of one's own identity, the experience of being molded by forces outside one's control, the attempt to fashion other selves."[28] The intersection of Ronsard's self-representations acquires heightened color from his preoccupation with self-proclamation and self-definition. His roles as "prince of poets" and "poet of princes," both flagrantly public, are both at the same time built on his representations of a private self constructed in emulation of and in conflict with a dominant literary model for which Petrarch is the authority.

The following chapters sound the diverse ways in which Ronsard's poetic persona is characterized, with heightened self-consciousness, by his relation to the poetic persona of the *Rime sparse*. In the 1552–53 collection of the *Amours*, reenactment of the elements of Petrarch's sequence that help to define a "story" is accompanied by a use of mythological allusion that insistently recalls the structure of allusions created in the Italian collection. The imitative strategy is neither simple nor innocent: some poems promote assimilation of the two lyric personae while others invite distancing and the appreciation of contrast, reconfiguring a relation between the French and the Italian poet in lines that are restlessly redrawn. In the *Sonets pour Helene*, following Ronsard's emphatic disavowal in the intervening years of Petrarch's authority in matters amatory and poetic and his abandonment of the Petrarchan vein in the poems eventually combined in the *Second Livre des Amours*, he returns to that authority and that vein. Now, however, he paradoxically offers both a Petrarchan and an alternative casting of himself as poet and lover, as well as a dual projection of his lady as object of his love and subject of his poetry.

The relation woven between the poetic personae of the *Rime* and the *Amours* is nowhere more apparent than in the poems "Sur la mort de Marie," the only one of Ronsard's collections to engage the Petrarchan theme of the death of the beloved and the lover's response. The return to the Petrarchan vein in these poems, proclaimed by some readers to be no more than a "passing resurrection,"[29] is seen here, on the contrary, to afford the essential key to the coherence of this highly idiosyncratic small collection.

In each of these chapters will be found reaffirmation of what Thomas Greene termed "the interplay of two imaginations strangely and radically dissimilar,"[30] and ample confirmation too that Ronsard, throughout his poetic career, engaged Petrarch in a rivalry and a challenge whose nature may be cast in the agonistic terms of a textual conflict.[31] This reappraisal seeks, then, not to contest many of the contrasts to the Petrarchan model often identified as constitutive of Ronsard's "newness," but rather to reposition his originality as love poet in terms of his dialogue with Petrarch. It concludes with further evidence, in revisions in the successive collective editions of his *Oeuvres*, of the enduring formative imprint of the "story" of the *Rime sparse* for his self-definition as both poet and lover.

1

Lyric Self-Fashioning

From "le Gaulois Apollon" to "le Pétrarque français"

When Hélène de Surgères identified Pierre de Ronsard as "the Apollo of our age, the Homer of France," her double nomination was hardly original. In fact, it inscribes itself—appropriately enough, in a poem—as a move in the poet's own game.[1] The second element of the compliment, of course, responds to the onomastic play through which Ronsard often represented Hélène herself, celebrating the dedicatee of his last collection of love lyrics through her name, "so fatal a name" "sung by Homer so many times" (*SH* I, 3; 16, 9).[2] The double title bestowed by Hélène upon her poet, however, reminds us also that Ronsard's game was fundamentally one, not only of representation, but of self-representation, a game in which, many years before the publication of the *Sonets pour Helene*, he had not hesitated to designate himself as the "Gaulois Apollon."[3]

It is easy to pass over such a gesture, to read it as merely typical of an age of hyperbolic eulogies.[4] In what was also an age of patronage, moreover, this particular variety of antonomasia was virtually ubiquitous, as poets vied for prestige and often for more substantial reward.[5] From a fortuitous convergence of humanist enthusiasm for the *gloire* of the classical age with the aspirations of the French nobility and their courtier-poets, there emerged what might well be characterized as a culture of impersonation, one rich in affinities with the Elizabethan court and destined to reach its apogee in the following century in the adulation of the Roi Soleil.[6] Not only were royal patrons or potential patrons compared in terms of their virtue and their heroism to the gods and heroes enthusiastically proclaimed by the humanists as the standards of glory. They might also be rendered, in a sort of ascribed impersonation, with all the attributes and even the costume of the classical personage in question; in a particularly remarkable example, François I is represented in a miniature with the combined attributes of Mars, Minerva, Mercury, and Diana, an iconography made explicit in the accompanying poem.[7] Or they might be cast as divinities in royal pageantry, as in Hugues Salel's *Chant poétique présenté au Roy le premier jour de l'an 1549* in which the gods of Olympus dance before Henri II, whose own role is that of Jupiter replacing Saturn.[8]

Ronsard was an enthusiastic participant in this culture, bestowing titles with a largesse equal to that which he hoped to inspire through his encomia. In "La Lyre," the poem in which he identifies himself as the "Gaulois Apollon," his patron Belot, praised for his eloquence, is "a true Socrates"; the Cardinal de Lorraine, praised too for his eloquence as royal emissary, is the "Mercury of the French"; Montmorency and the Duc de Guise are celebrated as "two new Achilles."[9] Mythological figures, divinities, exemplary historical personages are all reborn under his pen in the powerful men and women of sixteenth-century France, a phenomenon appropriate to the poet's task as Ronsard defined it in the preface to his *Odes:* "C'est le vrai but d'un poëte Liriq de celebrer jusques à l'extremité celui qu'il entreprend de louer" [It is the true objective of a Lyric poet to celebrate to the limit the one he undertakes to praise].[10] Read in this light, Ronsard's self-promotion may appear as no more than evidence that poets could undertake to praise themselves just as they undertook to praise patrons, could reward themselves even as they rewarded patrons; as Henri II was portrayed as now one god, now another, and as Catherine de Médicis was praised as the "Juno of France" and the Duchess of Savoie as "the new Pallas,"[11] so the "Gaulois Apollo" could be recognized in Pierre de Ronsard.

It should not be overlooked, however, that this latter self-titling, advanced during the years when Ronsard was the rising poet of a generation, was also a gesture of entitlement. Apollo was much invoked in the period as the presiding deity of poetic *fureur,* and many were the poets who declared themselves the beneficiaries of his inspiration.[12] So too Ronsard, as in the Apolline *fureur* that he associates with his poetic project in the *Hymne de l'Esté:*

Nouveau Cygne emplumé je veux voller bien hault,
Et veux comme l'Esté avoir l'estomaq chaut
Des chaleurs d'Apollon, courant par la carriere
Des Muses . . .[13]

A new feathered swan, I want to fly high, and, like Summer, feel my breast warmed with Apollo's heat, coursing along the path of the Muses . . .

But while others sought variously to valorize their status as "enfanz des dieuz" and as recipients of "quelque divine afflation" such as that claimed for poets by Sébillet in his *Art poétique* of 1548,[14] Ronsard in his self-styling as the "Gaulois Apollon" laid a more direct, and unmediated, claim to lyric preeminence. Not only would he, as he repeatedly vaunted, conceive his works under the sway of the furies of both love and prophecy:[15] he would *be* a new Apollo, one in whom the Gallic muse was incarnate.[16]

France, it seems, had for some time been looking for a new Apollo, or so one might conclude from the public musings on the renewal of poetry that appeared close upon each other in a period beginning some thirty years before Hélène's compliment to Ronsard. And Ronsard, as early as 1550, was looking for a title. In that year, publishing the first book of his *Odes*, he announced his restoration of the lyre to its former glory, by which he was now honored in his turn: "C'est toy," he tells the instrument, "qui fais que Ronsard soit esleu / Harpeur François" [It is you who bring about Ronsard's selection as French Harpist] ("A sa lyre," L I, p. 162). The title doubles that which he unambiguously claimed for himself in the preface to that same work, where he declared to his reader: "quand tu m'appelleras le premier auteur Lirique François . . . lors tu me rendras ce que tu me dois" [when you call me the first French Lyric author . . . then you shall render me what is my due]—a declaration concerning which Marc-Antoine de Muret felt obliged to defend him against the accusation of excessive self-praise.[17] Muret's defense, that such claims were almost conventional, may appear somewhat disingenuous: "cette coutume de se loüer est commune aveques tous les excellans poëtes qui jamais furent" [this custom of self-praise is common among all the excellent poets of all time].[18] In fact, however, it was, like Ronsard's pronouncement, part of a project of cultural initiation directed toward the reader that would render the latter capable of awarding the title to its legitimate claimant.[19]

The title that Ronsard here presents for the reader to confer upon him signals not only his renewal in French of a poetic form highly esteemed in antiquity but also that the form in question is closely associated with music.[20] Its emphasis, quite obviously, was both a reflection of and an appeal to reigning fashion at court. Court poets as well as professional musicians in concert accompanied themselves in song, and numbers of courtiers both played and sang. So did ladies: the poet of the *Amours* will twice recall Cassandre's song on the occasion of his *innamoramento*, first her "chant marié gentiment / Avec mes vers animez de son poulce" [song gracefully married to my verses given life by her thumb] (*A* 38), and again that song "lors qu'à son luth ses doits elle embesongne, / Et qu'elle dit le branle de Bourgogne, / Qu'elle disoit, le jour que je fus pris" [when she sets her fingers to her lute and sings the "branle de Bourgogne," that she was singing the day I was captured] (*A* 108).[21] In Lyon, Louise Labé penned memorable portraits of both herself and her beloved as skilled players of the instrument.[22] The fashion, like many others at the French court in the mid-sixteenth century, was set in Italy, and it was no doubt not for purely musical reasons that Ronsard called attention to "l'usage de la lire aujourd'hui resuscitée en Italie, laquelle lire seule peut et doit animer les vers, et leur donner le juste poi de leur gravité" [the use, revived today in Italy, of the lyre, which alone can and must give life to the verses, and give them the full weight of their solemnity] (*L* I, p. 48).

Against this background, Ronsard's self-styling as the "Gaulois Apollon" comes into better focus. Among the poets of the sixteenth century, as in other eras, lute and lyre take on a sense that is metaphoric, metapoetic, or metatextual.[23] Petrarch offered a precedent in a well-known poem, imitated by Du Bellay, in which he proclaims his inadequacy to speak of Laura:

> sì dirà ben: "Quello ove questi aspira
> è cosa da stancare Atene, Arpino,
> Mantova et Smirna, et l'una et l'altra lira." (*R* 247, 9–11)

> then he will say: "What this man aspires to would exhaust Athens, Arpinum, Mantua, and Smyrna, and both one and the other lyre."

Du Bellay expands this catalog in which the two lyres stand for the Greek and Latin lyric traditions by placing Petrarch himself at its head, a gesture that serves in turn as preparation for his reference to a Ronsard who would, along with other "modern"—French—poets, be unable to capture successfully the beauty of Olive:

> Ne cetuy là qui naguere a faict lire
> En lettres d'or gravé sur son rivage
> Le vieil honneur de l'une et l'autre lire. (*O* 62, 12–14)[24]

> Nor that one there who once gave us to read, in letters of gold engraved upon his bank, the ancient honor of both one and the other lyre.

The lyre, along with the lute with which it was sometimes interchangeable, figured in common but considerably imprecise usage to designate a variety of poetic modes; it could also be invoked to distinguish between pagan and Christian poetry, as in Du Bellay's *La Lyre Chrestienne*.[25] The instrument, as Terence Cave notes, "occupies a privileged place in the

Ronsardian corpus as a figure of poetry."[26] Striking in the case of Ronsard, however, is his recurrent representation not only of the instrument but of the poet in the act of playing it. He may well, in fact, have played the lyre, and possibly also the lute and the guitar.[27] But for our purpose the emphasis is important because it draws the attention of the reader, not to the imitative or competitive relation between the original text and the new text, but to the figure of the poet, who assumes the posture of the imitated master, be he ancient—as Pindar or Homer—or, like Apollo, divine.

Here the practice of imitation promulgated in the poetics of Ronsard and his contemporaries is deflected from the written to the performative act, to take on a new meaning as impersonation. Highly theatrical in this context, it is fully in keeping with a theatrical age in which, as Gilbert Gadoffre reminds us, the poet might claim for himself a privileged place in a world peopled by heroes as "the demiurge of this universe of mirrors," able to deify mortals as well as resuscitate the dead.[28] Ronsard, particularly insistent in this form of self-representation, was also particularly versatile in his self-casting as actor in this theater. Already in 1550, the year of his much-vaunted renewal of the lyric lyre in the first collection of the *Odes*, he imagined other uses for the instrument. Was France awaiting a new Homer, or perhaps a new Virgil? He would respond in epic vein, announcing the ambitious project of a dynastic epic to celebrate the House of Valois.[29] In his *Franciade*, named for the putative founder of the line, Ronsard would, he told the Muses, "chanter mon Francion sur vostre lyre" [sing of my Francus upon your lyre]; he would, he promised the king's sister Marguerite, write of her "plus haultement . . . Lors que hardy je publiray le tige Troyen de [ta] race" [in a more exalted manner . . . when boldly I shall treat of the Trojan root of (your) race], reminding her that "mon luc premierement / Aux François montra la voie / De sonner si proprement" [It was my lute that first showed the French the way to sound it so well].[30]

To show the way: such, of course, was the announced project of Du Bellay's *Deffence et illustration de la langue françoyse* whose publication preceded that of the *Odes* by a single year, the immediately acknowledged manifesto in which imitation of preeminent earlier poets such as Homer was advanced as the avenue of renewal for French poetry.[31] Ronsard's early enthusiasm for the *Franciade* project, however, was not effectively matched by that of its intended patrons; nor did the early *Odes* meet with the resounding and enduring success of which he confidently boasted in his preface. Did the circumstances result in a crisis of orientation, as Dassonville suggests?[32] In any case, it resulted in a change of orientation. Disposed once again to alter his course, Ronsard took his cue from two very recent works that had been rewarded with considerable success. Both were Petrarchan collections: Du Bellay's *Olive*, the sequence of love lyrics for which the *Deffence et illustration* was intended to serve as preface, and Pontus de Tyard's *Erreurs amoureuses* of 1549.

Intent as ever to inscribe his own career into the poetic record of his time, Ronsard now explicitly locates his new orientation in the wake of Du Bellay and Tyard, attributing it, of course, not to poetic fashion but to love. In the poem "A Jean de la Peruse, Poete," which passes in review the poetic endeavors of recent decades, he recalls first his own early efforts to "marier les Odes à la Lyre," then the amorous verses recording "les passions" of an enamored Du Bellay and the "amoureux ennuy" of an enamored Tyard. Struck in his turn by Cupid's arrow, he affirms, he had turned, like them, to sing of love:

> Comme ces deux de mesme fleche attaint,
> (Tant peult amour) helas! je fu contraint
> Dessus le luth autres chansons apprendre,
> Pensant flechir l'orgueil de ma Cassandre. (*L* V, p. 259)

> Struck like those two by the same arrow, (so much can love do) alas!
> I was constrained to learn other songs to the lute, thinking to bend
> the pride of my Cassandre.

Soon thereafter he composed a variant of this story, again placing his adoption of the Petrarchan mode under the sign of love but setting it off now against his preparation of the *Franciade:*

> N'agueres chanter je voulois
> Comme Francus au bord Gaulois
> Avecq' sa troupe vint descendre,
> Mais mon Luth pincé de mon doy,
> Ne vouloit en despit de moi
> Que chanter Amour & Cassandre. (*L* VI, p. 133)

> In those days I wanted to sing of how Francus descended with his
> troops to the Gaulish border, but my Lute, strummed by my fingers,
> wanted despite myself only to sing of Love and Cassandre.

This version of his new poetic enterprise is given a more dramatic, indeed epic coloration in the *Amours* said to have been composed in response to that urging:

> Ja desja Mars ma trompe avoit choisie,
> Et, dans mes vers ja françoys, devisoyt:

Sus ma fureur ja sa lance aiguizoit,
Epoinçonnant ma brave poësie.
Ja d'une horreur la Gaule estoit saisie,
Et soubz le fer ja Sene treluisoit,
Et ja Francus à son bord conduisoit
L'ombre d'Hector, & l'honneur de l'Asie,
Quand l'archerot emplumé par le dos
D'un trait certain me playant jusqu'à l'os,
De sa grandeur le sainct prestre m'ordonne:
Armes adieu. Le Myrte Paphien
Ne cede point au Laurien Delphien,
Quand de sa main Amour mesme le donne. (*A* 71)

Already Mars had selected my trumpet, and in my verses now in
French was composing: in my furor he was sharpening his lance,
spurring on my brave poetry. Already Gaul was seized by horror
and the Seine sparkled beneath the blade, and already Francus led
to its bank the shade of Hector and the honor of Asia, when the
winged archer, wounding me to the bone with an unerring shot,
ordained me the sacred priest of his greatness. Arms farewell. The
Paphian Myrtle does not yield to the Delphic Laurel, when Love
himself awards it with his hand.

Here, with the evocation of his work on the *Franciade*, Ronsard effectively
rewrites the Petrarchan scene of the innamoramento, blending the figures
of a bellicose Mars and of Apolline fureur into that of Cupid as archer. The
gesture asserts his uniqueness while proclaiming his filiation, creating a
central component of his poetic autobiography in progress.

The change might not, of course, be definitive. In the "Elegie à Cas-
sandre," included in the *Pièces du Bocage* of 1554, he protested the neces-
sity to abandon his newly successful love poetry in favor of more martial
matters, at the king's behest: "& si faut que ma lyre / Pendüe au croc ne
m'ose plus rien dire" [my lyre, stored upon its hook, no longer dares tell
me anything] and the new collection of *Odes* published in 1555 defines
itself as a farewell to the lyre, abandoned now in favor of the martial trum-
pet:[33]

Mais or,' par le commandement
Du Roi, ta Lyre j'abandonne
Pour entonner plus hautement
La grand' trompette de Bellonne ... (*L* VII, pp. 66–67)

But now, by the King's command, I abandon your Lyre to sound
more forcefully the great trumpet of Bellonne . . .

Not only the lyre but the lute as well: both must be set aside, he tells
Cassandre in an "Elegie," as he takes up the trumpet to sing of the king's
prowess:

> Donques en vain je me paissois d'espoir
> De faire un jour à la Thuscane voir
> Que nôtre France, autant qu'elle, est heureuse
> A soupirer une pleinte amoureuse . . .
> Mon oeil, mon coeur, ma Cassandre, ma vie,
> Hé! qu'à bon droit tu dois porter d'envie
> A ce grant Roi, qui ne veut plus soufrir
> Qu'à mes chansons ton nom se vienne ofrir.
> C'est lui qui veut qu'en trompette j'échange
> Mon Luc, afin d'entonner sa louange,
> Non de lui seul, mais de tous ses aïeus
> Qui sont issus de la race des Dieus.
> Je le ferai puis qu'il me le commande . . . (L VI, pp. 57–58)

Thus in vain I nourished the hope to one day make Tuscany see that
our France, as much as she, is happy to sigh forth an amorous plaint
. . . My eye, my heart, my Cassandre, my life, Oh! by rights you must
envy this great King, who no longer wishes your name to inspire my
songs. He it is who wills that I exchange my lute for the trumpet, to
sound forth his praise; not his alone, but that of all his ancestors,
issued from the race of the Gods. I shall do it since he commands me
. . .

Yet Ronsard holds out hope for both his poetry and Cassandre, for the
king, having himself some experience in love, will surely allow him to
return to his more intimate theme:

> S'il l'a senti, ma coulpe est effacée,
> Et sa grandeur ne sera courroucée
> Qu'à mon retour des horribles combas
> Hors de son croc mon Luc j'aveigne à bas,
> Le pincetant, & qu'en lieu des alarmes
> Je chante Amour, tes beautés, & mes larmes . . . (53–58)

If he has heard it, my fault is erased, and his grandeur will not be
angered that on my return from the horrible battle I draw down my

lute from its hook, strumming it, and that instead of alarms I sing
Love, your beauties, and my tears . . .

Nor will this transposition signal a diminution of his own "heroic" status,
for he goes on to claim a remarkable precursor. Ferocious Achilles, he tells
Cassandre, upon returning to camp from battle, took advantage of just
such an interlude to take up the lute:

> Ainsi Achile apres avoir par terre
> Tant fait mourir de soudars en la guerre
> Son Luc doré prenoit entre ses mains
> Teintes encor de meurdres inhumains,
> Et vis à vis du fils de Menetie
> Chantoit l'amour de Briseis s'amie . . . " (61–66)

Thus Achilles, after casting so many soldiers dead to the earth in the
melee, took his gilded Lute in those hands still tinged with inhuman
carnage, and face to face with Menetie's son he sang the love of his
beloved Briseis . . .

then suddenly took up arms again to return to combat "plus vaillant." In
the same way, Ronsard assures his lady, as the king retires from combat
and disarms himself in his tent, her poet will find the occasion to sing her
praises: "De sur le Luc à l'heure ton Ronsard / te chantera" [your Ronsard
will sing of you upon the lute in time] (72–73).

"Ainsi Achile . . . Ainsi ton Ronsard": the passage testifies eloquently to
Ronsard's characteristic strategy of self-representation. The allusion, it
has been noted, is inaccurate, and its deflection is significant: in the pas-
sage of *Iliad* IX to which he refers, the hero sings not of love but of the
valiant deeds of the warriors.[34] In Ronsard's poem the fierce Achilles is
rewritten as a lyric poet; he is pressed into service as model for a new poet,
one who radically alters a canonized ancient text while at the same time
he invents a contemporary fiction offered to the reader as the historical
instance of his poem. In this extraordinarily flamboyant gesture, we find
what we might be tempted once again to characterize, not as imitation,
but as impersonation.

A final example confirms the striking pliability of these representations
which Ronsard molded to the needs of his own poetic persona as he wove
the new thread almost seamlessly into the old, into the literary represen-
tation of what he repeatedly termed the web of his life, the "trame de sa
vie." For in fact, in abandoning the ode and the epic to devote himself to
the love sonnet currently in favor, he abandoned neither the lyre nor his
identification with Apollo. On the contrary, his stance as musician is cen-

tral to his adaptation of the Petrarchan posture to his own measure in his first lyric collection. The adaptation is readily carried out: in the *Rime sparse* now to be imitated, had not Petrarch himself established an identity with Apollo through the Ovidian myth of the laurel? Now, in the first poem of the 1552 *Amours* to allude to his poetic celebration of the lady, Ronsard writes to a Cassandre cast here as Medusa:

> Moy donc rocher, si dextrement je n'use
>   L'outil des Seurs pour ta gloire esbaucher,
>   Qu'un seul Tuscan est digne de toucher,
>   Non le changé, mais le changeur accuse. (*A* 8, 5–8)

> If I then, a stone, fail to use skillfully the instrument of the Sisters to set forth your glory, one that a single Tuscan is worthy to touch, accuse, not the transformed one, but the transformer.

But he is not to be deterred: "Bien mille fois & mille," he records, "j'ay tenté / De fredonner sus les nerfz de ma lyre . . . Le nom, qu'Amour dans le cuoeur m'a planté" [Thousands and thousands of times I have tried to hum to the strings of my lyre the name that Love implanted in my heart] (*A* 27, 1–4). The thematic thrust of the sonnet closely echoes Petrarch's declaration of his inability to record his lady's name, as Ronsard's editors routinely observe; like Petrarch's poet, Ronsard's lyric protagonist has been unable to inscribe the name on paper, and like him he remains without voice: "Più volte già per dir le labbra apersi, / poi rimase la voce in mezzo 'l petto" [many times already have I opened my lips to speak, but then my voice has remained within my breast] (*R* 20, 9–10); "la voix fraude ma bouche, / Et voulant dire en vain je suis béant" [the voice evades my mouth, and wishing to speak, in vain I am merely gaping] (*A* 27, 13–14). But Ronsard adds the instrumentality of the lyre, defining his desire to "dire" as an attempt at song.

For this song he claims as precursor a mythic Apollo presented in a later poem in the collection as "ce grand Dieu le pere de la lyre" [this great God the father of the lyre] (*A* 116). The god, we learn, also sang in vain:

> Pour la douleur, qu'amour veult que je sente,
>   Ainsi que moy, Phebus, tu lamentoys,
>   Quand amoureux, loing du ciel tu chantoys
>   Pres d'Ilion sus les rives de Xanthe.
> Pinçant en vain ta lyre blandissante,
>   Et fleurs, & flots, mal sain, tu enchantoys,
>   Non la beaulté qu'en l'ame tu sentoys
>   Dans le plus doulx d'une playe esgrissante. (*A* 36, 1–8)

On account of the pain that love wills me to feel, you, Phoebus, lamented just as I do, when, enamored, you sang far from the heavens on the banks of the Xanthe. Strumming your caressing lyre in vain, you enchanted flowers and waves in your distress, but not the beauty that you felt in your soul in the sweetest part of a keen painful wound.

Petrarch, drawing on Ovidian story for a configuration of mythological elements, had repeatedly presented an Apollo who laments his loss of the nymph Daphne. The Apollo who voices his amorous frustration to the accompaniment of his lyre, however, is not found in the *Rime sparse*, and that is highly suggestive. Here the lyre that distinguishes Ronsard's poet-persona of the early *Amours* from that of Petrarch in the *Rime* is placed in the hands of his mythological double as well, lending authority to the conversion of the poet's voice from the epic to the amorous mode, and status to the languishing figure playing a lyre that now is "blandissante."[35]

*   *   *

It was thus as part of a broader strategy of impersonation that Ronsard adopted his new Petrarchan posture, with an enthusiasm that hardly concealed his ambition. His French contemporaries, he declared in the "Elegie a Cassandre," were inept as love poets, some crude and licentious, others unable to master the master's art to sing of "les amours":

> L'on trop enflé les chante grossement,
> L'un enervé les traine bassement,
> L'un nous despaint une amie paillarde,
> L'un plus aus vers qu'aus sentences regarde
> Et ne peut onc, tant se sceut desguiser,
> Aprendre l'art de bien Petrarquiser. (*L* VI, p. 59)

> One, too puffed up, sings of them inflatedly, another, irritated, drags them low, another paints for us a bawdy lover, yet another attends more to verse than to meaning and can never, however he covers it up, learn the art of Petrarchising well.

But Ronsard . . . Ronsard would be different. If only he could sing of Cassandre as he wished, he assured her and his reader in a poem to which we shall return, he would surpass poets both classical and modern:

> Que n'ay-je, Dame, & la plume & la grace
> Divine autant que j'ay la volonté,

Par mes escritz tu seroys surmonté,
Vieil enchanteur des vieulx rochers de Thrace.
Plus hault encor que Pindare, ou qu'Horace,
J'appenderoys à ta divinité
Un livre enflé de telle gravité,
Que Du Bellay luy quitteroyt la place.
Si vive encore Laure par l'Univers
Ne fuit volant dessus les Thusques vers,
Que nostre siecle heureusement estime,
Comme ton nom, honneur des vers françoys,
Hault elevé par le vent de ma voix
S'en voleroyt sus l'aisle de ma rime. (*A* 73)

Lady, had I but pen and grace as sublime as my will, in my writings you, ancient enchanter of the ancient rocks of Thrace, would be surpassed. Higher still than Pindar or than Horace, I would append upon your divinity a book swelled with such solemnity that Du Bellay would abandon the field to it. As live as the name Laura flies through the Universe borne upon the Tuscan verses that our century happily esteems, so your name, honor of French verses, raised on high by the wind of my voice would take flight on the wing of my rhyme.

It is interesting that while the name of Homer is prominent elsewhere in the first collection of the *Amours*, introduced through the mythological associations of the name of Cassandre, Ronsard makes no mention here of the ancient poet. But it is sufficiently evident that the master against whom Ronsard measures himself is not only, not principally, Homer.[36] Instead we find not only Du Bellay, successful imitator of Petrarch, but Petrarch as well.

This latter suggestion of incipient rivalry, like the avowedly new orientation of Ronsard's poetic enterprise, was not wholly unprepared. For if Ronsard clearly aspired to the title of "Homère de la France," the title which Hélène in a playful key and others with far more solemnity were to award him, his poetic aspirations from a very early date had taken on an alternative cast. And that cast is suggested in his early self-designation as the "Gaulois Apollon," which began our exploration of his poetic self-fashioning. For it can hardly have escaped his notice, attentive as he was to gestures of poetic entitlement, that Maurice Scève, in a famous dizain, had identified Petrarch as the "Tuscan Apollo."[37] Adopting the stance of the "Gaulois Apollon," Ronsard created the formula for an equation through which he might hope one day to distinguish himself as "le

Pétrarque français." It was a calculated ratio whose significance was not to be lost on his contemporaries, among them Etienne Jodelle, who succinctly defined its strategy as one of impersonation:

> Pétrarque Italien, pour un Phébus se faire,
> De l'immortel laurier alla choisir le nom;
> Notre Ronsard Français ne tâche aussi sinon
> Par l'amour de Cassandre un Phébus contrefaire.[38]

> The Italian Petrarch, to make himself a Phoebus, chose the name of the immortal laurel; our French Ronsard strives for nothing else than to impersonate a Phoebus through the love of Cassandre.

Thus Ronsard was to lay claim not only to the role of the mythical Apollo but also to parity with the most admired "modern" poet, the Petrarch who had for more than a century dictated the dominant poetic mode in Italy and who had, in the generation preceding Ronsard's, come to be acknowledged as the model of lyric poetry in France as well.[39]

To be the "French Petrarch": to some of Ronsard's contemporaries, and especially to his fellow aspirants to poetic glory, it may have seemed an odd ambition on his part, for he was a relative latecomer to the Petrarchan mode. Although the *Odes* contain much love poetry, that poetry is hardly Petrarchan, underlining instead the intensity of the lover's desire and postulating several ladies as its object; here, concludes Paul Laumonier, we are "at the Antipodes" of Petrarch.[40] Ronsard's earliest mentions of Petrarch in fact occur in comments not on his own poems but on those of others, and in them "Petrarch" is clearly a "text." Before 1545, to Peletier du Mans, who was attempting to translate Petrarch, Ronsard advanced as part of his portrait of his ideal *amie* "Qu'el'seust par cueur tout cela qu'a chanté / Petrarcque en Amours tant vanté / Ou la Rose par Meun décritte" [that she know by heart all that Petrarch, so highly esteemed in Love, had sung, or the Rose depicted by Meun] ("Ode a Jacques Peletier des beautez qu'il voudroit en s'amie"; *L* I, p. 6). This "amie" herself is far from the Petrarchan mistress; most of Ronsard's poem is explicit physical description, a list of desiderata for a mistress not only young but "inconstant & volage, / Follatre, & digne de tel age" [inconstant and flighty, playful, and worthy of her age]. Does her knowledge of Petrarch's love lyrics and of Jean de Meun's *Roman de la Rose* attest to her literary culture, or instead to her amatory inclination, like that of the young female reader whose acquaintance with Petrarch Ronsard had indicted as serving only "fins de coquetterie"?

La fille preste à marier, accorde
Trop librement sa chanson à la corde
D'un pouce curieus:
Et veut encore Petrarque retenir
Affin que mieus ell' puisse entretenir
L'amant luxurieux. (*L* II, pp. 190–91)

The young girl ready to marry tunes her song too freely to the string with a curious thumb: and seeks too to remember her Petrarch in order better to entertain a lustful lover.

In any case, here the ladies—imaginary or real—are perhaps only responding in kind to the attentions of their lovers. Those attentions were denounced with varying proportions of ridicule or indignation, whether real or feigned, by observers of the courtly scene at mid-century, some of whom were at the same time ardent participants in its poetic rituals.[41] In a more serious vein, Théodore de Bèze, in the preface to his *Abraham sacrifiant* (1550), opposes the solemnity of Christian praise of God to the frivolity of poets who flattered their patrons or their ladies—their "idoles"—by attempting to "petrarquiser un sonnet,"[42] an enterprise whose dubious issue is acknowledged by the impatient poet in the *Amours* who pleads with his lady either to reward or to reject his suit outright because he is unable to conduct it according to fashion, to "petrarquiser" sufficiently:

Dy l'un des deux, sans tant me desguiser
  Le peu d'amour que ton semblant me porte:
  Je ne scauroy, veu ma peine si forte,
  Tant lamenter ne tant petrarquiser.
Si tu le veulx, que sert de refuser
  Ce doulx present dont l'espoir me conforte?
  Si non, pourquoy, d'une esperance morte
  Pais tu ma vie affin de l'abuser? (*A* 123, 1–8)[43]

Say one or the other, without so much disguising the scant love that your manner shows me: I could not, given the intensity of my pain, lament or Petrarchize so much. If you want it, what use is it to refuse that sweet gift whose hope comforts me? If not, why sustain my life with a dead hope in order to disappoint it?

To readers familiar with Ronsard's *Odes*, his professed ambition to rival Petrarch may have seemed odd for other reasons as well. Those accustomed to his emphatic pronouncements of poetic intent would surely have recalled that only two years before the publication of the *Amours* dedicated to Cassandre, in the preface to the *Odes* and at the same time that he vaunted his accomplishments in the lofty vein of a Pindar, Ronsard had taken the offensive in his own defense: "Je ne fai point de doute que ma Poësie tant varie ne semble facheuse aus oreilles de nos rimeurs, & principalement des courtizans, qui n'admirent qu'un petit sonnet petrarquizé, ou quelque mignardise d'amour qui continue tousjours en son propos" [I have no doubt whatever that my often-varied Poetry will seem unwelcome to the ears of our rhymers, and especially our courtiers, who admire only a little "petrarchized" sonnet or some affected bit of amorous flattery that is invariable in its intention] (*L* I, p. 47)—those unable to "aprendre l'art de bien Petrarquiser" of whom he was scornfully to complain.

But already Ronsard was writing verses inspired by and in imitation of Petrarch, verses that disclose a project far more ambitious than that of producing a "petit sonnet petrarquizé." Already he takes aim at an entitlement and at a title: that of the French Petrarch.[44] He was not unprepared to undertake such a venture, for his early, extensive, and direct acquaintance with a number of Italian poets has been amply chronicled.[45] And there is textual evidence of Ronsard's attentive reading of Petrarch during that formative period in which we find, in Laumonier's phrase, "the stammerings of his Muse" (*L* I, p. xxi)—evidence found in his earliest lyric practice, even before the first collection of the *Amours* in 1552.

As Laumonier discovered, the publication of the *Hymne de France* in 1550 included at its end two love lyrics, a "Fantaisie à sa dame" and a "Sonnet à elle-même."[46] The latter poem, Ronsard's first published sonnet, is a close imitation, for the most part a paraphrase, of Petrarch's sonnet 220, "Onde tolse Amor l'oro e di qual vena" [Where and from what mine did Love take the gold] praising the beauteous attributes of the beloved. It is something of a set piece and unremarkable of its type, differing little from the efforts of other French poets who were already engaged in translating and imitating the Italian master. The "Fantaisie," however, more complex and more original, affords a pertinent test case for a reconsideration of Ronsard's early response to Petrarch's lyrics.

Ronsard's "Fantaisie" is cast in the form of a dream-vision for which a well-known Petrarchan source has been easily identified: canzone 323 of the *Rime sparse*, "Standomi un giorno solo a la fenestra," already translated by Clément Marot as "Visions de Pétrarque." The speaker of *R* 323 represents the death of his beloved lady through six allegorical visions, in each of which an object of contemplation—a noble wild creature, a laden ship, a laurel plant, a fountain, a phoenix, a lady—is fatally transformed and destroyed before the eyes of the poet, who is present merely as spectator.[47] In Ronsard's "Fantaisie" it is the poet himself who is subjected to a series of transformations, which allow the dreamer to penetrate unobserved into the chamber of a lady who remains very much alive; at their conclusion, he boasts of having witnessed the unsuspecting object of his desire

> Montrer la jambe & la cuisse charnue,
> Ce corps, ce ventre & ce sein coloré,
> Ainçois ivoire en oeuvre elaboré,
> Où j'avisoy une & une autre pomme,
> Dans ceste neige aller & venir, comme
> Les ondes font se jouant à leur bord,
> Quand le vent est ne tranquille ne fort.

show a leg and a well-fleshed thigh, that body, that belly and that flushed breast like well-worked ivory, where I observed one and another apple rise and fall within that snowiness, like the waves do in playing on their shore when the wind is neither still nor strong.

Read against Petrarch's canzone 323, these verses are entirely unexpected, and their effect is not attenuated by the fact that Ronsard here closely imitates another Italian source to which he would frequently return, Ariosto's portrait of Alcina in the *Orlando Furioso*.[48] The contrast is the more startling because the representations of the lady throughout Petrarch's R 323 are among the most distanced of the entire Italian collection: she appears in human rather than allegorical guise only in the final stanza, and here too, "sì leggiadra et bella Donna" [a Lady so joyous and beautiful], she is not fully revealed to the observer's view, her "parti supreme," or highest parts, being "avolte d'una nebbia oscura" [wrapped in a dark mist]. Not surprisingly, the contrast between the two poems figures large in the debate that opposes an "erotic" Ronsard to a "chaste" Petrarch: this erotic pretext, Dassonville exclaims, alters the tone, the object, and the meaning of the model poem.[49]

The relation merits reexamination, however, for despite the affinities suggested by the casting of both R 323 and Ronsard's "Fantaisie" as visions, the primary Petrarchan inspiration of Ronsard's poem is not the allegorical "canzone delle visioni" but another canzone, R 23, "nel dolce tempo de la prima etade" [in the sweet time of my first age].[50] In this poem, as in Ronsard's, the successive metamorphoses are not those of allegorical images to which the poet is witness but those of the subject himself. All of these transformations have direct Ovidian models: as the poet becomes a laurel, a swan, a stone, a weeping fountain, a disembodied voice, and finally a stag, they recall the fates of Daphne, Cygnus, Battus, Biblis, Echo, and Acteon.[51] Ronsard's persona finds himself carried away through the skies to become first a cloud, then a shower of rain, a rock, a fountain, a swan, a flower, a disembodied shade. Each transformation preceding the sight of the lady, exactly as in Petrarch's canzone, prompts the expression of his subjugation to the will of the beloved, his impotent lament at her rejection of his suit, his attempt to pronounce her name and to praise her. Only the final transformation in Ronsard's poem, the single one that follows the vision of the lady's nakedness cited above, departs from this pattern, conforming instead to *Rime* 323: here, in an image derived from that of a ship's destruction that figures the lady herself in Petrarch's poem, the poet is finally transformed into a ship threatened with disaster.

Among these metamorphoses, it is the swan image that has attracted the particular attention of readers because, in this very early poem, it sets out a claim to poetic fame, indeed to poetic immortality:

Et tout ainsi que j'avoy dans ce monde
Fait éternel vostre nom par mon onde,
Voulant remplir tout le ciel de son loz,
La plume aux flans, l'aesle me creut au doz:
Et nouveau cygne aloy par l'univers,
Chantant de vous les louanges en vers . . . . (31–36)

And just as I had made your name eternal in this world by my wave, wishing to fill all heaven with its praise, feathers sprouted on my body, and wings on my back: and, new swan, I went through the universe singing your praises in verse . . .

The image has also attracted critical attention as evidence of Ronsard's departure from the Petrarchan model: here he follows the example of classical precursors who had identified the poet with the swan as the creature able to exalt to the heavens the name of a person worthy of celebration and commemoration. The image was early adopted by others among the classicizing young poets of the Pléiade;[52] Du Bellay's *Olive* again affords numerous examples, as in his praise of Scève as "Cygne nouveau, qui voles en chantant / Du chault rivage au froid hiperborée" [new Swan, who flies in singing from the warm shore to the farthest northern cold] (*O* 105)[53] and in the apostrophe of the final poem: "Quel cigne encor' des cignes le plus beau / Te prêta l'aele?" [What swan again most beautiful of swans lent you his wing?] (*O* 115). The passage in Ronsard's "Fantaisie" clearly reflects this tradition, anticipating the claim to poetic immortality that he was shortly to advance in the ending of Book IV of his *Odes:* "J'ai fini mon ouvrage . . . Toujours toujours, sans que jamais je meure / Je volerai tout vif par l'univers" (*L* I, p. 152) [I have finished my work . . . Forever and ever, without ever knowing death, I shall fly alive through the universe].[54]

Ronsard's triumphant soaring swan, whose transformation results from the success of his enterprise to praise the lady's name, stands in almost complete contrast with the swan transformation of Petrarch's metamorphosis canzone:

Né meno ancor m'agghiaccia
l'esser coverto poi di bianche piume
allor che folminato et morto giacque
il mio sperar che tropp'alto montava;
che perch'io non sapea dove né quando
me 'l ritrovasse, solo, lagrimando,
là 've tolto mi fu, dì et notte andava
ricercando dallato e dentro a l'acque;
et giamai poi la mia lingua non tacque
mentre poteo del suo cader maligno,
ond'io presi col suon color d'un cigno. (*R* 23, 50–60)

Nor do I fear less for having been later covered with white feathers, when thunderstruck and dead lay my hope that was mounting too high; for, since I did not know where or when I would recover it, alone and weeping I went night and day where it had been taken from me, looking for it beside and within the waters; and from then on my tongue was never silent about its evil fall, as long as it had power; and I took on with the sound of a swan its color.

Petrarch here adapts another classical motif, that of the lamenting swan whose song is sweetest as it approaches death, which was also to be adopted by some of Ronsard's contemporaries, Du Bellay among them, as early as 1549.[55] Du Bellay's poet, protesting his inability to express his "martyre," may appear to present a contradictory opinion as he exclaims, "Je mourroy' cygne, où je meurs sans mot dire" [I shall die a swan, where I die without speaking a word] (*O* 8),[56] but he foretells in a later poem that "De cest oyseau prendray le blanc pennaige, / Qui en chantant plaingt la fin de son aage / Aux bordz herbus du recourbé Mëandre" [I shall take on the white plumage of that swan that, singing, lamented the end of its life on the grassy banks of the winding Meander] (*O* 59). The swan form in *R* 23, unlike Ronsard's and Du Bellay's, is the result of an unwitting and unwilling transformation, a figure of frustration whose movement is represented now, not as flight but as a fruitless search "beside and within the waters," and its song, not the praise of the beloved, but a wordless lament.

Are we then to conclude that Ronsard is here "unfaithful . . . to Petrarch's lesson" and that by this gesture he deliberately distances himself from the *Rime sparse*?[57] That ready conclusion would lead us to neglect a connection that has far-reaching implications for his later imitation of Petrarch. For once again closer examination is required, because the swan metamorphosis in Petrarch's canzone is doubled in that same poem by that of another bird, one that appears not in the series of the poet-lover's transformations but in the *commiato*, in the confident boast that he has been "l'uccel che più per l'aere poggia / alzando lei che ne' miei detti onoro" [the bird that rises highest in the air raising her that in my words I honor].

The presence of this source text is critical for our reading of Ronsard's claim of poetic triumph in the "Fantaisie à sa dame," for in the commiato of *Rime* 23 the context is quite specific and quite unlike that of the series of metamorphoses of the frustrated poet-as-victim in the body of the poem. Here each transformation alludes to one of the metamorphoses through which an enamored Jupiter takes on a mortal form, bird or animal, so as to possess the human object of his desire; in the verses cited, the god assumes the form of an eagle to carry Ganymede off to Olympus. Of this image of triumphant flight Petrarch makes a figure of triumphant poetry, as the speaker of his poem raises to the skies the lady honored in his verse. And Ronsard's poem follows Petrarch's lead, with a highly suggestive innovation: while his description of avian metamorphosis follows that of the lover's swan transformation in the Italian poem, it is the bird of the commiato of *R* 23 that inspires his own claim of poetic achievement. This is the Petrarch to whose achievement Du Bellay had early aspired, as he recalls in his "Complainte du Desesperé":

> Alors que parmy la France
> Du beau Cygne de Florence
> J'alloys adorant les pas,
> Dont les plumes j'ay tirées,
> Qui des ailes mal cirées
> Le vol n'imiteront pas. . . .[58]

while I went through France adoring the traces of the handsome swan of Florence, whose feathers I have plucked, whose flight my poorly waxed wings will not imitate. . . .

And it is the soaring Petrarch repeatedly evoked by Ronsard.[59] His assimilation of the bird images is confirmed in the "Elegie ou Amour Oyseau," where he identifies Petrarch as "ce Florentin, / Que Cygne par ses vers surmonta le Destin" [this Florentine who as a Swan overcame Fate by his verses] (*L* XV, p. 210), taken up again in his "Elegie Au Sieur Barthelemi Del-Bene" (*L* XVIII, pp. 253ff.) to whom he accords the title of

> . . . second Cygne apres le Florentin
> Que l'art, & le sçavoir, l'Amour, & le Destin,
> Firent voler si haut sur Sorgue la riviere,
> Qu'il laissa de bien loing tous les autres derriere

> . . . second Swan after the Florentine, whom art, knowledge, Love, and Fate made to fly so high above the river Sorgue that he left all others far behind.[60]

*   *   *

Ample evidence exists, then, that in this early phase of his lyric production Ronsard was not a dilatory and servile imitator of the current poetic mode; on the contrary, he was an excellent reader of Petrarch. But what he found in the *Rime sparse* was more than the affectation of a poetic fashion implied in his declaration of an inability to "tant petrarquiser" to win his lady's favors. The definitions that proliferated in the period are in this regard suggestive: Théodore de Bèze, for example, had added to his deprecation of poets devoting themselves only to the attempt to "petrarquiser un sonnet" that of a posturing that was affective as well as poetic, to "faire l'amoureux transy" [play the transfixed lover]; a more sympathetic or at least ostensibly neutral Muret annotates Ronsard's verb "Petrarquiser" in a sonnet from the first collection of the *Amours* (*A* 123) with the identical phrase: "faire de l'amoureus transi, comme Petrarque" (*L* IV, p. 96), and J. Lemaire suggests something very similar, to imitate "'le bon Petrarque, en amours le vrai maistre.'"[61] While these *gloses* appear to emphasize the sense of affectation—"une hypocrisie ou une imposture," as Yvonne Bellenger comments, "l'idée d'un amour tout en tromperie, tout en feintes, en somme d'un mensonge"[62]—the suggestion of role-playing in these substitutions of "faire" for "écrire" may have particular implications, especially in the case of Ronsard, for the practice of writing as well.

The latter verb, of course, is implicit, for all of these author-commentators are attempting to define modes of lyric writing. A particularly suggestive example of the many possibilities of "writing like Petrarch" is a poem by Jodelle that takes as its point of departure this version of the *innamoramento* in the *Rime sparse:*

> Era il giorno ch'al sol si scoloraro
> per la pietà del suo fattore i rai

quando i' fui preso, et non me ne guardai,
ché i be' vostr'occhi, Donna, mi legaro.
Tempo non mi parea da far riparo
contr'a' colpi d'Amor; però m'andai
secur, senza sospetto, onde i miei guai
nel commune dolor s'incominciaro.
Trovommi Amor del tutto disarmato,
et aperta la via per gli occhi al core
che di lagrime son fatti uscio et varco.
Però al mio parer non li fu onore
ferir me de saetta in quello stato,
a voi armata non mostrar pur l'arco. (*R* 3)

It was the day when the sun's rays turned pale with grief for his Maker when I was taken, and I did not defend myself against it, for your lovely eyes, Lady, bound me. It did not seem to me a time for being on guard against Love's blows; therefore I went confident and without fear, and so my misfortunes began in the midst of the universal woe. Love found me altogether disarmed, and the way open through my eyes to my heart, my eyes which are now the portal and passageway of tears. Therefore, as it seems to me, it got him no honor to strike me with an arrow in that state, and not even to show his bow to you, who were armed.

Very early in the *Rime*, Petrarch's sonnet recontextualizes Love's assault on the unsuspecting poet within a collective Christian frame. The quatrains of Jodelle's sonnet, opening with the "communes douleurs" that make the reader's identification of the source poem inevitable and immediate, paraphrase the Italian poem in the third person while affording its explication in the insistence on the common experience, both of the universal grief appropriate to Good Friday—for "tous coeurs chrétiens"—and of vulnerability to Love's ruses, that "dépourvus nous surprennent."

Aux communes douleurs qui poindre en ce jour viennent
Tous coeurs chrétiens, Pétrarque alla chanter qu'il prit
De ses douleurs la source, et par là nous apprit
Que les ruses d'Amour dépourvus nous surprennent.
En ces jours où les cieux, la mort, les pleurs retiennent
Nos coeurs ardents, quel lieu reste au feu qui l'éprit?
Il ne se gardait pas du lacs qui le surprit
Non plus que moi des rets qui plus fort me reprennent.

In the communal sorrows that pierce all Christian hearts on that day, Petrarch was to sing that he took the source of his own sorrows, and by that he taught us that the ruses of Love take us by surprise. On such days when the heavens, death, and tears occupy our ardent hearts, what place is left for the fire that took him? He was not on guard against the snare that surprised him, no more than I was against the snares that hold me stronger still.

The last of these verses effectively identifies the poet's experience with that of Petrarch within this common vulnerability, but only to set up a contrast that will at last imply that Jodelle's suffering in love transcends even that of its famous exemplar:

Bien qu'Amour sache assez qu'il est en moi trop fort,
Pour croître du tourment, non du désir, l'effort,
Il arme la peur froide, et l'aigre défiance.

Although Love knows full well that he is too strong within me, it is to heighten the force of the torment, not of desire, that he arms my cold fear and my sharp mistrust.

The concluding tercet then justifies the insertion of the Petrarchan episode in his own "story," in that it serves to render, in highly dramatic terms, not the innamoramento but the fear of losing a love already known:

Pétrarque à l'heur eût pu perdre sans grand'douleur
L'heur inconnu; ma perte aurait, las! ce malheur
D'avoir de l'heur perdu si haute connaissance.[63]

Petrarch could have lost the happiness he had never known without great pain; my loss, alas! would have the misfortune of knowing the lost happiness so very well.

Jodelle's evocative retelling of a well-known Petrarchan scene reminds us that from its earliest circulation, and despite the fact that it was not always circulated or, eventually, published in the same form, Petrarch's collection of *rime sparse* was associated with a story. In fact, the history of the early reception of the collection is bound up with story-making. Biographical annotations proliferated in the editions circulating widely in Italy and Europe;[64] Petrarch's Italian commentators, well known to Ronsard, contributed substantially to a reading of the collection in which Petrarch as protagonist of an exemplary love story took priority over considerations of form and style.[65] Vellutello's extremely influential commentary in fact intervenes in the sequence as Petrarch determined it, reordering the poems to project a unified narrative corresponding to events in Petrarch's life.[66] The popular 1528 edition of the *Rime* contained not only the commentary by Vellutello and, like most other editions, a *vita* of Petrarch, but also a half dozen pages entitled "Origine di Madonna Laura con la descrittione di Valclusa e del luogo ove il poeta a principio di lei s'innamorò" [The origins of my lady Laura with the description of Vaucluse and of the place where the poet first fell in love with her], along with a map of the Vaucluse.[67]

The story, of course, is in one sense illusory, in the very form of the lyric collection: it is belied first by the designation of the poems as "scattered rhymes" in the first verse of the proemial sonnet, and then by the formally independent status of the lyrics themselves.[68] But the poems read in sequence nonetheless induce in the reader a presumption of story. Since the appearance of Pierre de Nolhac's 1886 edition based on the partially autograph manuscript containing the poet's last revisions, readers have probed the rich variety of ways in which the individual poems are organized into the sequence.[69] But during the intervening centuries too, Petrarch's poems "read together" provoked and teased his readers toward that presumption of story, one that received a justification from Bembo well over a century after Petrarch's death. Bembo's emphasis was critical in defining a mode of lyric *imitatio* that would be vastly influential throughout the sixteenth century: it insisted on the form of the vernacular *canzoniere* as testimony to the poet's *vicenda sentimentale*, which is in turn the text's fictional substratum, its structural justification.[70]

The result was readily exported to France. Petrarch's vernacular lyrics had been accessible to the cultivated public in manuscript form in the preceding century, but from the early years of the sixteenth century the large numbers of printed editions of the *Rime* contributed substantially to the dissemination of the canzoniere as lyric model.[71] In 1552–53, Luigi Alamanni published his own collection of love poems commemorating a "destin amoureux" enacted near Avignon and Vaucluse. With these *Opere Toscane* written in Tuscan and published in Lyon, observes Olivier Millet, Alamanni already effects a symbolic implanting of a poetic culture, based on the Petrarch of the *Rime*, that united Italy and France.[72] His dedication of the poems to the glory of a receptive François I both responded and contributed to a "royal culture" in which François I took an interest that was not only direct but active.[73] The presumed discovery of Laura's burial site by Scève in 1533 in a church in Avignon generated sufficient interest that the king, passing through the city, arranged a visit to the tomb, where he was reported to have immediately composed an epitaph for Laura.[74]

Some fifteen years later, Vasquin Philieul published a translation of Petrarch's poems "in vita di Madonna Laura" under the title of *Laure d'Avignon*.[75] The collection, the only integral French translation undertaken in the sixteenth century, was not only immensely influential in its experimentation with the sonnet form;[76] it also affords telling evidence of the particularized reception of the *Rime* as "story." Philieul based his translation on Vellutello's edition and ordering, and like Vellutello, he accompanied the poems with frequent and occasionally detailed commentary, appearing now as brief prose passages or "arguments" preceding the translated texts. And those passages, taken together, represent the Petrarchan collection as a story of which each poem is to be read as an episode. Philieul frequently offers a precise place and circumstance to account for the composition in question. The explanation that prefaces the translation of *Rime* 108, "Aventuroso più d'altro terreno" [Luckier than any other ground] is suggestive of the degree of his imaginative involvement: "Estant Petrarque ainsi solitaire à Vaucluse, fut visité d'une compagnie d'Avignon, qui estoit allée veoir la fontaine de la Sorgue, et en icelle compagnie estoit madame Laure. Or ne fault dire si l'on y fit grand chere. Icy Petrarque escript à son amy Senuce, benissans le lieu, qui avait eu la grace que sa dame y fust" [Thus Petrarch, when alone in Vaucluse, received the visit of a group from Avignon who had gone to see the fountain of the Sorgue, and among them was madame Laura. It hardly needs be said that there was a warm welcome. Here Petrarch wrote to his friend Sennuccio, blessing the place that had been graced with his lady's presence].[77]

Ronsard was not the first among Petrarch's French successors to demonstrate a keen awareness not only of the Italian poet's status as master of the individual lyric but of his status as protagonist in a "story" as well. Marot had published, in 1539, a translation of *Six sonnets de Pétrarque*, sonnets which, Jean Balsamo observes, were of seminal importance particularly in their attestation to the structure of Petrarch's collection as a whole.[78] But Marot did not appear eager to exploit the potential of his innovative gesture,[79] and Scève, whose name was repeatedly associated with Petrarch's following the presumed discovery of Laura's tomb,[80] chose for his own lyric collection a form foreign to the Italian: the *dizain* whose very grammar and syntax, as Rigolot observes, appear to block the perception of a narrative continuity to which the *Rime* invites the reader.[81] But the *Délie* is a substantial collection, and it acquires its coherence as recueil in large part from what Doranne Fenoaltea terms the "narrative pre-text," a love story never narrated but accessible to the reader—indeed, formulated by the reader—through logical and pragmatic presupposition. And the reader familiar with the rhetoric of Petrarchan poetry will recognize in the first verse of the first poem of the *Délie*, in the evocation of the poet's "ieunes erreurs" corresponding to the "primo giovenile errore" of *Rime* 1, the particular type of love story to be expected.[82]

In fact, Scève's strategy of situating himself in relation to the poet's story in the *Rime sparse* is called explicitly to the reader's attention in several references in the *Délie* to Petrarch and his Laura/laurel. These may establish contrast: *D* 388 invokes both the impotence of reason to resist Love's assault in the staging of the innamoramento (*R* 2) and Petrarch's account of his frustrated pursuit leading only to "[il] lauro onde si coglie / acerbo frutto" [the laurel, whence one gathers bitter fruit] (*R* 6) to convey the contrast between Petrarch's recall of youthful vulnerability and his own more advanced age:

> Donc ce Thuscan pour vaine vtilité
> Trouue le goust de son Laurier amer:
> Car de ieunesse il aprint a l'aymer.
> Et en Automne Amour, ce Dieu volage,
> Quand me voulois de la raison armer,
> A preualu contre sens, & contre aage.[83]

> Thus it is in vain that this Tuscan finds the taste of his Laurel bitter: for he learned in his youth to love it. And in Autumn Love, that inconstant god, when I sought to arm myself with reason, prevailed against sense and against age.

Other poems too, alluding to Apollo's pursuit and ultimate celebration of an unyielding Daphne, evoke Petrarch's adaptation of the myth of the laurel to his own poet's story.[84] In the last of these, the well-known poem in which he entitles Petrarch the "Thuscan Apollo," he addresses the Rhone that flows through "mainte riue amoureuse,"

> Baingnant les piedz de celle terre heureuse,
> Ou ce Thuscan Apollo sa ieunesse
> Si bien forma, qu'a iamais sa vieillesse
> Verdoyera a toute eternité; (*D* 417)

> Bathing the feet of that happy land, where that Tuscan Apollo formed his youth so well that his old age will be verdant through all eternity;

and now, to the story of this poet who had won his own poetic immortality, is added that of Maurice Scève,

> . . . ou Amour ma premiere liesse
> A desrobée a immortalité.

> . . . there where Love stole away my first happiness from immortality.

Scève's dizain, as has been often noted, is a rewriting of *R* 208, playing, like the Italian original, on the name of the river Rhone: "rapido fiume ... rodendo intorno (onde 'l tuo nome prendi)" [swift river ... gnawing a way for yourself (whence you take your name)], "fleuue rongeant pour t'attiltrer le nom / De la roideur ... " [river gnawing away to gain yourself the name of rapidity].[85] But with the introduction of his own lyric persona, of course, we read as well the desire to replace Petrarch's love poetry with his own.[86]

For Du Bellay, the poetic lineage here suggested opened further possibilities for succession. His praise of Scève, as Jerry Nash points out, is frequently related, through the symbolism of the Rhone and its confluence with the Saône, to his praise of Petrarch and is central to his own claim to poetic immortality:

> L'Arne superbe adore sur sa rive
> Du sainct Laurier la branche tousjours vive,
> Et ta Delie enfle ta Saone lente.
> Mon Loire aussi, demydieu par mes vers,
> Bruslé d'amour etent les braz ouvers
> Au tige heureux, qu'à ses rives je plante. (*O* 105, 9–14)[87]

> The proud Arno adores on its bank the ever green branch of the sacred Laurel, and your slow-running Saone nurtures your Delie. My Loire too, demigod through my verses, scalded by love extends its open arms to the favored sapling that I plant on its banks.

Du Bellay, who assured his place in literary history with the doctrine of imitation published in the *Deffence* of 1549, avowed in that same year, in the first preface to the *Olive*, his own imitation of Italian poets, Petrarch first among them: "Vrayment je confesse avoir imité Petrarque" [In truth I confess having imitated Petrarch].[88] But Du Bellay in practice goes beyond his own ambitious theory, for with regard to the *Olive* the phrase "to imitate Petrarch" does not render adequately the relation between the new poet and the old. In a poem (*O* 84) otherwise inspired by another source (Sannazaro's *Arcadia*), the initial verse "Seul et pensif par la deserte plaine," translated from the opening of *R* 132, assumes the function of an exordium which, as Caldarini points out, proposes a type of assimilation of the poet to Petrarch.[89] Here the experience of the poet of the *Rime sparse* is no longer evoked as that of another; instead, the third-person allusion and the first-person speaker's voice are collapsed into one.

Du Bellay's ambition is, of course, to *equal* Petrarch: Olive against Laura, olive against laurel, explicit in the opening sonnet as the poet addresses the garland of olive branches from which the collection draws its title: "Orne mon chef, donne moy hardiesse / De te chanter, qui espere te rendre / Egal un jour au Laurier immortel" [Bedeck my head, give me the boldness to sing of you, hoping to render you one day equal to the immortal Laurel].[90] Some years later, that ambition was to be mocked by Du Bellay himself, in a poem addressed to a lady with all the beauty of Laura:

> Pourquoy de moy a vous donc souhaitté
> D'estre sacree à l'immortalité,
> Si vostre nom d'un seul Petrarque est digne?
> Je ne sçay par d'où vient ce desir là,
> Fors qu'il vous plaist nous monstrer par cela
> Que d'un Corbeau vous pouvez faire un Cygne.[91]

> Why have you then hoped to be consecrated to immortality by me, when your name is worthy of Petrarch alone? I know not what prompts that desire, unless it pleases you to show us thereby that you can make a Swan of a Crow.

But in the unbounded optimism of the poetic climate of 1549–50, Du Bellay's advertisement of his imitative strategy is suggestive, and so is Ronsard's recorded response, for it is in these terms that Ronsard promptly sends Du Bellay his encouragement:

> Si tu montres au jour tes vers
> Entés dans le tronc d'une olive,
> Qui hausse sa perruque vive
> Jusque à l'egal des lauriers vers. (*L* II, p. 39)

> If you one day show your verses grafted in the trunk of an olive tree, that raises its living leafy crown as high as the laurel verses.

It is not surprising, then, that it was by invoking not the style but the "story" of the *Rime sparse* that a supportive Ronsard had responded to his friend's professed ambition before the publication of the *Olive*, to predict for that recueil the glory of the canzoniere written for Laura:

> Une Laure plus heureuse
> Te soit un nouveau souci,
> Et que ta plume amoureuse
> Engrave à son tour aussi
> Des contens l'heur & le bien,
> A celle fin que nostre siecle encore
> Comme le vieil, en te lisant t'honore,
> Pour gaster l'encre si bien.

that a happier Laura be your new concern, and that your amorous pen engrave too in turn the happiness and good fortune of its contentment, to the end that our century again, like the former, honor you in reading you for having expended your ink so well.

And here Ronsard characterizes that relation in a way that foreshadows his own strategy of assimilation, as he praises the Du Bellay who shows him some verses as having "l'âme de Pétrarque":

> . . . son livre antiq' tu ne leus onques,
> Et tu écris ainsi comme lui, donques
> Le méme esprit est en toi. (L II, pp. 65–66)

. . . you never read his ancient book, and you write thus like him, therefore the same spirit is in you.

It would be difficult to overestimate the importance of this declaration. This is not a rhetoric of imitation; it is the opposite, a denial of imitation, in that it is ostensibly prompted by Du Bellay's *not* having read Petrarch—although Du Bellay, as we have seen, belies that suggestion in his 1549 preface to the *Olive*. We might even call it instead a rhetoric of reincarnation, the same rhetoric that Du Bellay himself employs in the negative sense when he evokes the Homer who had immortalized the Greek heroes:

> Puis que les cieux m'avoient predestiné
> A vous aymer, digne object de celuy
> Par qui Achille est encor' aujourdjuy
> Contre les Grecz pour s'amye obstiné,
> Pourquoy aussi n'avoient-ilz ordonné
> Renaitre en moy l'ame et l'esprit de luy? (O 20, 1–6)

Since the heavens had predestined me to love you, object worthy of him through whom Achilles is still relentless against the Greeks today for his beloved, why did they not also ordain his soul and his spirit reborn in me?

Here Du Bellay's theoretical meditation in the *Deffence* is suggestive in a rather unusual way. In a famous passage, the young poet explains the success of the revered Latin masters:

> Immitant les meilleurs aucteurs Grecz, se transformant en eux, les devorant, & apres les avoir bien digerez, les convertissant en sang & nouriture, se proposant, chacun selon son naturel & l'argument qu'il vouloit elire, le meilleur aucteur, dont ils observoint diligemment toutes les plus rares & exquises vertuz . . .

Imitating the best Greek authors, transforming themselves into the
Greeks, devouring them, and after having well digested them, con-
verting them into blood and nourishment, they proposed the best
author as a pattern, each according to his natural bent and the argu-
ment he wished to elect; they diligently observed all of the rarest
and most exquisite virtues of the model author . . .[92]

Metaphors for the process of imitation abounded in the Renaissance;
Petrarch himself had advanced one that, drawn from Seneca, was to have
a long posterity, likening the poet to the bee that makes sweet new honey
from many flowers.[93] Du Bellay's metaphor of innutrition in this passage
is more carnal, more violent, than many others representing the process in
similar ways: the devouring of the target author and that author's conver-
sion through the digestive process into the very substance, the very blood
and nourishment, to feed the hunger of the aspiring new author. But the
essential paradox of his recommendation lies in its opening, not with the
process of innutrition, but with its contrary: that of the new author trans-
forming himself into the model author.[94] As Thomas Greene comments,
this figurative account is something of an offense to logic: "The imitator
simultaneously and paradoxically becomes his model and makes the
model part of himself by innutrition"; in contrast, in Ronsard's own writ-
ing about poetry, the apian metaphor is present but reduces or suppresses
the element of transformation, and the innutrition metaphor is absent.[95]
But the transformation of the self into the other remains, and it is highly
suggestive for a poet who aspired to be known as a "new"—a French—
Petrarch.

The suggestion of reincarnation in Du Bellay's rhetorical posturing in
O 20 goes beyond his source from the Giolito anthology readily identified
through other elements of the poem.[96] It also goes well beyond the figura-
tion of the poet—Scève, Du Bellay, Petrarch, or another—who self-con-
sciously poses with lyre or lute or has himself portrayed as crowned with
laurel, as Ronsard is portrayed in the frontispiece of the *Amours*. The con-
ventional nature of their postures was fully apparent; they were adopting
a common literary role. Etienne Pasquier wrote in 1555, in response to the
question of the "sincerity" of the love experience apparently common to
Petrarch and so many of his imitators: "Ainsi ne fault-il trouver trop es-
trange, si accommodans leurs escrits au subject qui semble estre du tout
voüé à la jeunesse (en laquelle à present ils vivent) ils se sont proposez
faire les passionez dans leurs oeuvres pour servir d'un bon miroüer à tout
le monde?" [Thus must we find it terribly strange, if in adjusting their
writing to the subject that seems wholly devoted to the time of youth (in

which they are at present living) they have proposed to play the enam-
ored in their works to serve as an accurate mirror of all around them?]
Many years later, Ronsard would invoke this same commonsense prin-
ciple in his own defense, going on to mock his accusers with the accusa-
tion of a naive reading:

> Je suis fol, Predicant, quand j'ay la plume en main,
> Mais quand je n'escri plus, j'a le cerveau bien sain . . .
>   Tu sembles aux enfans qui contemplent es nues
> Des rochers, des Geans, des Chimeres cornues,
> Et ont de tel object le cerveau tant esmeu,
> Qu'ils pensent estre vray l'ondoyant qu'ils ont veu,
> Ainsi tu penses vrais les vers dont je me joüe.[97]

> I am quite mad, Preacher, when I have my pen in hand, but when I
> stop writing, my brain is quite healthy . . . You are like the children
> who see in the clouds rocks, Giants, horned Chimera, and have their
> brains so moved by such objects that they think the shifting shape
> they have seen to be true; in the same way you think true the verses
> with which I play.

But Ronsard had attracted the criticisms addressed to him in part because
of the manner of his own response to Petrarch, a response that fully ex-
ploited the recognition that the poetic voice of the lyric collection, speak-
ing in the first person to tell his own story, was a poetic persona with a
particular story to tell—a realization with far-reaching consequences for
his own lyric collections. Much recent reexploration of Renaissance writ-
ing has demonstrated that, as the editor of a recent volume concludes, "it
is in and through fiction(s) that the most adventurous (and sometimes
precarious) conceptualizations of the self appear,"[98] and the fiction-
making that Ronsard found in the lyric collection of *Rime sparse* took a
characteristically idiosyncratic turn, with far-reaching consequences, in
the development of his own poetic "self."

2

"M'approprier quelque louange"
Les Amours, 1552–1553

Ronsard's first collection of his *Amours* opens with an invitation, albeit an indirect one:

Qui voudra voyr comme un Dieu me surmonte,
    Comme il m'assault, comme il se fait vainqueur,
    Comme il r'enflamme, & r'englace mon cuoeur,
    Comme il reçoit un honneur de ma honte,
Qui voudra voir une jeunesse prompte
    A suyvre en vain l'object de son malheur,
    Me vienne voir: il voirra ma douleur,
    Et la rigueur de l'Archer qui me donte.
Il cognoistra combien la raison peult
    Contre son arc, quand une foys il veult
    Que nostre cuoeur son esclave demeure:
Et si voirra que je suis trop heureux,
    D'avoir au flanc l'aiguillon amoureux,
    Plein du venin dont il fault que je meure.

He who would see how a God masters me, how he assaults me, how he gains victory, how he inflames and then freezes my heart, how he acquires an honor from my shame—he who would see a youth quick to follow in vain the object of its misfortune, let him come to see me: he will see my pain, and the rigor of the Archer who overcomes me. He will know how much reason can do against that bow, when the archer is determined that our heart remain his slave: and he will see too that I am only too happy to have the amorous dart in my side, full of the poison of which I must die.

"Qui voudra voyr . . . ": both this opening formula and the rhetorical strategy of the poem as a whole, as has often been noted, are drawn from Petrarch; by general consensus, their model is sonnet 248, "Chi vuol veder," of the *Rime sparse*. *R* 248 was among the best-known sonnets of the Italian collection, one of the first six translated into French by Clément Marot; it had been the object of particular attention by both Scève and Du Bellay.[1] The placement of this recall at the outset of his first lyric collection is carefully calculated by Ronsard, and it is far more than a signal that, in the poems to follow, the practice of imitation—much in the air in 1552—is in evidence. With this opening, the invitation to the poem's inscribed *destinataire* is doubled by an invitation to the reader; as Gisèle Mathieu-Castellani observes, "On pourrait lire dans ce discours un autre discours en creux: 'Qui voudra voir comme je m'approprie la parole pétrarquienne vienne voir mes Amours.'"[2]

This invitation resonates with Ronsard's explicit self-explanation in his earlier "Au Lecteur" (*L* I, p. 43), where he had affirmed his study of "bonnes lettres" in terms of his desire to "m'approprier quelque louange, encores non connue, ni atrapée par mes devanciers, & ne voiant en nos Poëtes François, chose qui fust suffisante d'imiter: j'allai voir les étrangers" [appropriate for myself some praise, not yet known nor captured by my precursors, and not seeing in our French Poets anything that was worthy of imitation, I turned to foreigners]. Now, in the unlikely event that his reader might not recognize the foreign source to which the opening poem alludes, more explicit signals will follow, and soon. In a poem whose thematic importance was noted in the preceding chapter, he alludes to "a single Tuscan" worthy to sing his lady's praises (*A* 8, 5–8). Later, as we have seen, in the association of Cassandre with Laura in "Que n'ay-je, Dame, & la plume & la grace" (*A* 73) he proclaims that had he only the ability to celebrate her as he would wish, the couple Cassandre-Ronsard, beloved and poet, would be equal to that of Laura-Petrarch. And later still, in a return to the motif of the dance of the Muses and the feet of Pegasus to which he had alluded in the liminal "Voeu," he denies that it was from them, from Parnassus, that he drew his inspiration.[3] "Et si ma lyre, ou si ma rime agrée," he tells Cassandre, "Ton oeil en soit, non Parnase, estimé" [if my lyre, or my rhyme be found pleasing, it is your eye, not Parnassus, that is to be esteemed] and he continues:

Certes le ciel te debvoit à la France,
Quand le Thuscan, & Sorgue, & sa Florence,
Et son Laurier engrava dans les cieux. (*A* 170, 9–11)[4]

Certainly heaven owed you to France, when the Tuscan engraved
Sorgue and Florence and his Laurel in the heavens.

The reader who examines Ronsard's opening sonnet more closely,
however, soon finds that the nature of the appropriation here suggested
will not take the form of similarity but that of difference; for while
Petrarch's poem urges the reader to witness the unique qualities of the
beloved lady—an invitation frequently imitated by Italian Petrarchists as
well as by Scève and by Du Bellay—Ronsard's sonnet calls attention not
to the lady but to the speaker of the poem himself.[5] The lady, in fact, is
absent from the poem except as presumption, and the space left vacant by
her absence is filled by the poet-lover. His appropriation of the space re-
served for the object of the invited spectator's gaze is established through
the proliferation of first-person object pronouns that accompany the first-
person possessives throughout the quatrains: the spectator will observe
"comme un Dieu me surmonte, / comme il m'assault . . . / . . . mon cuoeur,
. . . ma honte, / . . . Me vienne voir: il voirra ma douleur . . . / l'Archer qui
me donte." It is only in the final tercet that the speaker as object gives way
to the speaker as subject, although one still subordinated to the
spectator's gaze: "Et si voirra que je suis trop heureux . . . Plein du venin
dont il fault que je meure."

The invitation to the reader adapted by Ronsard from *Rime* 248 was to
serve similarly as introduction for several later French collections.[6] Yet the
Petrarchan recall in "Qui voudra voyr" is more complex, for at the same
time that Ronsard's opening poem flagrantly deflects the comparison
with *Rime* 248 suggested by its rhetorical matrix, its emphasis on the pro-
tagonist as object of the addressee's attention relates it to a second Petrar-
chan model, one that is particularly significant because it is the poem
chosen by Petrarch to open his own lyric collection:

Voi ch'ascoltate in rime sparse il suono
di quei sospiri ond'io nudriva 'l core
in sul mio primo giovenile errore,
quand'era in parte altr'uom da quel ch'i'sono:
del vario stile in ch'io piango et ragiono
fra le vane speranze e 'l van dolore,
ove sia chi per prova intenda amore
spero trovar pietà, non che perdono.
Ma ben veggio or sì come al popol tutto
favola fui gran tempo, onde sovente
di me medesmo meco mi vergogno;
et del mio vaneggiar vergogna è 'l frutto,

e 'l pentirsi, e 'l conoscer chiaramente
che quanto piace al mondo è breve sogno.

You who hear in scattered rhymes the sound of those sighs with
which I nourished my heart during my first youthful error, when I
was in part another man from what I am now: for the varied style in
which I weep and speak between vain hopes and vain sorrow,
where there is anyone who understands love through experience, I
hope to find pity, not only pardon. But now I see well how for a long
time I was the talk of the crowd, for which often I am ashamed of
myself within; and of my raving, shame is the fruit, and repentance,
and the clear knowledge that whatever pleases in the world is a brief
dream.

Petrarch's opening, like Ronsard's, is an invitation, here direct—"you,"
not "anyone who"; "voi," not "qui"—and this poem, like Ronsard's, in-
vites an inscribed audience to attend to the suffering of the poet as lover.
Here too the personal pronouns are insistent, culminating in the rein-
forced alliterative stress of the often-cited "di me medesmo meco mi
vergogno." As this verse suggests, however, Petrarch's concentration of
first-person markers establishes in the progression of the poem an inti-
mate meditation on human experience, in keeping with his invitation to
his addressee to listen to the sound of his sighs, "il suono / di quei sospiri
ond'io nudriva 'l core."

Proemial poems reproducing the schema of *Rime* 1 or containing a va-
riety of other obvious resonances were very frequent in Italian Petrarchist
collections.[7] The proemial sonnet on the Petrarchan model imposed itself
as a decisive moment of the canzoniere in which the poet not only pre-
sents the work to follow but offers the reader the warrant that that work,
though composed of multiple lyrics, is not a miscellaneous collection.[8] In
France, the major recueils of love poetry in the sixteenth century all re-
spond to Petrarch's preoccupation with the poet's inner experience.[9]
Marot's translation of *Rime* 1 already underlines the nature of the appro-
priation in setting aside the reference to the poet's "rime sparse" in favor
of "mes rymes," usurping the ownership of all that follows.[10] And in this
sense Ronsard's sonnet at once defines his own stance, his own claiming
of the status of poetic subject, in the striking nature of its contrast to the
posture assumed by the speaker: the opening of "Qui voudra voir," Marc
Bensimon comments, is "d'abord et surtout invitation à un spectacle: ce
n'est pas un hasard si Ronsard utilise trois fois le verbe *voir* dans ces
quatre vers: alors que dans toute son oeuvre le verbe *entendre* ne revient
que 236 fois, *voir* s'y rencontre près de trois mille!"[11]

Significantly, the single use of the verb *vedere* in Petrarch's poem indicates not literal sight but insight, not spectacle but self-recognition—"ben veggio or sì come al popol tutto / favola fui gran tempo . . ."—and the poem turns inward upon his own meditation on the experience. Ronsard's lyric protagonist too proposes his suffering as Love's victim as exemplary—the observer "cognoistra combien la raison peult / Contre son arc, quand une foys il veult / Que nostre cuoeur son esclave demeure"— but there is none of the "vergogna" to which Petrarch's speaker confesses and none of the ambivalence introduced by the Italian poet's location of the experience in terms of his own affective development, "in sul mio primo giovenile errore / quand' era in parte altr'uom da quel ch'i' sono." Ronsard's speaker suggests no change, partial or otherwise; no shame, no regret, no reflection; no hope that his inscribed audience may accord him pity and pardon. On the contrary, his declaration at its end that "je suis trop heureux, / D'avoir au flanc l'aiguillon amoureux," while in itself an extreme expression of that *voluptas dolendi* that frequently characterizes his response to the Petrarchan motif of the tormented lover,[12] concludes in the exhibitionist mode that marks the poem as a whole.[13]

That the intertextual triangle relating Ronsard's poem to *R* 1 and *R* 248 is drawn along such lines of tension and opposition would seem to establish at the outset of the *Amours* that it is contrast, not likeness, that is offered up emphatically, even aggressively, for the attention of the reader.[14] The reader will find nonetheless that those lines may be repeatedly redrawn and the relation repeatedly reconfigured. The thematic concerns of both "Voi che ascoltate" and "Chi vuol veder" that are suppressed in Ronsard's opening sonnet emerge later in the collection in a poem that not only offers insistent resonances with *A* 1 but duplicates both its opening formula and its rhetorical structure:

Qui vouldra voyr dedans une jeunesse,
    La beaulté jointe avec la chasteté,
    L'humble doulceur, la grave magesté,
    Toutes vertus, & toute gentillesse:
Qui vouldra voyr les yeulx d'une deesse,
    Et de noz ans la seule nouveauté,
    De ceste Dame oeillade la beaulté,
    Que le vulgaire appelle ma maistresse.
Il apprendra comme Amour rid & mord,
    Comme il guarit, comme il donne la mort,
    Puis il dira voyant chose si belle:
Heureux vrayment, heureux qui peult avoyr

Heureusement cest heur que de la voyr,
Et plus heureux qui meurt pour l'amour d'elle. (*A* 64)

He who would see beauty conjoined with chastity in a youthful age, the humble sweetness, the grave majesty, all virtues, and all courteousness: he who would see the eyes of a goddess, and the unique novelty of our time, let him cast his eyes on the beauty of this Lady, whom the vulgar call my mistress. He will learn how Love laughs and bites, how he heals, how he gives death; then he will say before such a lovely thing: Truly happy, happy he who can happily have this happiness to see her, and more happy still he who dies for love of her.

What are we to make of this new poem, whose "ton inaugural" seems to announce a new beginning? Are we to conclude, retrospectively, that the beginning of the collection is thus "un faux début, redoublé et annulé par ce redoublement après qu'on ait [*sic*] lu plus du quart des poèmes"?[15] In fact, the interplay of the Petrarchan subtexts in both *A* 1 and *A* 64 allows us to assess differently the relationship between the two poems. Now, to Petrarch's opening "Chi vuol veder quantunque può Natura / e 'l ciel tra noi, venga a mirar costei," Ronsard responds, "Qui vouldra voir dedans une jeunesse / La beauté jointe avec la chasteté … ," echoing the celebration of beauty conjoined with chastity—"come è giunta onestà con leggiadria" [how chastity is joined with gaity]—of *R* 261, and the poem continues as a concatenation of echoes of Petrarchan formulations. Its first tercet, "Il apprendra comme Amour … guerit, comme il donne la mort," adapts *R* 159, "non sa come Amor sana e come ancide / chi non sa come dolce ella sospira … " [he does not know how Love heals and how he kills who does not know how sweetly she sighs …]. And from *R* 261 Ronsard adapts yet another invitation to observe the unique lady. Petrarch writes:

Qual donna attende a gloriosa fama
di senno, di valor, di cortesia,
miri fiso nelli occhi a quella mia
nemica che mia donna il mondo chiama. (*R* 261, 1–4)

Whatever lady hopes to have glorious fame for wisdom, virtue, courtesy, let her look fixedly into the eyes of that enemy of mine, whom the world calls my lady.

And as his editors regularly observe, Ronsard follows: "De ceste Dame oeillade la beaulté, / Que le vulgaire appelle ma maistresse."
In this last echo the relation between the two texts is particularly inter-

esting, not least because Ronsard's sonnet accords the public denomina-
tion of the lady—"ma maitresse"—a strong pivotal position by placing it
at the close of the first movement, at the midpoint of the poem.[16] In
Petrarch's sonnet, the imitated verse occurs at the end of the first quatrain
and is followed by a crescendo of praises of the lady—exemplar of honor
and of "qual è diritta via / di gir al Ciel, che lei aspetta et brama" [what is
the straight way to go to Heaven, which awaits and desires her] (7–8)—
which condition the reception of the single mention of her beauty in the
poem, the "infinita bellezza ch'altrui abbaglia" [infinite beauty that
dazzles us] of its closing. Petrarch's identification of the lady as she "che
mia donna il mondo chiama," moreover, is introduced by the stress of the
enjambment on "nemica" in the opening of the verse and suggests that
the two terms are to be read in a relation of opposition; it contrasts Laura's
resolute resistance to the poet's suit, a resistance lamented in other poems
and one that exemplifies the virtues celebrated in this poem, with the
ironic sense of the public awareness of the love he has so openly professed
in his verse. Ronsard's poem, while it explicitly refers to the lady's
"chasteté" conjoined with her beauty, nonetheless eliminates this tension:
the terms now juxtaposed, "Dame" and "maitresse," invert the relation
between public designation and private relation in a way suggestive, not
of distance, but of intimacy.

   A 64 is not, of course, unique in the collection in its juxtaposition and
blending of elements of multiple Petrarchan sources. It merits special at-
tention with regard to the Petrarchan presence in the first collection of the
Amours, however, because it illustrates an imitative strategy that is central
to Ronsard's self-representation as protagonist. In this poem, the mosaic
composed of fragments found in widely scattered poems of the *Rime
sparse* composes a version of the lyric persona's experience, which, rather
than resulting in a dissimulatory dilution of the effect of imitation, con-
centrates the relation between the two texts to a particular end. Character-
izing Cassandre as she "que le vulgaire appelle ma maistresse," Ronsard
not merely imitates Petrarch. He appropriates Petrarch's voice and at the
same time appropriates the "story" of the *Rime* as it were from within.

   We would be mistaken to assume that this appropriation is limited to
poems such as *A* 64 in which Ronsard appears intent upon its immediate
recognition by the reader. Its formative function emerges, on the contrary,
only from a reading of the collection as a whole, just as the "story" of the
Rime sparse emerges only from a sequential reading of the entire sequence.
How might such a story be constructed of a collection of formally inde-
pendent lyrics? Like his Petrarchan precursors and contemporaries,
Ronsard makes use of a substantial repertoire of what may be described

as "situations": the lover, for example, reenacts the plight of the wounded roe-buck or the entrapped bird.[17] Among these, a relatively small number lend themselves to a narrative elaboration or a suggestion of narrative: the lady's greeting withheld or bestowed; the lady before her mirror or her weeping observed; the lover's temporary possession—or his coveting—of an object belonging to her; his professed desire for vengeance occasioned by amorous frustration. It is partly because of their presence that the pieces the reader is invited to fit together implicate not only the individual poem but the collection as a whole.

Particularly striking in this regard is the commentary by Marc-Antoine de Muret, "approved" in that it accompanied the second edition of the *Amours* in 1553.[18] Several commentaries to the *Rime sparse* were well known in France; indeed, it has been noted that the composition of commentary on the *Amours* is the logical consequence of the theoretical choices of the Pléiade: Petrarch having imposed himself as the inevitable model, the imitation of that model "doit être poussée jusqu'à l'imitation de cette exégèse qui est la sanction même, et le signe le plus tangible, de son statut de modèle."[19] In the case of Muret, his preface to the 1553 edition is followed by Jean Dorat's verses acclaiming him as the "digne interprète" who will clarify the profundities of Ronsard's poems, with oracles both "profonds et obscurs."

Not only is Muret, as celebrated humanist, equal to the task; he also enjoys the privileged position of a contemporary who is party to Ronsard's intentions. And indeed, his particular status qualifying him to mediate between poems and readers is suggested not only in his preface and in Dorat's tribute but in the contrast between his image, inserted before the preface, and the portraits of Ronsard and Cassandre that precede the "Privilège" of the edition. "Présent dans l'organisation du recueil," François Rigolot observes, "il connaîtra du dedans le lyrisme de son ami poète; absent du texte des sonnets, il observera du dehors ce qui fait l'essence de leur inspiration poétique."[20] But Muret not only offers the reader the service of his erudition, enabling an understanding of the obscure allusions of the poems; significantly, his commentary not infrequently emphasizes narrative.

A particularly suggestive example is the commentary to *A* 87. Ronsard writes:

Oeil, qui portrait dedans les miens reposes,
    Comme un Soleil, le dieu de ma clarté:
    Ris, qui forçant ma doulce liberté
    Me transformas en cent metamorfoses:

Larme, vrayment qui mes soupirs arroses,
  Quand tu languis de me veoir mal traicté:
  Main, qui mon cuoeur captives arresté
Parmy ton lis, ton ivoyre & tes roses,
Je suis tant vostre, & tant l'affection
  M'a peint au vif vostre perfection,
  Que ny le temps, ny la mort tant soit forte,
Ne fera point qu'au centre de mon sein,
  Tousjours gravéz en l'ame je ne porte
  Un oeil, un ris, une larme, une main.

Eye, remaining portrayed within mine like a Sun, the deity of my illumination: laugh, transforming me in a hundred metamorphoses while forcing my sweet liberty: tear, in truth watering my sighs when you weary of seeing me so badly used: hand, holding my heart captive within your lily, ivory, and roses, I am so much yours, and so much has affection depicted your perfection deep within me, that neither time nor death, however powerful, will ever prevent that I bear, always engraved in my soul, an eye, a laugh, a tear, a hand.

One might, with some of Ronsard's editors (Weber, André Gendre), point out that all four of the aspects of the lady summarized in the final verse of this poem are among those featured in the *blasons* of the female body popular in the period, or cite the motif of the lady's portrait imprinted in the lover's heart from *R* 96: "il bel viso leggiadro che depinto / porto nel petto" [that lovely smiling face, which I carry painted in my breast]. One might also cite this poem as a curiously particularized example of one of the *schémas* that Françoise Joukovsky identifies in the collection, in which, in a variety of ways, "le poète subit les assauts d'une autre réalité."[21] Muret, however, approaches the poem differently; in his explanation Ronsard's juxtaposed images are linked together into a sequence, a linear narrative:

Quelquefois sa Dame luy avoit fait tant de faveur, que de le regarder avec un doux souris, & luy tendre amoureusement la main. Parquoy il print la hardiesse de luy descouvrir une partie des passions qu'il enduroit pour elle: ce qu'il fit avecques tant de grace, qu'elle mesme esmeuë à pitié, se print à larmoyer. Ceste privauté luy donna tant de plaisir, qu'il dit que le temps ne la mort ne sçauroient faire qu'il n'ayt tousjours en memoire l'oeil, le ris, la larme & la main de sa Dame.

Sometimes his Lady did him so much favor as to look upon him with a sweet smile and extend her hand affectionately. Thus he became bold enough to reveal to her a part of the passion that he endured for her: which he did with so much grace that she herself, moved to pity, began to weep. This intimacy gave him so much pleasure that he said that neither time nor death could prevent him from bearing always in memory the eye, the laugh, the tear, and the hand of his Lady][22]

In this passage Muret elaborates expansively on his frequent explanatory formula "il dit que," which appears here only in the closing clause. He constructs the narrative of an episode by introducing elements absent from this sonnet although present in other poems of the collection—the lady extends her hand to the poet, and he was emboldened to speak. Not only does Ronsard's poem, conforming in this to much Petrarchan verse, render the lady as a composite of beautiful parts—an icon—captured in the recapitulative enumeration of the closing verse while Muret gives us the lady in active response, showing affection for the lover and extending her hand "amoureusement."[23] Muret gives us a quite different scenario, in which the lady is indeed moved to pity, to tears, by his declaration of his suffering.

Here we find early evidence that Ronsard's first collection of his *Amours* promoted a reading not entirely dissimilar from the reception of the *Rime sparse*, in which both commentators and readers privileged narrative elements, attempted to identify lyric personae and give shape to "situations" or events, and attempted—or were tempted—to conjoin them into a "story." This is of course not to suggest that the *Amours* have either a "clear narrative structure" or a "coherent progression in a moral or spiritual dimension," both of which Grahame Castor rightly denies them in the attempt to distinguish Ronsard's collection from Petrarch's;[24] it is in fact highly debatable that such are found in the *Rime sparse*. The connection, however, is more direct than may immediately appear. Not only does Ronsard, like Petrarch, claim for his lyric persona the exemplary singularity of one for whom the experience of love transformed a mortal life into a unique destiny.[25] In the working out of that destiny, his response to the *Rime* in the first collection of his *Amours* distinguishes itself at once from that of his contemporaries in its close adherence to those elements of Petrarch's sequence that help to define a story.

Let us begin with a poem that, though highly suggestive for Ronsard's self-representation as lyric protagonist, is not immediately suggestive of his recall of the *Rime*.

Avant le temps tes temples fleuriront,
De peu de jours ta fin sera bornée,
Avant ton soir se clorra ta journée,
Trahis d'espoir tes pensers periront.
Sans me fleschir tes escriptz flétriront,
En ton desastre ira ma destinée,
Ta mort sera pour m'amour terminée,
De tes souspirs tes nepveux si riront.
Tu seras faict d'un vulgaire la fable,
Tu bastiras sur l'incertain du sable,
Et vainement tu peindras dans les cieulx:
Ainsi disoit la Nymphe qui m'affole,
Lors que le ciel pour séeller sa parolle
D'un dextre ésclair fut presage à mes yeulx. (*A* 19)

Before their time your temples will blossom white, your end will be delayed for not too long, your day will come to a close before your evening, betrayed by hope your thoughts will perish. Your writings will fade without bending me, my destiny will be in your disaster, your death will be the result of loving me, and your nephews will laugh at your sighs. You will become the laughingstock of the common people, you will build on the uncertainty of sand, and you will paint in vain in the heavens: thus was speaking the Nymph who drives me mad, when the heavens, to seal her words, showed me the omen of a lightning flash on the right side.

The importance of this poem, which Alfred Glauser terms one of the best "poèmes-symboles" of the recueil, is considerable within the collection as a whole; as Nathalie Dauvois remarks, "Dans cette mise en scène qui ravit exemplairement au poète jusqu'à la parole . . . convergent les contradictions textuelles et métatextuelles du recueil."[26] The sonnet is unique in the 1552–53 *Amours* in its rhetorical structure, a succession of predictions whose origin and addressee are not disclosed until the opening verse of the final tercet. That tercet, recalling to the reader both the identification of the poet's lady with the Trojan Cassandre promoted early in the sequence (*A* 4) and the prophetic gift of that Cassandre to which other poems allude (notably *A* 24 and 33), has led commentators early and late to seek in Ronsard's familiarity with Greek and Roman oracular tradition the key to the poem as a whole.[27] Yet at the poem's end nothing is confirmed: the celestial omen that accompanies the augury is not ratification but *présage*, intensifying with its solemnity the portentious opening onto the future of the poet-lover's relation with Cassandre.

The key to the poem as a whole may be sought instead in Ronsard's reading of the *Rime sparse*, for in the Petrarchan poem in which he found the verse he translated as the opening of *A* 19 he found also an allusion to omens and foretelling:

> Qual destro corvo, o qual manca cornice
> canti 'l mio fato, o qual Parca l'innaspre? (*R* 210, 5–6)

> What crow on the right or raven on the left may sing my fate? or what weird Sister enspool it?

Rigolot, who notes the allusion to the ominous presage in Petrarch's poem, points out that here "le thème . . . retrouve une motivation frappante lorsqu'il est encodé corrélativement avec les prédictions de la vaticinante Troyenne."[28] If, following the prompting of this correlation, we examine Ronsard's poem more closely for Petrarchan resonances, we find that they are abundant. The fate predicted by Cassandre, beginning with the premature graying of the lover, is closely modeled on the vision of his own fate achieved only retrospectively by Petrarch's lyric persona: "Avant le temps tes temples fleuriront" directly renders Petrarch's "del fiorir queste inanzi tempo tempie" [these temples are blossoming white before their time] (*R* 210, 14). The implication of premature aging is intensified by that in verses 2 and 3 of an early death—"De peu de jours," "Avant ton soir"—echoing a recurring motif of the *Rime* as the poet-lover proclaims the effect of his love: "i raggi d'Amor sì caldi sono / che mi fanno anzi tempo venir meno" [the rays of love are so hot that they kill me before my time] (*R* 37, 84–85).[29] The prediction that "trahis d'espoir tes pensers periront" echoes another motif omnipresent in the *Rime*, one introduced in the proemial sonnet as Petrarch proposes to his reader his "rime sparse" composed "fra le vane speranze e 'l van dolore," and repeated at frequent intervals, of which "più veggio il tempo andar veloce e leve / e 'l mio di lui sperar fallace e scemo" [the more I see that Time runs swift and light and that my hope of him is fallacious and empty] (*R* 32, 3–4) is but one example. The echoes are clearer still when this poem is read against the revised 1584 version of Ronsard's opening sonnet cited above, which effectively intensifies the thematic concentration on the love experience as a *déception amoureuse*.[30]

Now consider Cassandre's prediction that Ronsard's outpouring of verses will not succeed in overcoming her resistance: "Sans me fleschir tes escriptz flétriront." Petrarch's poet is explicit in his fantasy that his verses might move Laura:

Io canterei d'Amor sì novamente,
ch'al duro fianco il dì mille sospiri
trarrei per forza, e mille altri desiri
raccenderei ne la gelata mente . . . (*R* 131, 1–4)

I would sing of love in so rare a way that from her cruel side I would draw by force a thousand sighs in a day, and a thousand high desires I would kindle in her frozen mind.

In another poem, his sighs are dispatched as envoys—"Ite, caldi sospiri, al freddo core, / rompete il ghiaccio che pietà contende . . . " [Go, hot sighs, to her cold heart, break the ice that fights against pity . . .] (*R* 153, 1–2)— and late in the poems *in vita* he exclaims: "Temprar potess'io in sì soavi note / i miei sospiri ch'addolcissen Laura," dedicating them to "umiliar quell'alma" [Could I but tune in such sweet notes my sighs that they would sweeten the breeze . . . to humble that soul] (*R* 239, 7–8, 13–15). But all, of course, is in vain, and the failure of these attempts condemns him to the same fate that Cassandre predicts for Ronsard.

We have not yet exhausted the threads in Cassandre's augury that weave the poet's story into that of the protagonist of the *Rime sparse*. Petrarch's poet-lover had foreseen his own ridicule: "I' sarei udito / e mostratone a dito" [I would be heard of and pointed out for it] (*R* 105, 83– 84); Ronsard's poet's sighs, instead of achieving their private objective of winning Cassandre, will merely expose him to public ridicule: "De tes soupirs," she proclaims, "tes nepveux se riront." The following verse, Cassandre's prediction that "Tu seras faict d'un vulgaire la fable," con- firms the relation between the two texts. This verse has been read as an expression of Ronsard's pessimism concerning the fate of his own po- etry,[31] a pessimism apparently confirmed in the verses that follow: "tu bastiras sur l'incertain du sable, / Et vainement tu peindras dans les cieulx."[32] The augury itself, however, is Ronsard's transposition of the confession of the speaker of *R* 1 concerning his own amorous adventure, that "al popol tutto / favola fui gran tempo"; he will later confirm its accuracy in similar terms, as he addresses a Cassandre "chaste prophete":

D'un abusé je ne seroy la fable,
    Fable future au peuple survivant,
    Si ma raison alloyt bien ensuyvant
L'arrest fatal de ta voix veritable. (*A* 33, 1–4)

I would not be voiced about as an example of one deceived, a future laughingstock to those who remain, if my reason were to follow well the fatal sentence of your truth-speaking voice.

With this dark vision of his fate attributed to Cassandre, Ronsard constructs early in the 1552–53 collection a prospective view that promotes the assimilation of his protagonist's experience to that of the poet-lover of the *Rime sparse*. For a retrospective view, consider the version of his youthful experience in a poem added in 1553:

> Depuis le jour que mal sain je soupire,
>   L'an dedans soi s'est roüé par set fois.
>   (Sous astre tel je pris l'hain) toutefois
>   Plus qu'au premier ma fievre me martire:
> Quand je soulois en ma jeunesse lire
>   Du Florentin les lamentables vois,
>   Comme incredule alors je ne pouvois,
>   En le moquant, me contenir de rire.
> Je ne pensoi, tant novice j'étoi,
>   Qu'home eut senti ce que je ne sentoi,
>   Et par mon fait les autres je jugeoie.
> Mais l'Archerot qui de moi se facha,
>   Pour me punir, un tel soin me cacha
>   Dedans le coeur, qu'onque puis je n'eus joïe. (*A* 216)

Since that day that I sigh for afflicted, the year has come round seven times. (Beneath such a star I took the hook) and still my fever torments me more than on the first occasion. When I used to read in my youth the lamenting voice of the Florentine, incredulous then I could not refrain, mocking him, from laughing. I was so inexperienced that I did not think any man could feel what I did not feel, and by my own case I judged all others. But the Archer, becoming angry with me, as punishment embedded such a care in my heart that never since have I known joy.

The second quatrain of this well-known sonnet, with its explicit reference to his reading of "the Florentine," has been routinely cited as testimony to Ronsard's negative attitude toward his Italian precursor.[33] The speaker's recall of the scorn and ridicule with which he reacted to his early reading of Petrarch's verses led Dassonville, for example, to remark that "antipétrarquiste de tempérament, [Ronsard] ne pouvait concevoir qu'un amoureux pût être si longtemps malheureux et fidèle," and others have found in the passage not only the charge of lack of verisimilitude but that of lack of sincerity in those "lamentables vois" of the Italian poet.[34]

Such conclusions, however, are based on the assumption that these verses are to be read as autobiographical, as a pronouncement by the poet Ronsard concerning the poet Petrarch. If we evaluate their status instead as a pronouncement by Ronsard's poetic persona, as a retrospective comment in the voice of the fiction, we find that only in a relational reading does the perspective relating this affirmation to the work of his predecessor fully emerge. The principal subtext of the quatrain is found in Petrarch's metamorphosis canzone, the poem that, of all the poems of the *Rime sparse*, offers the most comprehensive self-portrait of the poet as lover, a retelling of his amorous experience from his "primo etade" to the moment of composition:

> canterò com'io vissi in libertade
> mentre Amor nel mio albergo a sdegno s'ebbe;
> poi seguirò sì come a lui ne 'ncrebbe
> troppo altamente e che di ciò m'avenne . . . (R 23, 5–8)
> ché sentendo il crudel di ch'io ragiono
> infin allor percossa di suo strale
> non essermi passato oltra la gonna,
> prese in sua scorta una possente Donna . . . (32–35)

> I shall sing how then I lived in liberty while love was scorned in my abode; then I shall pursue how that chagrined him too deeply, and what happened to me for that. . . . For that cruel one of whom I speak, seeing that as yet no blow of his arrows had gone beyond my garment, took as his patroness a powerful Lady . . .

Ronsard's sonnet, like the canzone, gives the circumstances of his *innamoramento*. Its temporal indication of that event, that "L'an dedans soi s'est roüé par set fois," recalls not only Virgil (*Georgics* II, 402) but more specifically Petrarch's similar formulation of the occasion that "dicesette anni à già rivolto il cielo / poi che 'mprima arsi" [the heavens have already revolved seventeen years since I first caught fire] (*R* 122). Its statement of the consequences—"ma fievre me martire"—echoes Petrarch's designation of "i martiri" in *R* 23, whereas the final tercet recalls Petrarch's description of Love's armed attack provoked by the poet's youthful indifference.

Ronsard's poem, like Petrarch's, presents a version not only of the earliest phase of the protagonist's experience of love but of its prehistory. Petrarch identifies the youthful innocence of love, that preceding the misfortunes of the young lover, as characterizing the "dolce tempo de la prima etade," which corresponds to Ronsard's "en ma jeunesse." Ronsard was later to revise these verses, replacing "en ma jeunesse" in 1578 with "en mon estude."[35] In the 1553 poem, however, the further indication of his earlier self as "tant novice" develops the analogy:

> Je ne pensoi, tant novice j'étoi,
>> Qu'home eut senti ce que je ne sentoi,
>> Et par mon fait les autres je jugeoie.

This confession identifies the poet's incredulous reaction with that of Petrarch's poet-protagonist who, innocent of Love's power like Ronsard's protagonist two centuries later, will be subjected to Love's assault:

> . . . lagrima ancor non mi bagnava il petto
> né rompea il sonno, et quel che in me non era
> mi pareva un miracolo in altrui. (27–29)

> . . . no tear yet bathed my breast nor broke my sleep, and what was not in me seemed to me like a miracle in others.

If the speaker of Ronsard's poem had mocked Petrarch in his youth, it was in that same way and for the same reason that the speaker of Petrarch's poem had mocked others; and experience was to teach both that to mock lovers was to incur the punitive wrath of Amor. From a certain speculative perspective of literary history it may not be inaccurate to remark, with Michel Dassonville, that "ce n'est pas l'Archerot qui lui fit changer d'avis, comme il le prétend à la fin de ce sonnet, mais bien le succès qu'obtint dès 1549 *L'Olive* de Joachim du Bellay."[36] But this misses the point of the self-representation in the poem in question. The often-cited mention of Petrarch in the French sonnet, the recalled scorn for the "lamentables vois" of the Italian poet's *rime*, is neither an authentic critique of Petrarch on the part of Ronsard nor a candid profession of Ronsard's sometime anti-Petrarchan vein. It functions instead in a more general allusive strategy, to locate his persona's early experience in relation to the story of the young poet-lover recorded in the *Rime sparse.*

The story begins, conventionally, with the *innamoramento*, an event repeatedly rendered by Ronsard through the accumulation and synthesis of elements drawn from poems by Petrarch, his successors, or both. *A 3*, "Dans le serain de sa jumelle flamme" [in the serenity of her twin flame] may stand as example, in that the poem derives its effect, as Daniela Boccassini remarks, from its summation of "tutte le figure dell'innamoramento estratte dal repertorio della lirica tradizionale."[37] In the

1552–53 *Amours* the fatal event occurs in April (*A* 14 and 89), in an echo of Petrarch's initial encounter with Laura that has not escaped the attention of Ronsard's editors. And like Petrarch, Ronsard will record anniversaries of the occasion.[38] *A* 14 recalls the "vingtuniesme jour / Du mois d'Avril" [twenty-first day of the month of April] to record its first anniversary, and *A* 124, marking that same anniversary, opens with the indication of the year, "L'an mil cinq cent contant quarante & six" [the year one thousand five hundred forty-six], together recalling the calendrical precision of Petrarch's "mille trecento ventisette, a punto / su l'ora prima, il dì sesto d'aprile" [one thousand three hundred twenty-seven, exactly at the first hour of the sixth day of April] (*R* 211, 12–13).[39] *A* 164, "Hà, Belacueil," marks the fifth year, *A* 115 the sixth. The latter poem is particularly rich in Petrarchan resonances:

> Le seul Avril de son jeune printemps,
> Endore, emperle, enfrange notre temps,
> Qui n'a sceu voyr la beaulté de la belle,
> Ny la vertu, qui foysonne en ses yeulx:
> Seul je l'ay veue, aussi je meur pour elle,
> Et plus grand heur ne m'ont donné les cieulx. (9–14)

The very April of her youthful springtime gilds, empearls, and bedecks our age, that has not known how to see the beauty of this beauty, nor the power that abounds in her eyes: I alone have seen it, thus do I die for her, and the heavens have granted me no greater happiness.

Editors have noted that the conclusion of this poem echoes Petrarch's proclamation *in morte di Laura* of a singular destiny: "Non la conobbe il mondo mentre l'ebbe: conobbil'io . . ." [the world did not know her while it had her; I knew her . . .] (*R* 338, 12–13). But there are more echoes, some of them strong: the curious series of verbs in the second of these verses, as Muret commented, are "mots faits à l'imitation de Pétrarque" [words invented in imitation of Petrarch] rendering Petrarch's praise of Laura's physical beauty: "quant' arte dora e 'mperla e 'nostra / l'abito eletto e mai non vista altrove" [how much skill has gilded and impearled and incarnadined that noble body never seen elsewhere] (*R* 192, 5–6). And the poem cited above for its identification of Ronsard's lyric protagonist with that of the *Rime sparse*, "Depuis le jour que mal sain je soupire" (*A* 216), is associated with the seventh anniversary, its parenthetical indication "sous astre tel je pris l'hain" echoing one of Petrarch's anniversary poems, "in tale stella presi l'esca e l'amo" [under such a star I took the bait and the hook] (*R* 212, 14). Here as in the *Rime sparse,* these notations suggestive of an overall referential chronology contribute to the reader's perception of a story in the collection as a whole. And to the privileged reader well versed in the Italian collection—Ronsard's fellow poets, at least, if not his larger courtly audience—it contributes to the perception of a story that is in many respects "the same."[40]

Or take the other element, that of setting, fundamental to that perception. The setting of the story of Ronsard and Cassandre in a natural landscape conforms to the Petrarchan model, as Fernand Desonay points out: "Ronsard, contrairement à la réalité des faits, s'il est vrai qu'il a rencontré pour la première fois Cassandre Salviati dans la ville de Blois, veut nous persuader qu'il s'agit d'une idylle champêtre. . . . Rappelons . . . que la Laura du *Canzoniere* est une créature de plein air."[41] And while Ronsard's use of landscape in the 1552 *Amours* unquestionably creates a "unity of place" which is of central importance to the collection—as Dassonville observes, "si elle favorise l'unité de l'oeuvre et justifie le dialogue entre le poète et ce petit monde qui lui était si familier, elle garantit la relation qu'il dit exister entre sa dame et le pays où elle vivait elle aussi"[42]—the comment could equally well be made of the *Rime sparse.* It is worthy of note that Ronsard's explicit references to Petrarch very frequently include reference to place, to the setting that helps to identify the Italian poet's "story"; it is quite clear that he reads the natural setting of Vaucluse, upon which Petrarch insists, as an essential part of the myth of Laura.[43]

Ronsard's use of nature, some readers have suggested, distances his collection from the *Rime sparse* through its frequent recourse to concrete detail in which we readily recognize the landscape, however stylized, of Vendôme. The suggestion is valid, even though the poems most often cited as illustrative of this decor contain imitative elements.[44] But those differences of descriptive detail aside, the experience of Ronsard's lover-in-landscape repeatedly replicates that of the Petrarchan protagonist. Take a poem in which that experience is played out in solitude, a consequence of the alienation of the lover from human society as a result of the *innamoramento.* Although the theme of the melancholy retreat into nature was not new with Petrarch, who probably knew its incarnation in the myth of Bellerophon,[45] Ronsard's adaptation furthers the identification of his protagonist with that of the *Rime sparse:*

> Je te hay, peuple, & m'en sert de tesmoing,
> Le Loyr, Gastine, & les rives de Braye,
> Et la Neuffaune, & l'humide saulaye,
> Qui de Sabut borne l'extreme coin.

Quand je me perdz entre deux montz bien loing,
   M'arraissonnant seul à l'heure j'essaye
   De soulager la douleur de ma playe,
   Qu'Amour encherne au plus vif de mon soing. (*A* 119, 1–8)

I hate you, people, and the Loir and Gastine and the shores of the
Braye be my witness, and the Neuffaune, and the damp stand of
willows that marks the farthest corner of Sabut. When I lose myself
far between two mountains, reasoning with myself all alone I try to
ease the pain of my wound that love implants in the very quick of
my care.

The poem combines an echo of *R* 259, "Cercato ho sempre solitaria vita, /
le rive il sanno e le campagne e i boschi . . . " [I have always sought a
solitary life—the riverbanks know it and the meadows and the woods
. . .] (1–2), with the recall of "Solo e pensoso i più deserti campi" [Alone
and filled with care . . . the most deserted fields] (*R* 35). The latter poem,
one of the best known of the *Rime,* is echoed with extraordinary density in
the *Amours* of 1552, suggestive, as Luzius Keller proposes, that it assumes
a structural function within the sequence as a whole.[46] Again and again
Ronsard combines echoes of Petrarch's evocation of the lover in nature to
create his own persona's experience: the recall in the *Rime* of a passage
through the forest of Ardennes, "Raro un solenzio un solitario orrore /
D'ombrosa selva mai tanto mi piacque . . . " [Rarely has the silence, the
solitary chill of a shady wood pleased me so much . . .] (*R* 176, 12–13)[47]
combines with the conclusion of "Solo e pensoso" in the closing of an-
other poem in which Ronsard confides to Baïf:

Ores un antre, or un desert sauvage,
   Ore me plaist le segret d'un rivage,
   Pour essayer de tromper mon ennuy:
Mais quelque horreur de forest qui me tienne,
   Faire ne puis qu'Amour tousjours ne vienne,
   Parlant à moy, & moy tousjours à luy. (*A* 161, 9–14)

Now a cave, now a wild desert, now the seclusion of a riverbank
pleases me, to try to distract me from my cares; but no matter what
fearful forest holds me, I cannot prevent Love from coming always,
speaking to me, and I always to him.

ma pur sì aspre vie ne sì selvagge
cercar non so, ch'Amor non venga sempre
ragionando con meco, et io con lui. (*R* 35, 12–14)

but still I cannot seek paths so harsh or so savage that Love does not always come along discoursing with me and I with him.

The nature in which the lover takes refuge, however, is not devoid of the image of the beloved. On the contrary, it takes on that image through his obsessive projection: "pur nel primo sasso / disegno co la mente il suo bel viso . . . " [and in the first stone I see I portray her lovely face with my mind . . .] (*R* 129, 28–29); "Puis figurant ta belle idole feinte / Dedans quelque eau . . . " [then imagining your lovely feigned form within the water . . .] (*A* 119, 9–14). But it figures also in his recall of her observed presence in nature, from which it is inseparable. Take a poem in the *Rime* that affords one of the many versions of the *innamoramento*:

> Qual miracolo è quel, quando tra l'erba
> quasi un fior siede! ovver quand'ella preme
> col suo candido seno un verde cespo!
> Qual dolcezza è ne la stagione acerba
> vederla ir sola coi pensier suoi inseme,
> tessendo un cerchio a l'oro terso e crespo! (*R* 160, 9–14)

What a miracle it is, when on the grass she sits like a flower! or when she presses her white breast against a green tree trunk! What sweetness it is in the spring to see her walking alone with her thoughts, weaving a garland for her polished curling gold!

Now Ronsard:

> Dedans des Prez je vis une Dryade,
> Qui comme fleur s'assisoyt par les fleurs,
> Et mignotoyt un chappeau de couleurs,
> Eschevelée en simple verdugade. (*A* 62, 1–4)[48]

In the Meadows I saw a Driad, who was sitting among the flowers like a flower and fondling a hat of many colors, her hair tousled, in a simple billowing skirt.

Petrarch recalls an almost hallucinatory moment in which he viewed Laura receiving the tribute of nature:

> Da' be' rami scendea,
> dolce ne la memoria,
> una pioggia di fior sovra 'l suo grembo . . . (*R* 126, 40–42)

From the lovely branches was descending (sweet in memory) a rain of flowers over her bosom . . .

and Ronsard makes the tribute explicit in his version of the scene, as Cassandre's song—whose transformative sweetness recalls here as in other poems that of Laura[49]—produces a "beau printemps" in the midst of winter's chill:

> Le ciel ravy, que son chant esmouvoyt,
>> Roses, & liz, & girlandes pleuvoyt
>> Tout au rond d'elle au meillieu de la place. (*A* 107, 9–11)

> The enchanted heavens, moved by her song, rained down roses, and lilies, and garlands all round her amid that place.

Or take the well-known poem in which Cassandre, like Laura alone with her thoughts—"coi pensier suoi inseme"—moves through this landscape:

> Voyci le bois, que ma sainte Angelette
>> Sus le printemps anime de son chant.
>> Voyci les fleurs que son pied va marchant,
>> Lors que pensive elle s'esbat seullette.
> Iö voici la prée verdelette
>> Qui prend vigueur de sa main la touchant,
>> Quand pas à pas pillarde va cherchant
>> Le bel esmail de l'herbe nouvelette.
> Ici chanter, là pleurer je la vy,
>> Ici soubrire, & là je fus ravy
>> De ses beaulx yeulx par lesquelz je desvie:
> Ici s'asseoir, là je la vi dancer:
>> Sus le mestier d'un si vague penser
>> Amour ourdit les trames de ma vie. (*A* 159)

> Here is the wood that my holy young angel animates in springtime with her song, here the flowers trodden by her feet when she wanders pensive and all alone. Ah! here the meadow of delicate green that draws vigor from the touch of her hand, when step by step, pillaging, she seeks out the lovely enamel of the fresh young grass. Here I saw her singing, there in tears, here she smiled, and there I was enrapt by her lovely eyes on whose account I stray: here I saw her sitting, there dancing: upon the loom of such varying thought Love weaves the web of my life.

The poem is exceptionally rich in Petrarchan resonances, initiated by the echo of Laura "nova angeletta" and "angioletta" in *R* 106 and 201. Laura too is observed in her landscape in a variety of moods, among them pensive, as when Petrarch evokes the "fresco ombroso fiorito e verde colle / ov'or pensando et or cantando siede . . . " [fresh, shady, flowering green hill, where, sometimes thoughtful, sometimes singing, she sits . . .] (*R* 243, 1–2) or the "lieti fiori e felici, et ben nate erbe / che Madonna pensando premer sòle" [happy and fortunate flowers and well-born grass, whereon my lady is wont to walk in thought] (*R* 162, 1–2); and the insistent "voici," "ici," "là" of Ronsard's poem, identifying the various points in the common landscape that activate the recall of her presence, echoes the rhetorical structure of another Petrarchan sonnet:

> Qui cantò dolcemente, et qui s'assise,
> qui si rivolse, et qui ritenne il passo,
> qui co' begli occhi mi trafisse il cuore,
> qui disse una parola, e qui sorrise,
> qui cangiò il viso. In questi pensier, lasso,
> notte e dì tiemmi il signor nostro Amore. (*R* 112, 9–14)[50]

Here she sang sweetly and here sat down; here she turned about and here held back her step; here with her lovely eyes she transfixed my heart; here she said a word, here she smiled, here she frowned. In these thoughts, alas, our lord Love keeps me night and day.

Also frequently cited as a subtext of Ronsard's poem is another sonnet from the *Rime:*

> Come 'l candido piè per l'erba fresca
> i dolci passi onestamente move,
> vertù che 'ntorno i fiori apra e rinnove,
> de le tenere piante sue par ch'esca. (*R* 165, 1–4)

As her white foot through the green grass virtuously moves its sweet steps, a power that all around her opens and renews the flowers seems to issue from her tender soles.

The inspiration for this depiction of the lady whose presence and touch animate the landscape is equally apparent in *A* 43, "Avec les liz, les oeilletz mesliez" [the carnations mingled with the lilies] in which her passage causing the meadow to flower—"un pré de fleurs s'esmaille soubz ses piedz" [a field of flowers paints itself beneath her feet]—recalls from *Rime* 42 the western breeze that awakens the flowers in every meadow, "desta i fior tra l'erba in chascun prato" [awakens the flowers in the grass in every meadow]. Hesiod's description of Venus may be in the background here, as Bensimon suggests in his note to this verse, but the echo of Petrarch is more immediate, and it is confirmed by other elements in the poem. Not only does Petrarch's poem open with the "dolce riso" [sweet laugh] of Laura, which becomes the "doulx ris" of Cassandre; the Petrarchan original is readily identified from the final tercet of Ronsard's sonnet, where the lady's beauty can calm Jupiter's wrath—"De Juppiter rasserener la dextre, / Ja ja courbé pour sa fouldre eslancer" [to calm the right hand of Jupiter, already poised to hurl his lightning]—echoing Petrarch's assertion that "a Giove tolte son l'arme di mano" [Jove's arms have been taken from his hand] with the appearance of Laura.

There is a difference between these representations, by Petrarch and by Ronsard, of an essentially passive protagonist. Each seeks the solitude of nature, recalls scenes of the lady's presence in nature, and in her presence is immobilized in contemplation or mesmerized as if by enchantment in these privileged moments: "Ce chant qui tient mes soucis enchantez . . . " [this song that holds my cares enraptured . . .], writes Ronsard (*A* 137, 6).[51] Ronsard's reveries nonetheless, as Thomas Greene has masterfully demonstrated, introduce subtle but telling changes: *A* 159 cited above, for example, suggests a "pleasurably melancholy errancy of the body and sensibility," a willing surrender to an insubstantial mood. The "willed and fecund" passivity suggested by Ronsard's representations may lack "the formidable emotional intensity" of the state of the speaker in the Petrarchan subtexts, but it achieves "precisely an opening out of that relentless enclosing power."[52]

But in both collections the protagonist is at other moments restive, active, engaged in pursuit of the lady. Thus Petrarch, in a poem already closely imitated by Du Bellay:[53]

Sì traviato è 'l folle mi' desio
a seguitar costei che 'n fuga è volta,
e de' lacci d'Amor leggiera e sciolta
vola dinanzi al lento correr mio . . . (*R* 6, 1–4)

So far astray is my mad desire, in pursuing her who has turned in flight and, light and free of the snares of Love, flies ahead of my slow running . . .

Petrarch's sonnet develops as an allegory in which the lover's desire is figured as a steed that carries him away, in a frenzied chase whose anticipated conclusion is not the attainment of its object but his death:

che quanto richiamando più l'envio
per la secura strada men m'ascolta;
né mi vale spronarlo, o dargli volta,
ch'amor per sua natura il fa restio;

e poi che 'l fren per forza a sé raccoglie,
i' mi rimango in signoria di lui,
che mal mio grado a morte mi trasporta. (5–11)

that when, calling him back, I most send him by the safe path, then
he least obeys me, nor does it help to spur him or turn him, for Love
makes him restive by nature; and when he takes the bit forcefully to
himself, I remain in his power, as against my will he carries me off to
death.

It is this frenzy, this helpless state of the lover caught up in his hopeless
pursuit, that is defined in the opening of Ronsard's sonnet 113: "Franc de
raison, esclave de fureur, / Je voys chassant une Fére sauvage" [Freed of
all reason, a slave of my fury, I go pursuing a wild creature]. Petrarch had
repeatedly depicted the lady as "fera," a wild creature.[54] Here again, as
Boccassini notes, Ronsard rereads and rewrites precisely those myths that
Petrarch had raised to the status of emblems of his condition as unhappy
lover and as poet in search of his own identity, to render now the un-
bridgeable gap between lover and beloved.[55] Thus Ronsard: "Puissé-je
avoir ceste Fére aussi vive / Entre mes bras, qu'elle est vive en mon
cuoeur . . . " [Would I could have this wild Creature as alive in my arms,
as she is alive in my heart . . .] (*A* 157, 1–2).

Object of the lover's pursuit, the lady figured as "fére" is here also his
prey, the "chasse" as pursuit becoming the literal hunt. Ronsard's alle-
gorical development makes explicit the cynegetic motif:

J'ay pour ma lesse un cordeau de malheur,
    J'ay pour limier un trop ardent courage,
    J'ay pour mes chiens, & le soing, & la rage,
    La cruaulté, la peine & la douleur. (*A* 113, 5–8)

I have as my lead a cord of misfortune, I have as my bloodhound a
too ardent courage, as my pack of dogs I have care and rage, cruelty,
pain, and suffering.

The conclusion of the failure of the dogs to take the prey is unexpected
and violent:

Mais eulx voyant que plus elle est chassée,
    Loing loing devant plus s'enfuit eslancée,
    Tournant sur moy la dent de leur effort,
Comme mastins affamez de repaistre,
    A longz morceaux se paissent de leur maistre,
    Et sans mercy me traisnent à la mort. (9–14)

But they, seeing that the more she is pursued the more she flees far far ahead, turning the teeth of their striving on me like mastiffs hungry for prey, they feed upon their master with deep bites, and drag me without mercy on to death.

In a free play with Petrarchan topoi, the amorous hunt yields here to the projection of an actual hunting scene, one that has its counterpart in popular allegories such as *La chasse et le depart d'amours.*[56]

A passage of a canzone from the *Rime sparse* has often been proposed as the source of Ronsard's poem:

> Ahi crudo Amor, ma tu allor più m'informe
> a seguir d'una fera che mi strugge
> la voce e i passi et l'orme,
> et lei non stringi che s'appiatta et fugge. (*R* 50, 39–42)

> Ah cruel Love! but you then most shape me to pursue the voice and the steps and the footprints of a wild creature who destroys me, and you do not seize her, she crouches and flees.

Petrarch's poem, however, lacks the violence of Ronsard's conclusion in which the hunter's own dogs "a longz morceaux se paissent de leur maistre." The contrast has been invoked to underline the imaginative distance between the two poets; "entre le chasseur aggressif et frustré de Pétrarque et le chasseur attaqué et victime de lui-même que représente Actéon," concludes André Gendre, "il n'y a strictement que l'imagination de Ronsard."[57] But in fact Ronsard closely models his Acteon on a Petrarchan version of the amorous hunt found in another poem, for the casting of the lover as Acteon, along with the violence of his fate resulting from his pursuit of the "fera," is suggested by the final metamorphosis of the protagonist in *Rime* 23, where the speaker of the poem, following his desire and "cacciando" as Ronsard's will be "chassant," pursues his usual object, "quella fera bella e cruda," and comes upon her naked in a fountain.[58] She, like her prototype Diana, splashes water over the intruder, effecting his transformation:

> ch'i' senti' trarmi de la propria imago
> et in un cervo solitario et vago
> di selva in selva ratto mi trasformo,
> et ancor de' miei can fuggo lo stormo. (157–160)

> for I felt myself drawn from my own image and into a solitary wandering stag from wood to wood quickly I am transformed and still I flee the belling of my hounds.

Petrarch's version, in which the Ovidian source is more directly evoked, anticipates Ronsard's in depicting the consequences of too great an ardor in approaching the forbidden presence of the lady.

The function of mythological story in the *Rime sparse* and the 1552–53 *Amours* affords a particularly pertinent test case for Ronsard's adaptation of Petrarchan models, not least because the two major derivative currents in his poetry, the mythological and the Petrarchan, have long been described and evaluated as relatively free of mutual influence or contamination. The mythological current in Ronsard's early collection has itself been somewhat neglected, perhaps, as I. D. McFarland suggests, because the "partial randomness and apparent freedom of the mythological cross-references" found here have been overshadowed by the later emergence, in the practice of the poet's maturity, of major figures adapted to ambitious allegorizing patterns.[59] But the possible relevance of Petrarch's *Rime* to that domain has been more neglected still. Helmut Hatzfeld, describing the "mythologie retrouvée" prominent in much sixteenth-century French poetry, makes no mention of Petrarch as intermediary in that recovery;[60] considering the use of mythology by the poets of the Pléiade, Guy Demerson identifies Petrarch's contribution through the representation of pagan divinities in his allegorical *Trionfi*, but to the *Rime sparse* is ascribed in this regard little more than "pagan reminiscences."[61] As Dassonville authoritatively summarized the distinction, mythology was already in 1550 on its way to becoming a code, and the Petrarchist tradition was another; and Petrarch's name is absent from Pierre Léonard's survey of the many and varied readings of the mythological component that occupies a privileged position in critical studies of Ronsard's oeuvre.[62]

Yet the theme of metamorphosis is fundamental in Ronsard's poetry, reiterated through a vocabulary that includes *transformation* and, more generally, *mutacion*.[63] And we have seen, in the preceding chapter, that the allusions to metamorphosis in the final section of the "Fantaisie à sa dame" attest to Ronsard's early, close familiarity with Petrarch's treatment of mythological subjects in several poems of the *Rime sparse*, from which he draws freely, as the thematic development of his own text suggests. Although the versions of metamorphosis in the "Fantaisie" do not directly evoke prototypes in mythological story, the function of those prototypes is not lost on the French poet: again and again in the *Amours* of 1552–53, when Ronsard's lyric protagonist assumes the role and reenacts the story of a mythological god or hero—in particular, but not exclusively, of Apollo or of Acteon—the mediation of the *Rime* is in evidence. If indeed, as Dassonville affirms, the mythological references allow the poet to achieve a maximum of signification with a great economy of means—

if the very allusion to Prometheus, Narcissus, or Sisyphus bears with it "a story, an atmosphere, and a destiny"[64]—very frequently we must be attentive also to the Petrarchan mediation.

It was in the "comparatively relaxed and elastic structure" of mythological narrative, Ann Moss suggests, that Ronsard "found most latitude for his manoeuvre" of distancing himself from his admired precursors and thereby addressing the anxiety of influence.[65] But that maneuver exists in the *Amours* in tension with another by which Ronsard finds in Petrarch's renewal of Ovidian story the composite paradigm for the representation of his contemporary lyric persona. Early in the 1552 collection, a poem in praise of Cassandre's beauty lays bare the fertile analogy of the poet as transformer, as maker of metamorphoses:

> Hé que ne suis je Ovide bien disant!
> Oeil tu seroys un bel Astre luisant,
> Main un beau lis, crin un beau ret de soye. (*A* 17, 12–14)

Alas that I am not well-spoken Ovid! Eye, you would be a lovely shining star, hand, a lovely lily, hair, a lovely silken net.

Now, in Ronsard's early exploration of the use of mythological figures for the creation of his own poetic persona, the mediation of the *Rime* emerges as critical. Far from affording a measure of the distance between the French poet and his Italian precursor, it figures in the allusive strategy by means of which Ronsard in his posture as the "French Petrarch" invites his reader to measure his achievement in relation to that of the celebrated poet of the *Rime sparse*.

Yet more significant is that Ronsard's recurrence to mythological models drawn from the *Rime* very often conforms closely to their particular function in the economy of Petrarch's collection as a whole. Here prominence must be accorded the figure of Apollo, to whom the central role as mythological prototype is awarded. To both evoke and invoke Apollo as suitor of the Trojan Cassandre is of course an obvious extension of Ronsard's identification of his lady with her homonymous mythological counterpart: attempting to win Cassandre, Apollo bestowed upon her the gift of prophecy; in retaliation for her rejection, he decreed that her prophecies would never be believed. The Trojan War topos variously developed in the *Amours* serves as further context for the adversative relation of poet to lady insinuated in Ronsard's formulas "ma guerriere Cassandre" [my warring Cassandre] (*A* 4) and "ma doulce guerriere" (*A* 185).[66] But the latter is a translation of *R* 21, "o dolce mia guerrera" [O my sweet warrior]—one already borrowed from Petrarch by Ronsard's precursors to designate the lady who offers opposition to the lover's suit[67]—and if Apollo lover of Cassandre affords an obvious prototype for Ronsard lover of Cassandre, there is frequently an intermediary identification, that in which Petrarch lover of Laura found his prototype in Apollo lover of Daphne and of the laurel into which she was transformed.

Take, for example, the opening of a famous sonnet by Petrarch:

Apollo, s'ancor vive il bel desio
che t'infiammava a le tesaliche onde . . . (*R* 34, 1–2)

Apollo, if the sweet desire is still alive that inflamed you beside the Thessalian waves . . .

It is in the name of this ardent desire, to be later replicated in the poet's own "accesa voglia" of *R* 73, that Petrarch's poet appeals to the god to favor the "honored and sacred plant":

dal pigro gelo et dal tempo aspro et rio
che dura quanto 'l tuo viso s'asconde
difendi or l'onorata et sacra fronde
ove tu prima et poi fu' invescato io. (5–8)

against the slow frost and the harsh and cruel time that lasts as long as your face is hidden, now defend the honored and holy leaves where you first and then I were limed.

This sonnet, grounded in Apollo's identity as sun god who can at will create conditions propitious for the laurel, couches its invocation of his protection in meteorological terms: "di queste impression l'aere disgombra" [disencumber the air of these impressions]. Ronsard, taking up the theme of the lady's illness to treat it in a manner that more closely resembles that of Tibullus,[68] will nonetheless follow Petrarch in casting his prayer for Apollo's aid in terms of the god's ardent love, his "ancient fire":

Dieu medecin, si en toy vit encore
L'antique feu du Thessale arbrisseau,
Las, pren pitié de ce teint damoyseau,
Et son lis palle en oeilletz recolore. (*A* 188, 5–8)

God of healing, if there still lives in you the ancient fire of the Thessalian brush, alas, take pity on this pallid complexion, and recolor its pale lily shade in carnations.

The connection has attracted little notice in this poem and even less in another, often-cited sonnet inspired by *R* 34 and added to the *Amours* in 1553, in which it is both more evident and more complex:[69]

Mets en obli, Dieu des herbes puissant,
    Le mauvais tour que non loin d'Hellesponte
    Te fit m'amie, & vien d'une main pronte
    Garir son teint palement jaunissant.
Tourne en santé son beau cors perissant,
    Ce te sera, Phebus, une grand'honte,
    Sans ton secours, si la ledeur surmonte
    L'oeil qui te tint si long tans languissant.
En ma faveur si tu as pitié d'elle,
    Je chanterai comme l'errante Dele
    S'enracina sous ta vois, & comment
Python sentit ta premiere conqueste,
    Et comme Dafne aus tresses de ta teste
    Donna jadis le premier ornement. (*A* 217)

Forget now, god of the powerful herbs, the deception that my beloved worked upon you not far from the Hellespont, and come with a ready hand to heal her pallid sallow complexion. Return to health her ailing lovely body; it will bring great shame to you, Phoebus, if without your aid ugliness overcomes the eye that held you languishing for so long. If in my favor you take pity on her, I shall sing of how the wandering Dela took root beneath your voice, and how Python felt your first conquest, and how Daphne long ago gave the first ornament to your tresses.

Here the appeal to Apollo to exercise his restorative powers is developed by Ronsard as both contrast and similarity. Now, however, the similarity lies only in the desired result of the intervention, to restore the lady's color and her health. And now, strikingly, the lady is no longer identified as the beloved both of the god and of the latter-day poet. Whereas Petrarch, and after him Ronsard in *A* 188, called upon Apollo in the name of the god's own love for the lady, now she is identified as the beloved of the poet alone, her designation as "m'amie" contrasting with the final image of *R* 34 in which she is "la donna nostra."

The alteration is in keeping with the evident allusion to the mythological Cassandre, who incurred Apollo's wrath and his punishment by her refusal of his love; hence the poet's gesture is not to attempt to reawaken Apollo's love for the lady but to assuage the god's anger at the "mauvais tour" to which he was once subjected. The opening verse, thus motivated, calls attention through the total reversal in the function of memory to Ronsard's rewriting of the Petrarchan poem: while the Italian poet beseeches Apollo to recall his love for Daphne—"se non ài l'amate chiome bionde, / volgendo gli anni, già poste in oblio" [if you have not forgotten, with the turning of the years, those beloved blond locks] (*R* 34, 3–4)— Ronsard's Apollo is urged to "mettre en obli" Cassandre's rejection of his desire. It is a strong gambit, one that reveals the strength of Ronsard's assertion of his own poetic persona even as he appropriates the gesture of the protagonist of Petrarch's sonnet. Its force is underscored by the intrusion of the lyric "je" in the anticipated consequences of Apollo's intervention. Now the god will not be rewarded by the lady's return to health and beauty but rather by Ronsard himself, who holds out the promise—"si tu as pitié d'elle"—of celebrating Apollo's already renowned exploits once again in his own song. But the relation to the Petrarchan source-text, from which Ronsard's poem thus far represents a deviation, receives a final turn at the poem's close. For though the sonnet opens with the evocation of Apollo's frustrated love for the Trojan Cassandre, it closes with the recall of the same god's frustrated love for the Daphne "who gave his tresses their first ornament."

In a considerable number of poems in the *Rime sparse* in which the poetic persona identifies with the Ovidian Apollo as lover of Daphne, the celebration of the beloved is at the same time a celebration not only of passion but of its sublimation. "If you cannot be my bride," Apollo declares while embracing the laurel, "you will at least be my tree!" But in the *Rime* this triumphant note is undercut by and subordinated to a darker reading that reminds us that Daphne was transformed into the laurel to escape the god's ardent pursuit, a pursuit doomed to failure by Cupid's vengeful arrow.[70] Apollo's love for Daphne as reenacted by the lyric protagonist results in rejection and ultimate loss. Any triumph that remains to him, that of rendering the vanished beloved immortal through his song, only superficially masks the failure of his suit: the song attempts, and repeatedly fails, to fill the void left by the lady's escape from his possession. Such, of course, is also the case of Ronsard's poet-lover: on the level of content, as Jean-Claude Moisan observes, it is this *échec amoureux* that unifies the 1552–53 collection.[71]

> Plus elle court, & plus elle est fuytive,
>   Par le sentier d'audace, & de rigueur,
>   Plus je me lasse, & recreu de vigueur,
> Je marche apres d'une jambe tardive.

Au moins escoute & rallente tes paz;
   Comme veneur je ne te poursuy pas,
   Ou comme archer qui blesse à l'impourveue. (*A* 157, 5–11)

The more she runs, the more she flees away along the path of bold-
ness and rigor, the more I weary, and lacking all vigor, I walk after
her with a slow leg. At least listen and slow your steps! I do not
pursue you as a hunter, or as an archer who inflicts sudden wounds.

The scene as a whole, "image de chasse où se lit la transcription cinétique
de son désir,"[72] recalls that other frustrated pursuit for which the passage
of the *Metamorphoses* serves as subtext, Petrarch's pursuit of an elusive
Laura, Daphne's avatar.

The pursuit is not only destined to failure; it is fraught with peril.
Ronsard, after recasting the protestation of benevolent intent—"comme
veneur je ne te poursuy pas"—that works a variant on that of the Ovidian
Apollo to the fleeing Daphne that "I am no enemy," returns to protest
again:

Apres ton cours je ne haste mes pas
   Pour te souiller d'une amour deshonneste:
   Demeure donq: le Locroys m'amonneste
   Aux bordz Gyrez de ne te forcer pas . . .
Il te voulut, le meschant, violer . . . (*A* 100, 1–4, 9)

I do not hasten my steps after your flight in order to defile you with
a dishonorable love: stay then: the Locroyan admonishes me on the
Gyrean shore not to force you . . . He, wicked one, wanted to violate
you . . .

The allusion to desired or attempted rape, unveiling the sexual violence
that the poem explicitly denies, in this poem as elsewhere distances Ron-
sard from Petrarch's depictions of amorous pursuit, as JoAnn DellaNeva
observes.[73] At the same time, however, in alluding also to the divine pun-
ishment meted out to Ajax "le Locroys," who had pursued the Trojan
Cassandre, it resonates with the threat of violence to be enacted upon the
lover as well and furthers the assimilation of Ronsard's persona with that
of the hapless lover of the *Rime sparse*. The lover predestined by the gods
to an unhappy end, the lover fearful of the punishment reserved by the
gods for their presumptuous rivals: in these readers have identified the
"personnage unique" that is the poet-lover of the early *Amours*.[74] But they
also characterize the poet-lover of the *Rime sparse*, for in the Ovidian

world of constantly renewed desire and divine retribution evoked by the use of mythological models, Petrarch's poet-lover is a fearful participant.

François Rigolot, observing that "le voeu le plus constant" of the *Amours* is that of metamorphosis, calls attention to Ronsard's elaboration of a lapidary myth in which the lover is transformed into a stone.[75] Consider then this transformation in Petrarch's metamorphosis canzone, a poem to which, as we have seen, Ronsard devoted careful study well before 1552:

> anzi le dissi 'l ver pien di paura;
> ed ella ne l'usata sua figura
> tosto tornando fecemi, oimè lasso!
> d'un quasi vivo et sbigottito sasso. (*R* 23, 77–80)

> rather I told her the truth, full of fear, and she to her accustomed form quickly returning made me, alas, an almost living and terrified stone.

Each metamorphosis of the speaker of this poem, it has been observed, results from an encounter with "the voice and the presence of the interdict against his desire and against his speaking";[76] while here it is the lady herself who effects the transformation, the motif is subject to numerous variations in Petrarch's collection, most prominent among them the agency of the transfixing and transforming Medusa. In the *Rime sparse* Medusa affords the most direct expression of the threatening aspect of desire: in each of her appearances in the collection (*R* 51, 179, 197, 366), as in the metamorphosis canzone, the lover is a victim turned to stone as a result of too bold an advance. Ronsard too makes repeated use of the figure of Medusa to render the relation between desire, interdict, and transformation.[77] Her first appearance in the *Amours* records the lover's transformation occurring "Comme au regard d'une horrible Meduse" [as in the gaze of a horrible Medusa] (*A* 8). Ronsard's lament that his lady's eye "Estrangement m'empierre en un rocher" [strangely turns me to stone within a rock] in fact adapts the curious verbal construct of *Rime* 37, "perchè pria, tacendo, non m'impetro?" [why do I not first turn to stone in silence?], in a poem in which the voice of the speaker is *not* silenced—the anguished lover is unable to abandon the lament that not only expresses but exacerbates his desire and hence his pain. Here Ronsard's disabling transformation is doubled by an unvoiced interdiction, betraying a poetic rivalry, against his attempts to celebrate the lady: the poem also contains the first direct allusion to Petrarch as the Tuscan who alone might be able to render due praise to Cassandre.[78]

There is, however, another prominent and often-noted aspect to Ronsard's depiction of metamorphosis, one antithetical to the pessimistic figuration of the helpless, suppliant lover. "Metamorphosis as imagined by Ronsard," as Terence Cave observes, "is most often a means of liberation from a sterile situation."[79] Consider a poem that explicitly thematizes liberation:

> Je veulx darder par l'univers ma peine,
>> Plus tost qu'un trait ne volle au descocher:
>> Je veulx de miel mes oreilles boucher
>> Pour n'ouir plus la voix de ma Sereine.
> Je veulx muer mes deux yeulx en fontaine,
>> Mon cuoeur en feu, ma teste en un rocher,
>> Mes piedz en tronc, pour jamais n'aprocher
>> De sa beaulté si fierement humaine.
> Je veulx changer mes pensers en oyseaux,
>> Mes doux souspirs en zephyres nouveaux,
>> Qui par le monde evanteront ma pleinte.
> Et veulx encor de ma palle couleur,
>> Dessus le Loyr enfanter une fleur,
>> Qui de mon nom & de mon mal soit peinte. (*A* 16)

I want to fire out my pain through the universe, faster than an arrow flies from the bow: I want to stop up my ears with honey, no longer to hear the voice of my Siren. I want to change my eyes into a fountain, my heart into fire, my head into a stone, my feet into a trunk, never to come near her beauty so proudly human. I want to change my thoughts into birds, my sweet sighs into new soft breezes that will blow my lament about the world. And I want too that my pallor give birth to a flower near the Loir, one painted with my name and with my pain.

The exhibitionism of this sonnet located early in the *Amours* immediately strikes the reader. In this it is similar to the opening sonnet: the insistent first-person markers, calling attention to the lover as object in that poem, impose him now as subject. Each stanza opens with an expression of his willfulness—"Je veulx"—and the poet as subject is in full possession of his own pain, as the proliferation of possessives makes clear. Following the dramatic thrust of the opening verse and the recall of the stratagem of self-preservation adopted by Ulysses, the remainder of the poem sets forth a series of imagined metamorphoses. In a particularly creative variant on the Petrarchan topos, Ronsard here repeats some of the transformations to which the poet-lover of the *Rime* is subjected in *R* 23—into a tree, a bird, a rock, a fountain, along with that into a flower, also suggested by Petrarch in other poems[80]—but attributes them not to the lady's coldness or harshness but to his own will, as metamorphoses that would render him invulnerable to her.[81]

It might also render him the victor in his erotic game. The *songe érotique*, as readers have often noted, affords an illusion of possession in some of the most frequently cited poems of the *Amours*, such as "Il faisoyt chault, & le somme coulant" [It was warm, and the flowing sleep] (*A* 186), of which Muret comments, with a discretion equal to its brevity, that "le sens n'est pas fort difficult à comprendre." In sonnet 127, "Quand en songeant ma follastre j'acolle" [When I embrace my playful one in my dreams], it is in terms of metamorphosis that the poem's speaker suggests the plenitude of sensual fulfillment in his dream of making love to Cassandre, "Changeant ma vie en cent metamorphoses: / Combien de fois . . . " [Changing my life in a hundred metamorphoses: how many times . . .].[82] And the dreaming state is not the only means of invoking such metamorphoses. "Je me transforme en cent metamorfoses": in the famous sonnet "Ha, seigneur dieu" (*A* 41) added to the collection in 1553, the lover who is no longer victim or martyr seeks in metamorphosis not only escape but fulfillment, and his will to metamorphosis is often rendered in erotically explicit images. For example, playfully: "Hé, que ne sui-je puce!" he exclaims in that same poem, so that "La baisotant, tous les jours je mordroi / Ses beaus tetins, mais la nuit je voudroi / Que rechanger en homme je me pusse" [Would that I were a flea! Kissing her, every day I would bite her beautiful breasts, but at night I would want to regain the form of a man]. Such poems appear flagrantly to subvert the decorum of the Petrarchan tradition,[83] and they are fundamental to an essential difference that readers have been at pains to identify between Ronsard's use of mythology and that of Petrarch: the "veine érotique" of the early *Amours* is very frequently contrasted to the poems of a Petrarch "chantre de l'amour chaste et constant."[84]

But as we have seen with the earlier "Fantaisie à sa dame," once again the question requires review, for there are other Petrarchan poems that figure in the intertextual play of Ronsard's representations of metamorphosis, poems in which Petrarch himself established the precedent for the evasion and indeed the subversion of those conventions that have long been associated with his transcription of the experience of desire. The poetic persona of the *Rime*, like that of Ronsard's sonnet, could fantasize an outcome opposite to that of Apollo's thwarted pursuit. At the close of a canzone early in the collection, lamenting his amorous frustration and the cruelty of the "aspra fera" who is his amorous prey, this poet exclaims:

> Con lei foss'io da che si parte il sole,
> et non ci vedess'altri che le stelle,
> sol una notte et mai non fosse l'alba,
> et non se transformasse in verde selva
> per uscirmi di braccia, come il giorno
> ch'Apollo la seguia qua giù per terra! (R 22, 31–36)

> Might I be with her from when the sun departs and no other see us but the stars, just one night, and let the dawn never come! and let her not be transformed into a green wood to escape from my arms, as the day when Apollo pursued her down here on earth!

That the verses build in the canzone toward an adynaton that acknowledges the futility of such a wish in no way alters the impact of its introduction into the imaginative world of the poet-lover: the sudden shift in referent, from the protagonist's wish-fulfillment fantasy to the mythological paradigm, effects the introduction of sexual content otherwise forbidden by the unalterable distance between Petrarch's enamored persona and his elusive lady.

Ronsard will repeat the wish for an unending night with the lady:

> Et vouldroy bien que ceste nuict encore
>   Durast tousjours sans que jamais l'Aurore
>   D'un front nouveau nous r'allumast le jour. (A 20, 12–14)

> And I would want this night to last forever, without Dawn rekindling the day for us with a new glance.

The preceding images of this famous sonnet, however, are among those that confirm for some readers the contrast between Ronsard's representation of love experience and that of Petrarch:

> Je vouldroy bien richement jaunissant
>   En pluye d'or goute à goute descendre
>   Dans le beau sein de ma belle Cassandre,
>   Lors qu'en ses yeulx le somme va glissant.
> Je vouldroy bien en toreau blandissant
>   Me transformer pour finement la prendre,
>   Quand elle va par l'herbe la plus tendre
>   Seule à l'escart mille fleurs ravissant.

Je vouldroy bien afin d'aiser ma peine
   Estre un Narcisse, & elle une fontaine
   Pour m'y plonger une nuict à sejour . . . (*A* 20, 1–11)

I would like, richly deepening in hue, to descend as golden rain, drop by drop, into the lovely lap of my lovely Cassandre, when sleep is descending into her eyes. I would like to transform myself into a seductive bull in order guilefully to take her, as she goes through the tenderest grass alone and apart, plucking a thousand flowers. I would like, to ease my pain, to be a Narcissus, and she a pool so that I could plunge into it for a night . . .

Thomas Greene characterizes this poem as "a willed escape from Petrarch"; Grahame Castor suggests that such verses allow Ronsard to represent the fulfillment of the poet's desire for Cassandre, a fulfillment "which, at the straightforward 'biographical' level, is impossible within the conventions of the petrarchan narrative."[85]

The question invites further examination, however, for the principal intertext of Ronsard's metamorphosis sonnet 20 is once again *Rime* 23. In the successive moments of Petrarch's metamorphosis canzone, as Bortolo Martinelli observes, "la pulsione erotica è il filo conduttore che collega la serie delle transformazioni ed esse altro non sono . . . che diverse forme emblematiche e figurative attraverso cui si esprime il libido petrarchesco."[86] And the series of transformations does not end with the last of the punitive metamorphoses to which the lover is subjected. Instead, its commiato extends the elaboration of mythological prototypes in the stanzas:

Canzon, i' non fu' mai quel nuvol d'oro
che poi discese in preziosa pioggia
sì che 'l foco di Giove in parte spense;
ma ben fui fiamma ch'un bel guardo accense,
et fui l'uccel che più per l'aere poggia
alzando lei che ne' mie detti onoro. (*R* 23, 161–66)

Song, I was never the cloud of gold that once descended in a precious rain so that it partly quenched the fire of Jove; but I have certainly been a flame lit by a lovely glance and I have been the bird that rises highest in the air raising her whom in my words I honor.

While the preceding, unwilled metamorphoses are patterned on the fates of ill-fated Ovidian lovers, these concluding transformations with which the poet negatively or positively identifies his own experience—like the two transformations longingly evoked in the octet of Ronsard's sonnet—are all accounts of metamorphoses of Jove. They differ radically from the metamorphoses to which the lover has been subjected in that they are willed by the subject: faithful to the Ovidian portrayal of Jupiter, they represent not amorous failure but amorous conquest.

The most suggestive difference between Ronsard's version and that of Petrarch is not that the French poem's verses, as so frequently noted, are sensually more explicit than any found in the *Rime sparse*. It lies, rather, in the role claimed for the speaker of the poem. While Petrarch's second allusion to Jupiter's amorous metamorphoses, introduced by the contrastive "ma," functions to asserts his own potency not with regard to sexual conquest but to poetry, those "detti" of celebratory verse with which he has exalted the beloved but inaccessible lady, the initial admission that he had never been—"i' non fu' mai"—the virile golden shower that had assuaged the desire of the god, is curiously devoid of affect. When Du Bellay, in a late sonnet, would reintroduce the affect to deny his desire to possess the lady against her will—

> Je ne souhaitte poinct me pouvoir transformer,
> Comme feit Jupiter en ploye jaunissante,
> Pour escouler en vous d'une trace glissante
> Cest ardeur qui me faict en cendres consommer—

> I do not at all wish to be able to transform myself, as did Jupiter in a yellowing rain, to pour into you with a gliding trace this ardor that consumes me into ashes—

his verses, as Rigolot points out, stand in marked contrast to Ronsard's "je vouldroy bien," as a refusal of the languid scene of seduction that the poet of the *Amours* would like to reenact with Cassandre.[87]

The fact that Ronsard, even while following Petrarch in adopting Apollo as prototype for his unsuccessful lover, most frequently introduces Jupiter as the deity whom the protagonist of the early *Amours* appears eager to imitate is not surprising. As Gendre observes, "mieux encore que le soleil personnifié, le maître des dieux a de quoi figurer le désir masculin"; the sonnet "Or que Juppin epoint de sa semence" (127) led the same critic to remark that "le désir de Jupiter fascine donc Ronsard!"[88] While Ronsard's Jupiter appears in a variety of contexts in which he is "associated with the themes of joy, love, abundance, triumph, light,"[89] again and again, in the early *Amours* as in the *Rime*, the powerful deity appears as a figure of sexual appetite, affording a paradigm of willful conquest to counter the fateful metamorphoses of unsuccessful Ovidian lovers evoked throughout the collection. Consider the allusions to his erotic exploits that recur in other poems of the *Amours:*

Belle est sa bouche, & son soleil jumeau,
 De neige & feu s'embellit son visage,
 Pour qui Juppin reprendroyt le plumage,
 Ore d'un Cygne, or le poyl d'un toreau. (*A* 183, 5–8)

S'Europe avoit l'estomac aussi beau,
 De t'estre fait, Jupiter, un toreau,
 Je te pardonne . . . (*A* 41, 9–11)

Beautiful is her mouth, and her twin sun embellishes her face with snow and fire, for which Jupiter would take on again the plumage of a swan, or the hide of a bull.

If Europa had so lovely a breast, I pardon you, Jupiter, for having made yourself a bull . . .

Ronsard draws, of course, on classical sources, as he had already done in the early ode "Défloration de Lède" published in 1550, in which he imitates the poem "Europe" published under the name of Theocritus.[90] Yet his representations of desire and its satisfaction may once again repay closer scrutiny, for while early commentators of the famous sonnet "Or que Juppin" in the 1552 collection pointed to its intertextual relations with classical texts, more recent commentators point also to the presence of echoes from poems of the *Rime sparse*. One of these, the motif "Seul, & pensif" that sets the lyric protagonist in a deserted landscape—"aux rochers plus segretz"—apart from the joyous plenitude of the new season, invites the reader to recall the opening of the celebrated Petrarchan sonnet "Solo e pensoso" (*R* 35), in which the lover measures with his steps "i più deserti campi," while at the same time inviting recognition of a different thematic charge in which Ronsard asserts his originality with regard to the Petrarchan model.[91]

Other segments of poems of the *Amours*, some less frequently examined, are closely modeled on Petrarch's representations of Jove. In the *Rime sparse*, as elsewhere in his poetic corpus, Petrarch attributes to the deity a strong affective response to the beauty of Laura.[92] The privileged relation between the lady and the most powerful of the gods is established in meteorological conceits that suggest the influence of the beloved on atmospheric phenomena: in two successive poems, Vulcan labors in the absence of Laura to prepare Jove's arrows, "il qual or tona or nevica et or piove," while with her return, as we have seen, the god's arms are taken away (*R* 41, 5; 42, 5). Now Cassandre, in a poem already cited:

> Que diray plus? J'ay veu dedans la plaine,
> Lors que plus fort le ciel vouloyt tançer,
> Cent fois son oeil, qui des Dieux s'est faict maistre,
>   De Juppiter rasserener la dextre
>   Ja ja courbé pour sa fouldre eslancer. (*A* 43, 10–14)

What more shall I say? I have seen in the plain, when the heaven sought to show its severity, her eye—which has gained mastery of the Gods—calm a hundred times the right hand of Jupiter already poised to lance his lightning bolts.

Editors note that in another poem, "Un voyle obscur par l'orizon espars" (*A* 142), Ronsard develops a more complete exposition of the relation between favorable or inclement weather and the lady's presence or absence, condensing into a single poem the elements of Petrarch's two sonnets.

Both poets invoke the god's intervention to punish the recalcitrant beloved. Petrarch's version, "L'arbor gentil che forte amai molt'anni," is the most vehement expression of frustrated passion in the collection of his *Rime*, for here the withdrawal of the privilege of immunity to lightning accorded the symbolic laurel would figure in the destruction of the beloved plant:

> "Né poeta ne colga mai né Giove
> la privilegi, et al sol venga in ira
> tal che si secchi ogni sua foglia verde!" (*R* 60, 12–14)

"Let no poet ever gather from it, nor let Jove favor it, and let it receive the sun's anger so that all its green leaves dry up!"

Ronsard's sonnet "En nul endroyt, comme a chanté Virgile" also registers a change of attitude on the part of the beloved, and it too calls upon Jupiter for the retribution of his lightning, in a cry that is characteristically more direct:

> Puisse le ciel sur sa langue envoyer
>   Le plus aigu de sa fouldre à troys pointes
>   Pour le payment de son juste loyer. (*A* 182, 12–14)

May heaven send the most piercing of its three-pronged lightning upon her tongue as the payment of what she has deserved.

In his initial allusion to Jupiter in the *Rime sparse*, in one of the recalls of his erotic conquests in the conclusion of the metamorphosis canzone, Petrarch deflects the Ovidian narration of the god's capture of his human prey into a claim for the status of his own poetry:

. . . fui l'uccel che più per l'aere poggia
alzando lei che ne' miei detti onoro. (*R* 23, 166–67)

I have been the bird that rises highest in the air raising her whom in
my words I honor.

The vaunt, which was to afford a constant thematic vein to later Petrar-
chan poets, is particularly suggestive for Ronsard's adoption of a poetic
persona in the early *Amours*. In yet another echo of that canzone already
evoked in the preceding chapter, he confides his desire to exalt his lady so
that her name,

. . . honneur des vers françoys,
Hault elevé par le vent de ma voix
S'en voleroyt sur l'aisle de ma rime. (*A* 73, 12–14)[93]

. . . honor of French verses, raised high by the wind of my voice
would take flight on the wing of my rhyme.

To the "detti" of Petrarch correspond the "vers" of Ronsard. The latter's
affirmation, however, is cast in the conditional, following the poet's im-
plied incapacity in its opening formulation: "Que n'ai je, Dame, & la
plume & la grace / Divine autant que j'ay la volonté" [Would that I had,
lady, pen and grace divine to equal my will]. Dassonville comments that
too little attention has been paid to such avowals, particularly rare in the
work of a man who does not suffer the sin of excessive modesty.[94] But we
need not conclude, as does the critic, that such passages signal Ronsard's
admission that he is temperamentally unsuited to the Petrarchan vein; for
closer attention frequently reveals that these protestations are closely
modeled on those of Petrarch's poet, who repeatedly proclaims his own
incapacity to capture the lady's beauty and her qualities adequately in
verse.

The model for this particular poem is Petrarch's lament that Laura's
star is an unlucky one, a "stella difforme," in that the celebration of her
name, worthy of the greatest ancient poets, had been entrusted to him
instead:

[nome] d'Omero dignitissima e d'Orfeo
o del pastor ch'ancor Mantova onora,
ch'andassen sempre lei sola cantando,
stella difforme e fato sol qui reo
commise a tal che 'l suo bel nome adora,
ma forse scema sue lode parlando. (*R* 187, 9–14)

for she is worthy of Homer and Orpheus and of the shepherd whom Mantua still honors, worthy to have them always singing only of her, but a deformed star and her fate, cruel only in this, have entrusted her to one who adores her lovely name but perhaps mars her praise when he speaks.

It was to the "beau nom" of Cassandre that Claude Binet, in his biography of Ronsard, attributed the motivation for the poet's amorous verse, "as he himself told me many times." Rigolot, who cites Binet's testimony, points out that it is particularly enlightening: "C'est le 'beau nom' de 'Cassandre' qui fascine l'onomaturge en Ronsard et lui donne de nouvelles raisons de suivre l'inimitable 'Thuscan.' Car la trace graphique et phonique du 'Nome' est bien une invention pétrarquienne."[95]

Take then the first sonnet in the *Amours* to give thematic priority to writing, as the poet records his attempt to voice the name of the beloved:

> Mais tout soubdain je suis espovanté,
>   Car sa grandeur qui l'esprit me martyre
>   Sans la chanter arriere me retire
>   De cent fureurs pantoyment tourmenté. (*A* 27, 5–8)

But suddenly I am overcome with fear, for her grandeur that martyrs my spirit pulls me back without singing of her, panting and tormented by a hundred furies.

R 20 has been proposed by both Weber and Gendre as the source of the first part of this poem, followed by a Platonic reference to poetic *fureur*. In fact, however, it has a much closer connection with the *Rime:* it rewrites the confession, in an early sonnet of the Italian collection, of failed early attempts to record Laura's name. Petrarch's poem, which opens with "Quando io movo i sospiri a chiamar voi, / e 'l nome che nel cor mi scrisse Amore," succeeds only in framing the individual syllables of her name, and the poet confesses to both his own presumption and the failure that may be its consequence:

> se non che forse Apollo si disdegna
> ch'a parlar de' suoi sempre verdi rami
> lingua mortal presuntuosa vegna. (*R* 5, 12–14)

except that perhaps Apollo is incensed that any mortal tongue should come presumptuous to speak of his eternally green boughs.

Ronsard's version is in this case exemplary of the originality with which he adapts his Petrarchan models. The tercets of his sonnet also attribute to Apollo the abortive outcome of the attempt to "compose" or formulate the lady's name but link them to the classical resonances of the name of Cassandre to compose a highly dramatic scene in which the god's presence, possessing the Delphic priestess, results in the silencing of the voice that would be raised:

Je suis semblable à la prestresse folle,
  Qui bégue perd la voix & la parolle,
  Dessoubz le Dieu qu'elle fuit pour neant.
Ainsi picqué de l'Amour qui me touche
  Si fort au cuoeur, la voix fraude ma bouche,
  Et voulant dire en vain je suis béant.[96]

I am like the mad priestess, who stammering loses her voice and her speech, beneath the God that she flees in vain. Thus stung by the Love that touches my heart with such force, my voice eludes my mouth, and wishing in vain to speak, I am left gaping.

Writing as the "new" Petrarch, Ronsard again and again appropriates the voice of Petrarch's lyric protagonist to render his poetic as well as his amorous experience. Early in the collection, he reduplicates Petrarch's stance as he attempts to write of the lady, to record his praise of her beauty:

Amor in altra parte non mi sprona,
né i pie' sanno altra via né le man come
lodar si possa in carte altra persona. (*R* 97, 12–14)

Love does not spur me anywhere else, nor do my feet know any other road, nor do my hands know how on paper any other person can be praised.

D'autre esperon mon Tyran ne me poingt . . .
Ma main ne sçait cultiver aultre nom,
Et mon papier n'est esmaillé, si non
De vos beaultez que ma plume colore. (*A* 25, 9, 12–14)

My tyrant drives me with no other spur . . . my hand knows not how to cultivate another name, and my paper is not adorned except with your beauties colored by my pen.

So, too, editors have noted, does he adapt Petrarch's proclamation that Laura is worthy to be celebrated by the greatest poets of antiquity:

Se Virgilio et Omero avessin visto
quel Sole in qual vegg'io con gli occhi miei,

tutte lor forze in dar fama a costei
avrian posto, e l'un stil coll'altro misto:
di che sarebbe Enea turbato e tristo,
Achille, Ulisse, e gli altri semidei . . . (R 186, 1–6)

If Virgil and Homer had seen that sun which I see with my eyes, they would have exerted all their powers to give her fame and would have mingled together the two styles: for which Aeneas would be angry; and Achilles, Ulysses, and the other demigods . . .

Si l'escrivain de la mutine armée,
    Eut veu tes yeulx, qui serf me tiennent pris,
    Les faictz de Mars il n'eut jamais empris,
Et le Duc Grec fut mort sans renommée . . . (A 84, 1–4)

If the scribe of the rebelling host had seen your eyes, that hold me enslaved, he would never had undertaken to record the deeds of Mars, and the Greek Duke would have died with no renown. . .

But on closer consideration the latter echo is particularly suggestive, because the conclusion of Ronsard's poem for which the verses above function as subtext takes as subtext on a different level his rivalry with Petrarch:

Mais s'il advient ou par le vueil des Cieux,
    Ou par le traict qui sort de tes beaulx yeulx,
    Qu'en publiant ma prise, & ta conqueste,
Oultre la Tane on m'entende crier,
    Iö, Iö, quel myrte, ou quel laurier
    Sera bastant pour enlasser ma teste? (9–14)

But if it comes about through the will of the Heavens, or through the arrow that comes from your lovely eyes, that in making public my captivity and your conquest I am heard to cry beyond the Don "Io, Io," what myrtle or what laurel will suffice to encircle my head?

These verses, for all their pronounced classical ring, echo the end of another sonnet of the *Rime* concerning the fame that the poet-lover would desire for Laura's name:

. . . del vostro nome, se mie rime intese
fossin sì lunghe, avrei pien Tyle e Batteo,
la Tana e 'l Nilo, Atlante, Olimpo e Calpe.

Poi che portar nol posso in tutte e quattro
parti del mondo, udrallo il bel paese
ch'Appenin parte e 'l mar circonda e l'Alpe. (*R* 146, 9–14)

. . . with your name, if my rhymes were understood so far away, I
would fill Thule and Bactria, the Don and the Nile, Atlas, Olympus,
and Calpe. Since I cannot bear it to all four parts of the world, the
lovely country shall hear it that the Apennines divide and the sea
and the Alps surround.

Examples may be readily multiplied. Now Ronsard, on the beauty of
Cassandre:

A front baissé je pleure gemissant,
   De quoy je suis (pardon digne de grace)
   Soubz l'humble voix de ma rime si basse,
   De tes beaultez les honneurs trahissant.
Je cognoy bien que je devroy me taire,
   Ou mieux parler: mais l'amoureux ulcere
   Qui m'ard le cuoeur, me force de chanter.
Doncque (mon Tout) si dignement je n'use
   L'encre & la voix à tes graces vanter,
   Non l'ouvrier, non, mais son destin accuse. (*A* 66, 5–14)

With head bowed I weep quivering, because I am (a fault worthy of
grace) betraying with the humble voice of my so lowly rhyme the
honors due to your beauties. I know well that I should fall silent, or
speak better: but the amorous ulcer that burns my heart obliges me
to sing. Thus (my All) if I do not worthily use ink and voice to praise
your graces, blame not the worker but his destiny.

While critical comment on this poem has focused on the opening qua-
train, for its identification of Cassandre's "beau chef jaunissant" in appar-
ent contradiction to Ronsard's usual celebration of her dark hair,[97] the rest
of the poem cited above is a mosaic of phrases and images from the *Rime
sparse:* Petrarch's poet writes "non perch'io non m'avveggia / quanto mia
laude è 'ngiuriosa a voi" [Not that I do not see how much my praise in-
jures you] (*R* 71, 16–17) and continues to write as he had written, while
confessing that he finds in the task "peso non da le mie braccia, / né ovra
da polir colla mia lima" [a weight that is not for my arms, a work not to be
polished with my file] (*R* 20, 1–6). Yet he writes still, under love's con-
straint: "Poi che per mio destino / a dir mi sforza quell'accesa voglia . . . "

[Since through my destiny that flaming desire forces me to speak . . .] (*R* 73, 1–2). The closing verses of Ronsard's poem are modeled on the ending of two poems from the *Rime:*

> . . . onde vien l'enchiostro, onde le carte
> ch'i' vo empiendo di voi; se 'n ciò fallassi,
> colpa d'Amor, non già defetto d'arte (*R* 74, 12–14)

> . . . and whence comes the ink, whence the pages that I fill with words of you (if in that I err, it is the fault of Love, not at all a lack of art)

and a sonnet whose phrasing of "il mio dir troppo umile" informs Ronsard's "humble voix de ma rime":

> "Lingua mortal al suo stato divino
> giunger non pote; Amor la spinge e tira
> non per elezion ma per destino." (*R* 247, 12–14)

> "Mortal tongue cannot reach her divine state; Love drives and draws his tongue, not by choice but by destiny."

"Non l'ouvrier, non, mais son destin accuse": the poet is obliged by Love to sing the praises of his lady—"l'amoureux ulcere . . . me force de chanter"—and both the love and the song are fated, inscribed in the record of Ronsard and Cassandre that will, as he writes in other poems, ultimately be submitted to the judgment not of their immediate audience but of posterity.

The closing poem of the collection reinscribes that record into contemporary history, locating it against the background of a national struggle— "Lors que HENRY loing des bornes de France, / Vangeoyt l'honneur de ses premiers ayeulx . . . " [When Henry far from the borders of France avenged the honor of his first ancestors . . .]—that would have been well known to his immediate audience at court, reminding us that Ronsard was not only the Prince of Poets but the poet of princes. The terms of its opening, however, are an obvious reminder to the reader of the Petrarchan mode chosen for the recueil as a whole, that of the effusions of a lover torn between hope and doubt: "J'alloy roullant ces larmes de mes yeulx, / Or plein de doubte, ores plein d'esperance" [I went about with these tears pouring from my eyes, now full of doubt, now full of hope]. To the "larmes" correspond the sighs of the poem's closing, reminding us once again of Petrarch's collection characterized at its opening as "quei sospiri": "Soyt pour jamais ce souspir engravé, / Dans l'immortel du temple de Memoyre" [May this sigh be forever engraved in the immortal space of the temple of Memory].[98] In penning these final verses, Ronsard would appear to impose a definitive closure on a poetic experience evoked through the multiple allusions to the most conventional elements of the Petrarchan tradition as they are concentrated in the proemial sonnet of the *Rime sparse:* allusions to a Petrarch who offers up his sighs, in the "vario stile in ch'io piango e ragiono / fra le vane speranze e 'l van dolore."

Defending the Title

The *Sonets pour Helene*

There was something ironic about the recognition of Ronsard as the "Pétrarque Vandomois" in 1554. For already in 1553, the year he published the expanded collection of the *Amours* whose Petrarchan strategy had earned him that coveted tribute, the current of poetic fashion had begun to run swiftly against the Petrarchan mode: in that year Du Bellay, who had only four years earlier set the example of the Petrarchan recueil in French with his *Olive*, published a satirical piece that was later, reworked, to bear the title "Contre les pétrarquistes."[1] Ronsard himself, however, was neither proclaiming nor practicing an absolute fidelity to the once-favored master: in that same year, once again demonstrating his prodigious adaptability, he published the *Livret de Folastries*, which shows instead the strong influence of Catullus and the neo-Latin poets. Although the *Folastries* did not bear his name, in the following year his responsiveness to new poetic currents was more openly demonstrated: in 1554, following shortly upon the appearance of Henri Estienne's edition of *Anacreon*, he published two other miscellaneous volumes, the *Bocage* and *Meslanges*, whose poems are often inspired by the *Greek Anthology*.[2]

It is not surprising, then, that when he returned to the project of reorganizing and republishing his *Amours*, many of the new poems introduced have a markedly different tone. While the two *Continuations des Amours* published successively in 1555 and 1556—whose poems were to appear together, from the time of the first collective edition of 1560, in a new organization known as the *Second Livre des Amours*—contain numerous poems that closely imitate Petrarchan originals and others that incorporate widely recognized Petrarchan motifs, for this new poetry the inspiration is no longer primarily Petrarchan; there is critical consensus, as William J. Kennedy observes, that "after *Les Amours* Ronsard moves away from the Petrarchan model as his major imitative concern."[3]

Much of the new impulse is stylistic, as Ronsard makes plain in the long poem which, with the title "A son Livre," closes the *Nouvelle Continuation* (cited as *NC*) in 1555 and in 1560 becomes the "Elegie" that opens the *Second Livre des Amours*.[4] Here Tibullus is one of the authorities cited for a new style of writing, a style "bas, / Populaire & plaisant, ainsi qu'a fait Tibulle, / L'ingenieux Ovide, & le docte Catulle" [lowly, popular, and pleasing, just as Tibullus did, and ingenious Ovid, and learned Catullus] (*NC* 42, 174–76). And Ronsard himself offers an explanation for his adoption of this new style: the "grave premier style" of his poems for Cassandre is ill suited, he now declares, for his celebration of a beloved much different from the former object of his affection.[5]

Critics have often endorsed Ronsard's explanation, concluding that the humble status of the putative Marie was indeed a principal motivation in his movement away from the Petrarchan idiom.[6] The explanation, however, is deliberately disingenuous, for it has been repeatedly pointed out that if the prominence of the name Marie in the new recueil superficially suggests an ensemble organized as a pendant to that for Cassandre, a number of the poems included in the *Continuations* were evidently written for other ladies: Cassandre herself; another (Parisian) Marie; a Sinope to whom were dedicated fourteen sonnets from the *Meslanges* of 1559 worked into the 1560 collection. Other poets, moreover, were making very similar moves during the same period.[7] But with Ronsard the innovation is thematic as well as stylistic, for at the same time that he announced his opposition to a narrowly Petrarchan style, he was loudly proclaiming his opposition to Petrarchan ideals of sobriety and constancy. Considering the many and varied reflections on inconstancy in these poems, one may well wonder, as does Gendre, whether Ronsard actually modified his style because of having met Marie or whether instead, wanting to change his style, he developed the role for her.[8]

It is in his avowed intent to achieve a "stile apart, sens apart, euvre apart," Dassonville notes, that Ronsard distinguishes himself from "these knights of fidelity" by setting himself up as the champion of inconstancy.[9] And there were other proponents. Jodelle, for example, who like Ronsard would elsewhere explore the theme, prominent in contemporary philosophical thought, of inconstancy as a principal characteristic of the created universe,[10] could write to a lady whose disdain he had suffered:

Vostre injuste desdain affranchit ma jeunesse
L'Amour se paist d'amour, c'est n'avoir point de coeur
D'aymer les cruautez d'une ingrate maistresse.[11]

Your unjust disdain liberates my youth. Love feeds upon love, it is to have no heart at all to love the cruelties of an ungrateful mistress.

In contrast to this sententiousness, Ronsard in "A son Livre" offers the lover practical advice concerning the response of "quelque jeune fille . . . à son premier amant" [some young lady . . . to her first lover]. Patience is in order, he counsels, for time will perhaps improve her, "la rendra meilleure"; but, on the contrary,

> . . . quand elle devient de pis en pis tousjours,
> Plus dure, & plus cruelle, & plus rude en amours,
> Il la faut laisser là, sans se rompre la teste
> De vouloir adoucir une si sotte beste.

If she continues to become worse and worse, harder and more cruel, and more savage in love, one must leave her there, without breaking one's head through wanting to sweeten such a stupid beast.

Despite the absence of explicit reference, the antipetrarchism of these two declarations is obvious, and it is difficult to imagine a notion more opposed to the spirit of the *Rime* than "ce genre de calcul et d'exigence."[12]

Yet all of this may miss an important point, for the case of Ronsard is singular in that the reaction against the Petrarchan vein is attributed by the poet himself to his reading of Petrarch, not now as text but as "story." Whether the new direction to which he insistently calls the reader's attention in "A son Livre" be identified as a more humble style or as amorous inconstancy, that direction is still defined by Ronsard in terms of Petrarch as both author and poetic persona, although now negatively, and it is in these terms that he draws the lines of his justification for turning away from Cassandre.[13] Is his new book to be read by some honest and genteel lady who would rebuke him for having abandoned Cassandre, the beloved who first wounded him with Love's arrow, on the grounds that "le bon Petrarque un tel peché ne feist, / Qui fut trente & un an amoureux de sa dame, / Sans qu'une autre jamais luy peust eschaufer l'ame . . . " [the good Petrarch committed no such sin, remaining in love with his lady for thirty-one years without any other ever being able to warm his soul . . .]? ("A son Livre," 38–40). Such a lady would be appealing to the authority of what had come to be associated with the name of Petrarch to designate a *type* of loving, one whose continuing evolution away from carnality is evident in a treatise on the *Maladie d'Amour* of slightly later date that introduces into it the medieval lyric theme of *amour lointain*:

Quelques Italiens veulent assurer que l'excellent Poëte Pétrarque aima sa Laura avec passion extrême & long temps, sans l'avoir iamais veüe, & que depuis on appelle en Italie ceste espèce d'Amour *Amor Petrarchevole*.

Some Italians assure us that the excellent poet Petrarch loved his Laura with an extreme passion for a long time without ever having seen her, and that since then this type of love is called in Italy *Petrarchan Love*.[14]

Implicit in the response of this hypothetical female reader is the question of the relation between poetry and ethics—between Petrarch's love experience and his love poetry—and it is that question that forms the basis now for Ronsard's challenge to the Petrarchan authority, incorporated in the new volume that is instructed to reply on his behalf.

Ronsard's strategy is informed by a commentary-biography tradition that had concerned itself not only with the "story" of Petrarch and Laura but with the "reality" of Petrarch's relationship with Laura. Perhaps with Petrarch as with no writer before him, Giovanni Parenti observes, the interpretations of commentator-biographers imposed the idea of an aesthetic as the application and literary execution of an ideal of ethical conduct, one that, like a vow, bound both the man and the writer.[15] Roberto Fedi puts it this way: with Bembo, the "verity" of the poet's love was one with the "veritable" status of the text. Hence Bembo's response to a skeptical reader: "Se il Petrarca non v'ha potuto persuadere egli di essere stato veramente innamorato di Madonna Laura, con tanti suoi belli e cari scritti volgari, e spezialmente col primo suo sonetto, nel quale non è verisimile che egli fingesse a sua vergogna: e con tanti altri latini, ne' quali egli fa testimonio di ciò, io non presumerò già di poterlovi persuadere io" [If Petrarch himself has not been able to persuade you that he had truly been in love with Madonna Laura, with all those fine and precious vernacular writings of his, and especially with his opening sonnet in which it is not plausible that he should feign his own shame, and with all the other Latin works in which he bears witness to it, I shall not presume to be able to persuade you.][16]

Ronsard was among the skeptical, and he was not to be persuaded; it is the question of reality that, like a magnet, draws his attention and his refutation. The terms of his recall of Petrarch's celebration of Laura in "A son Livre"—as "admirable, / Chaste, divine, sainte . . . "—are faithful to those of the Italian poet:

"Parrà forse ad alcun che 'n lodar quella
ch'i' adoro in terra, errante sia 'l mio stile

faccendo lei sovr'ogni altra gentile,
santa, saggia, leggiadra, honesta et bella" (*R* 247, 1–4).[17]

It will perhaps seem to someone that, in my praise of her whom I adore on earth, my style errs in making her noble beyond all others, holy, wise, charming, chaste, and beautiful.

But Ronsard's echo is malicious, for it is couched as part of a challenge to the sincerity of Petrarch's declaration. There are only two credible options, Ronsard insists:

Ou bien il jouissoit de sa Laurette, ou bien
Il estoit un grand fat d'aymer sans avoir rien,
Ce que je ne puis croire, aussi n'est il croiable. (49–51)

Either he took pleasure in his Laurette, or else he was a great fool to love while receiving nothing, which I cannot believe, indeed it is not believable.

Here, in contrast to the critique of an insincerity of style and attitude that had been formulated by others—"J'ay oublié l'art de pétrarquizer, / Je veulx d'Amour franchement deviser, / Sans vous flatter, et sans me déguisez," wrote Du Bellay [I have forgotten the art of Petrarchizing, I want to treat of love frankly, without flattering you and without disguising myself] [18]—it is the standard of chastity celebrated by Petrarch that is held up to the measure of experience and found wanting. Later in the poem, Ronsard will cite as an example of amorous besottedness the Ulysses who abandoned "Circe la belle" to rejoin an unfaithful Penelope who "luy absent . . . faisoit l'amour" [in his absence . . . was making love] (115–26).[19] In a similar confrontation, Ronsard in an "Odelette a sa maitresse" invoked nature and common sense to renounce that standard and to ridicule the Petrarchan poets who contented themselves with it, not only as poets but as lovers:

Les amans si frois en esté
Admirateurs de chasteté,
Et qui morfondus petrarquisent,
Sont toujours sots, car ils meprisent
Amour . . . (*L* VI, p. 213)

The lovers so cold in summer, admirers of chastity, and who Petrarchize chilled to the bone, are always foolish, because they hold Love in contempt . . .

In "A son Livre" the attack on the presumption of chastity is different, however, in that it invokes the "case" of Petrarch himself. Here the presupposition of the sincerity of Petrarch's posture in the *Rime sparse* is sacrificed to the demands of common sense, not to attack the "real" Petrarch but to defend that Petrarch against his own book. Ronsard grounds his reasoning, paradoxically, in the book itself: "car à voir son escrit / Il estoit esveillé d'un trop gentil esprit / Pour estre sot trente ans" [because one can tell from his works that he was animated by too noble a spirit to remain foolish for thirty years] (45–47). Hence the conclusion concerning Petrarch and Laura—"Non, il en jouissoit, *puis* l'a faitte admirable, chaste, divine, sainte" [no, he had his pleasure of her, *then* he made her admirable, chaste, divine, holy]—and the general conclusion concerning lovers *qua* love poets: "aussi tout amant doit / Loüer celle de qui jouissance il reçoit . . . " [thus must every lover praise the one from whom he receives his pleasure . . .]. In Ronsard's rewriting of the dictates of gallantry, the cynicism of this "rule for lovers" requires little comment, as he disclaims Petrarch's

> . . . authorité pour me donner sa loy,
> Ny à ceux qui viendroient apres luy, pour les faire
> Si long temps amoureux sans s'en pouvoir deffaire:
> Luy mesme ne fut tel . . . . (42–45)

> . . . authority to impose his law on me, nor on those who would come after him, to render them so long enamored without any escape: he himself was not like that . . .

Thus even while announcing that he abandons both Cassandre and the Petrarchan celebration of a chaste but constant love—in both senses, that he will not now "write like Petrarch"—Ronsard situates his new enterprise once again in terms of Petrarch, in effect to rewrite Petrarch's own story. This affirmation of independence is curious indeed, however, for it once again aligns Ronsard with Petrarch, albeit with a Petrarch understood now to have separated "life" from poetry.[20] As Richard Regosin observes, the revision of Petrarch's "story" in keeping with a new schema in which the lack of reward justifies the lack of constancy allows the Italian master to regain his place, but in a new order.[21] Having publicly changed sides on the issue himself, in a move that would clearly have been understood to set him in contrast if not direct opposition to the eternally suppliant Petrarch, Ronsard now changes his public reading of Petrarch to bring the two once again into conformity.

Much was at stake for Ronsard in "A son Livre."[22] Its significance in defining a new poetic posture is confirmed by its inclusion—as "Elegie à son livre"—as the opening poem of the new collection taking shape as the *Second Livre des Amours,* whose departure from Petrarchan norms both thematically and stylistically is immediately evident and has been exhaustively detailed. In the self-representation of the poet, its reappearance is all the more interesting because it is now accompanied by a long note by Rémy Belleau. And this note, much like many of the commentaries of Muret to the *Amours* of 1553, mediates between poet and reader through an affirmation of the "truth" of Ronsard's own experience that stands behind the poem. Assembling the various details in the lyric into a narrative and adding information to which he had privileged access as the poet's friend, Belleau sets forth the chronology of the love affair and the circumstances that had inspired the poem.[23] And that genesis, once again, is re-referred for its authenticity to a "story," one in which a variability dictated by nature replaces the ideal of Petrarchan constancy.

Ronsard was to reaffirm the story in a variety of poetic contexts, as in the "Elegie à Genevre" that retells, in a "discours / Qui commence & finist nos premieres amours," the opening of another of its chapters.[24] That chapter had begun, he reminds Genèvre, as he walked with her, "nous esgarant tous deux d'amoureuses traverses" [both of us wandering along amorous paths], and she asked his name and whether he had loved other ladies. Indeed, he had replied: he had loved first "une jeune Maistresse, / Que ma Muse en fureur sa Cassandre appelloit" [a young Mistress that my muse in its furor called its Cassandre] and then "une belle Marie / Que j'aimay plus que moy" [a beautiful Marie whom I loved more than my own self] but lost to another suitor, "un autre serviteur." But at present, he had then declared to his interlocutrice, he was happily *disponible:*

> Maintenant je poursuy toute amour vagabonde:
> Ores j'aime la noire, ores j'aime la blonde,
> Et sans amour certaine en mon coeur esprover
> Je cherche ma fortune où je la puis trouver.
> S'il te plaisoit m'aimer, par tes yeux je te jure
> Que d'une autre amitié jamais je n'aurois cure. (151–56)

Now I pursue any vagabond love: now I love the dark-haired lady, now the blond, and without feeling certain love in my heart, I seek my good fortune where I can find it. If it pleased you to love me, I swear by your eyes that I would never care for another friendship.

Other poems suggest that the lady had accepted this rather curiously

framed invitation, but still more poems attest that his promise of endur-
ing fidelity to Genèvre—"me prendre a jamais pour serviteur fidelle," he
had pleaded [take me forever as your faithful servant] (v. 115)—was no
more binding than the fervent promises to Cassandre and to Marie.[25]

Even as he celebrated the freedom of the inconstant lover, however,
Ronsard was to experience the confirmation that poetic fashion was fickle
indeed. For by 1570 the mode was once again Italian; in 1573, a whole
series of works testify to a renewal of interest in Petrarchism.[26] It is a new
strain now, one closely reflecting the tastes of the aristocratic salons that
rapidly came to prominence in the period: the poetic generation of 1570
may fairly be labeled, Mathieu-Castellani comments, as "that of worldly
and *précieux* Petrarchism."[27]

And yet . . . Ronsard was not unprepared for the changing tide. Among
the *Septiesme Livre des Poèmes*, published in 1569, we find a group of five
sonnets (18–22) that are very closely modeled on poems in the *Rime sparse*,
faithful to its conception both of the lady and of the poet's love service.[28]
In the following years he continued to offer up liberally his own comple-
ment of "poésie courtesane," celebrating one and then another of the la-
dies in the royal retinue in poems that would form part, on the one hand,
of the *Sonets et Madrigals pour Astrée*, on the other of the *Amours
d'Eurymedon et de Callirée*, neither of them lacking in Petrarchan ele-
ments.[29] But it was with another collection, first published, like these, in
the new collective edition of 1578, that his own return to Petrarchism was
to be insistently reasserted, and it responded, at least in part, to a chal-
lenge to his poetic entitlement. Foremost among the spate of new works in
the "courtly" Petrarchan vein published in 1573 were two collections,
bearing the titles of *Amours de Diane* and *Amours d'Hippolyte*, by a young
poet now publishing his *Premières Oeuvres poétiques*. Philippe Desportes
had taken a lesson from the new generation of Italian poets who had re-
newed the Petrarchan vogue in Italy by reinfusing it with a modified
neoplatonism, and his new stripe of courtly Petrarchism made him the
new favorite at court.[30] And according to the author of the funeral oration
later pronounced for Desportes, it was the brilliant success of that collec-
tion that compelled Ronsard's return to his amorous vein:

Au renom de ces vers, vers les Rois de nos coeurs,
Ce grand Ronsard tressaut, jaloux de tels honneurs,
Des Muses les outils, que refroidy par l'age
Il laissait pendre au croc, reprend de grand courage,
D'un effort plus qu'humain reschauffant son beau sang.
Que ne fait un grand coeur pour ne perdre son rang?[31]

At the fame of these verses, toward the Kings of our hearts, this great Ronsard is jolted; jealous of such honors, with great courage he takes up again the instruments of the Muses that he, chilled by age, was leaving hanging upon their hook, rewarming his noble blood with a superhuman effort. What will a great heart not do to retain its rank?

Ronsard himself, of course, did not put it that way; once again, he declares, it is love that compels him to write: "Cassandre me ravit, Marie me tint pris: / Ja grison à la cour d'une autre je m'espris" [Cassandre enchanted me, Marie held me captive: now with gray hair I fall in love at court with another], he will recall in a poem added to the ambitious new collection in 1584 (*Amours diverses*, 46). But critics have generally agreed with the judgment of Desportes's eulogist that with the *Sonets pour Helene*, Ronsard apparently determined to combat Desportes on his own terrain.[32] The stakes were high for the aging poet well practiced in courting the courtly public and avid as always for applause.[33] Whether that intense motivation suggests that Hélène was not the object of genuine affection or admiration but merely a pretext—and especially a name—that he seized on to focus his rivalry with Desportes remains open to debate. There seems little doubt, however, that the new collection was intended, at least in part, to prove to current readers that he remained the legitimate pretender to the title of "French Petrarch."[34]

Although often cited as Ronsard's "return to Petrarchism," the *Sonets pour Helene* have in fact proven a particularly fertile ground for the demonstration of his deviations from Petrarchism. It is commonly acknowledged that the density of the reprise of Petrarchan elements is striking in this late collection; both sonnet 10 and sonnet 40 of Book I, to cite but two examples, are so largely a composite of poems from the *Rime* as to constitute almost a pastiche.[35] Many of the poems to which Ronsard now recurs are those already privileged, sometimes repeatedly, as loci of borrowings in his earlier, avowedly "Petrarchan" phase; and incontestably, as Weber comments, a certain number of Petrarchan formulas had been so assimilated into French poetic language since 1550 that it is difficult to be sure, when Ronsard uses them now, whether he is imitating Petrarch or imitating himself.[36] As with other questions of reception, however, there have been revisions and re-revisions of critical opinion concerning the nature and significance of the Petrarchan presence,[37] and often these have concluded in favor of its ambiguity. Grahame Castor, for example, observes that though the poems of the collection "place themselves very squarely and very clearly within the petrarchan tradition," we find here a Ronsard who "is both accepting the petrarchan conventions and simultaneously rejecting them";[38] Yvonne Bellenger identifies the same feature as "the paradox of the *Sonets pour Helene*."[39]

Ronsard's renewal of his claim to be the "French Petrarch" requires closer scrutiny. For while the new poetic mode appeared, in its attachment to the Italian poets of the Quattrocento—"pétrarquisante" or "néopétrarquiste"—to have largely forgotten Petrarch,[40] and though he would openly oppose the neoplatonist vogue to which Desportes owed much of his success,[41] Ronsard was in fact sounding out new resonances from the *Rime sparse*. In some of the sonnets of the new collection, as Donald Stone points out, we find an increasingly rich exploitation of the Petrarchan vein.[42] And it was in part through a reaffirmation of the Petrarchan persona that Ronsard once more entered the lists of poetic contenders.

Curiously, the two aspects that most convincingly confirm that reaffirmation are prominent among those that have been frequently invoked as evidence of his departure from the Petrarchan vein. The first concerns the choice of the object of love and of poetic celebration, the second the related emphases on the poet-lover's self-illusion and his aging. In both of these readers have discerned a Ronsard more "personal" than conventional, a Ronsard who proclaims his status as individual in confrontation with Petrarchan tradition; and it is incontestable that from the *Sonets pour Helene* there emerges a more individualized "portrait of the poet," a "volonté de se faire connaître à ses lecteurs," as Robert Garapon observes.[43] But we are again confronted with an apparent paradox. For while it is in large part through the addition of circumstantial detail—conversations, exchanges of gifts and letters, clear indications of places and occasions—that Ronsard creates this "new" persona,[44] the collection at the same time reveals a preoccupation with the "story" of Petrarch as poet in terms of which he now casts the "story" of Ronsard and Hélène.

The opening sonnet of the *Sonets* is addressed to Hélène:

> Ce premier jour de May, Helene, je vous jure
> Par Castor, par Pollux, vos deux freres jumeaux,
> Par la vigne enlassee à l'entour des ormeaux,
> Par les prez, par les bois herissez de verdure,
>
> Par le Printemps sacré, fils aisné de Nature,
> Par le sablon qui roule au giron des ruisseaux,
> Par tous les rossignols, merveille des oiseaux,
> Qu'autre part je ne veux chercher autre aventure.
>
> Vous seule me plaisez: j'ay par election,

Et non à la volee aimé votre jeunesse:
Ainsi je prins en gré toute ma passion.
    Je suis de ma fortune autheur, je le confesse:
La vertu m'a conduit en telle affection:
Si la vertu me trompe, adieu belle Maistresse.

This first day of May, Helene, I swear to you by Castor and Pollux, your twin brothers, by the vine enlaced around the elm trees, by the fields, by the woods bristling with green, by the sacred Springtime, eldest son of Nature, by the sand that rolls along the bed of the streams, by all the nightingales, marvel among birds, I desire to seek no other adventure elsewhere. You alone please me; I have by choice, not frivolously loved your youth: thus all my suffering pleases me. I confess that I am the author of my fortune; virtue brought me to such affection: should virtue deceive me, farewell fair Mistress.

Although few perhaps would accept these verses as conclusive evidence of a particular circumstance of patronage, that of a suggestion by Catherine de Medicis that Ronsard celebrate a young woman particularly admired in the circle of the court,[45] Ronsard's near-contemporaneous poetic celebration of other ladies indeed leads one to anticipate that the *Sonets* to follow will take shape in the context of royal favor and patronage.[46] And it is very likely, as Mary Morrison observes, that Ronsard's rivalry with Desportes may be at issue in this opening poem, to demonstrate his mastery in composing a sonnet swearing his lasting fealty to the lady.[47] "Et où rien de plus grand pourroit estre juré, / Je l'appelle à tesmoin de ce que je veux dire: / Jamais d'autres beautés mon oeil ne sera pris . . .," declares Desportes [and where nothing more grand could be sworn, I call upon her to witness to what I wish to say: My eye shall never be taken by other beauties . . .], and we might indeed conclude that Ronsard here takes up, deliberately and triumphantly, the weak phrase "rien de plus grand" to invoke an extraordinary array of highly particularized *témoins*, from Helen's mythological brothers Castor and Pollux to a personified Springtime "eldest son of Nature" and the images, at once singularly sharp and sensuous, drawn from nature, of the vine entwined around the elm and the fine sand rolling in the "lap" of the stream.

But whatever the more immediate circumstances of its composition, the poem also suggests that "to some extent, at least, this will be an 'antipetrarchan' collection—or rather that there will be clear variations from the standard petrarchan patterns."[48] Readers have found in its conclusion a particularly compelling indication of Ronsard's self-distancing from the Petrarchan model, and certainly the contrast with the Petrarchan verses inevitably recalled is marked indeed:

"Lingua mortale al suo stato divino
giunger non pote: Amor la spinge e tira
non per elezion ma per destino." (*R* 247, 12–14)

"Mortal tongue cannot reach her divine state; Love drives and draws his tongue, not by choice but by destiny."

It is crucial that both Ronsard's poem and Petrarch's foreground the question of choice and that their answers are radically opposed: to Petrarch's "non par elezion," Ronsard's "par election" responds with a resounding note of volition, of prideful self-mastery. Whereas Petrarch in numerous other poems of the *Rime sparse* will lament or celebrate the fated nature of his love for Laura, Ronsard will repeatedly reaffirm his willful choice: "Seule je te choisy" [I choose you alone], he tells Hélène, "seule aussi tu me plais" [you alone please me] (I, 15, 14); or he addresses her as "Beauté, que pour maistresse unique j'ay choisie" [Beauty, whom I have chosen as my only mistress].[49]

The final verses of Ronsard's opening poem are yet more emphatic. Affirming to Cassandre that virtue alone had led him to his deep affection, he continues—most unconventionally—with a warning to her against betrayal: "Si la vertu me trompe, adieu belle Maistresse." Can it be, the reader may wonder from the outset, that he is misguided, mistaken in his choice? The implication of a form of contract, moreover, anticipated in the oath he takes to Hélène in the first verse of this first poem—"Ce premier jour de May, Helene, je vous jure"—is made explicit very soon thereafter:

Naisse de noz amours une nouvelle plante,
Qui retienne noz noms pour eternelle foy,
Qu'obligé je me suis de servitude à toy,
Et qu'à nostre contract la terre soit presente. (I, 5, 5–8)

May a new plant be born of our love, that will retain our names in eternal witness that I have committed myself in servitude to you, and that the earth is present at our pact.

At some point—perhaps on the same occasion as that of sonnet 1, although not necessarily so—Ronsard and Hélène exchanged vows:

Dessus l'autel d'Amour planté sur vostre table
Vous me fistes serment, & je le fis aussi,
Que d'un coeur mutuel à s'aimer endurcy
Nostre amitié promise iroit inviolable.
Je vous juray ma foy, vous feistes le semblable . . . (I, 45, 1–5)

On the altar of Love set up on your table you made me an oath, and
I did the same, that resolute to love each other with mutual heart our
pledged friendship would be inviolable. I swore you my faith, you
did the same thing . . .

Such indications of reciprocity, although infrequent in the collection, radi-
cally alter the Petrarchan circumstance of the unattainable beloved. More
even than her inflexible resistance that fails to reward the poet's love ser-
vice—"Qui sert bien, sans parler demande son loyer" [he who serves well,
asks without speech for his reward] he objects to her reticence in a poem
added in 1584[50]—they afford the justification for the bitter reproaches lev-
eled at the lady in the present of the poem:

Je vous juray ma foy, vous feistes le semblable.
Mais vostre cruauté, qui des Dieux n'a soucy,
Me promettoit de bouche, & me trompoit ainsi:
Ce-pendant vostre esprit demeuroit immuable.
    O jurement fardé sous l'espece d'un Bien!
O perjurable autel! ta Deité n'est rien.
O parole d'amour non jamais asseuree! (5–11)[51]

I swore you my faith, you did the same thing. But your cruelty, that
fears not the Gods, was a promise merely spoken, and thus it de-
ceived me, while your spirit remained unmoved. Oh oath disguised
in a semblance of a Good! Oh altar of perjury! your Deity is nothing.
Oh word of love never sure!

Yet despite the prominence, achieved by the liminal position of this
sonnet, of Ronsard's insistence on his autonomous choice of Hélène as the
object of his love, we should hesitate in adopting it to define his overall
emphasis in the *Sonets pour Helene*. Nor should we be quick to generalize
from the emphasis on willful choice that "there is no longer an inna-
moramento,"[52] for elsewhere in the *Sonets* the innamoramento is repre-
sented—and repeatedly—on the Petrarchan model of the fatal blow in-
flicted by Amor. The distinguishing features of the model as he adapts it
are drawn prominently from two poems of the *Rime:* sonnet 2, in which
Petrarch makes use of the conventional imagery of the innamoramento as

a wounding inflicted by Amor cast as a stealthy adversary, and, from the celebrated "metamorphosis canzone" (*Rime* 23), the introductory passage that explains its circumstances. Both merit citation at length as points of reference:

Per fare una leggiadra sua vendetta
et punire in un dì ben mille offese,
celatamente Amor l'arco riprese,
come uom ch'a nocer luogo e tempo aspetta.
Era la mia virtute al cor ristretta
per far ivi et negli occhi sue difese
quando 'l colpo mortal là giù discese
ove solea spuntarsi ogni saetta;
però turbata nel primiero assalto
non ebbe tanto né vigor né spazio
che potesse al bisogno prender l'arme,
o vero al poggio faticoso et alto
ritrarmi accortamente da lo strazio
del quale oggi vorrebbe, et non po aitarme. (*R* 2)

To take a graceful revenge and to punish in one day a thousand offenses, Love took up his bow again secretly, like a man who waits for the time and place to hurt. My vital power was concentrated in my heart, to make there and in my eyes his defense, when the fatal blow fell where every previous arrow had been blunted; therefore, confused in the first assault, he lacked both strength and time to take up arms in this need, or to lead me up the weary high mountain away from the slaughter, out of which now he would wish to help me, but cannot.

Nel dolce tempo de la prima etade,
che nascer vide et ancor quasi in erba
la fera voglia che per mio mal crebbe,
perché cantando il duol si disacerba,
canterò com'io vissi in libertade
mentre Amor nel mio albergo a sdegno s'ebbe;
poi seguirò sì come a lui ne 'ncrebbe
troppo altamente e che di ciò m'avenne,
di ch'io son fatto a molta gente esempio . . . (*R* 23, 1–9)

In the sweet time of my first age, which saw born and still almost unripe the fierce desire which for my hurt grew—because, singing,

pain becomes less bitter—I shall sing how then I lived in liberty
while Love was scorned in my abode; then I shall pursue how that
chagrined him too deeply, and what happened to me for that, by
which I have become an example for many people . . .

I' dico che dal dì che 'l primo assalto
mi diede Amor, molt'anni eran passati,
sì ch'io cangiava il giovenil aspetto,
e d'intorno al mio cor pensier gelati
fatto avean quasi adamantino smalto
ch'allentar non lassava il duro affetto;
    lagrima ancor non mi bagnava il petto
né rompea il sonno, et quel che in me non era
mi pareva un miracolo in altrui.
Lasso, che son? che fui?
La vita el fin, e 'l dì loda la sera;
ché sentendo il crudel di ch'io ragiono
infin allor percossa di suo strale
non essermi passato oltra la gonna,
prese in sua scorta una possente Donna
ver cui poco giamai mi valse o vale
ingegno o forza o dimandar perdono;
ei duo mi trasformaro in quel ch'i sono,
facendomi d'uom vivo un lauro verde
che per fredda stagion foglia non perde. (*R* 23, 21–40)

I say that since the day when Love gave me the first assault many
years had passed, so that I was changing my youthful aspect; and
around my heart frozen thoughts had made almost an adamantine
hardness which my hard affect did not allow to slacken: no tear yet
bathed my breast nor broke my sleep, and what was not in me
seemed to me a miracle in others. Alas, what am I? what was I? The
end crowns the life, the evening the day. For that cruel one of whom
I speak, seeing that as yet no blow of his arrows had gone beyond
my garment, took as his patroness a powerful Lady, against whom
wit or force or asking pardon has helped and helps me little: those
two transformed me into what I am, making me of a living man a
green laurel that loses no leaf for all the cold season.

These are both well-known poems that had already attracted imitative
endeavors. Ronsard's own exceptionally close attention to the detail of

Petrarch's versions is readily evident in a poem in which he once again recalls Love as "the Archer" armed with fatal arrows:

Heureux le Chevalier, que la Mort nous desrobe,
Qui premier me fit voir de ta Grace l'attrait:
Je la vy de si loin, que la poincte du trait
Sans force demoura dans les plis de ma robe.
    Mais ayant de plus pres entendu ta parole,
Et veu ton oeil ardent, qui de moy m'a distrait,
Au coeur entra la fléche avecque ton portrait,
Heureux d'estre l'autel de ce Dieu qui m'affole. (II, 27, 1–8)

Happy the Knight, whom Death steals from us, who first made me see the appeal of your Grace: I saw it from so far away, that the point of the arrow remained without force in the folds of my robe. But having heard you speak from a closer distance, and seen your flashing eye that distracted me from myself, the arrow entered my heart along with your portrait, happy to be the altar of that God that drives me mad.

In this poem in which he attempts to reconcile the Petrarchan version of the instantaneous *innamoramento* in *R* 23 with the versions of his initial—although ultimately futile—resistance to Hélène's charms evoked in other poems of this collection, the image of the opening stanza may appear somewhat curious if we fail to recall the passage of *Rime* 23 of which Weber reminds us, depicting Amor's recognition that his initial efforts had been in vain: that, as his intended victim notes, the god's shafts had until then been without consequence.

    Or let us take the development of the suggestion, obligatory in the version of the *innamoramento* in the *Rime,* of the lover's earlier resistance to the charms of other ladies. That element, which figures prominently in the complex Ovidian intertext of Petrarch's collection, recalls Apollo's fated love for the nymph Daphne, imposed upon him by a vengeful Amor whose power had been mocked by the god.[53] And it would of course appear little less than incongruous in the case of the lover of the *Sonets pour Helene,* for not only had Ronsard in the course of his long poetic career published poems celebrating several ladies; he had also vigorously projected himself as the champion of inconstancy in defense of his successive affections. Poems to this effect appear in earlier collections, and in an often-cited poem of the *Sonets* he will remind his reader of his cumulative career as lover by declaiming his farewell to two of the *belles* to whom he had dedicated entire collections—"belle

Cassandre, & vous belle Marie"—because Love has now ordered him to pursue Hélène in turn:

> Maintenant en Automne encore malheureux,
> Je vy comme au Printemps de nature amoureux,
> A fin que tout mon âge aille au gré de la peine:
>   Et ores que je deusse estre exempt du harnois,
> Mon Colonnel m'envoye à grands coups de carquois
> R'assieger Ilion pour conquerir Heleine. (II, 10, 9–14)

Now in Autumn, still unhappy, I live as I did in Springtime amorous by nature, such that my entire life be ruled by the distress: and now that I should be freed from the harness, my Colonel dispatches me with great laying on of quivers to lay siege again to Ilion to conquer Helen.

Let us look more closely at the version of the *innamoramento* in the Premier Livre of the *Sonets:*

> J'avois desja passé le meilleur de ma vie,
> Tout franc de passion, fuyant le nom d'aimer.
>   Je soulois maintenant ceste Dame estimer,
> Et maintenant cest'autre, où me portoit l'envie,
> Sans rendre ma franchise à quelqu'une asservie:
> Rusé je ne voulois dans les retz m'enfermer.
>   Maintenant je suis pris . . . (I, 31, 3–9)

I had already passed the best part of my life, quite free of passion, fleeing the name of loving. I used to esteem first this Lady, then this other, as I fancied, without putting my liberty in the service of anyone: clever, I did not want to fall into the nets. Now I am caught . . .

Now his earlier loves are represented as passion-free, as a pastime in which he had bestowed his "esteem" on first one and then another lady. For the reader of his earlier *Amours,* this self-definition as "franc de passion, fuyant le nom d'aimer" [free from passion, fleeing the very name of love] might well ironically recall, for example, the dramatic opening of a poem concerning Cassandre, "Franc de raison, esclave de fureur, / Je voys chassant une Fére sauvage" [free of reason, a slave to madness, I go chasing a wild creature] (*A* 113); and that reader is likely to find the poet's declaration to Hélène early in the Premier Livre, that "Je suis du camp d'Amour pratique Chevalier: / Pour avoir trop souffert, le mal m'est familier" [I am an experienced Knight in Love's army: through having suffered over much, pain is familiar to me] (I, 14, 9–10), to be an entirely appropriate summary, not only of the *Sonets* but of the entire succession of Ronsard's amorous recueils. But that reader is now apparently to understand that all those protestations of the frenzied extremes of ardor, all those paroxysms of suffering, were the mere feint of a *rusé* poet and that only now has his resistance to the snares of love at last proved inadequate—because of the fatal charm of Hélène.

Equally fundamental in Petrarch's representation of the innamoramento is the failure of Reason to defend against Love's attack. While Petrarch's early Italian commentators, as Kennedy notes, unanimously respond in a moralistic vein, reading such confrontations as "the impersonal drama of a psychomachia, a battle of the senses against reason, flesh against spirit,"[54] Ronsard's focus remains steady on the dramatic potential of the metaphor. The explanation, touched upon often in a minor key in the *Amours* of 1552–53—for example, in "Qui voudra voyr" that opens the first collection of the *Amours*, the spectator of Ronsard's plight as Love's victim "cognoistra combien la raison peult / Contre son arc, quant une foys il veult / Que nostre cuoeur son esclave demeure"—is one of the most frequent in the *Sonets pour Helene*. At the first sight of Hélène, the poet confides, "Ma Raison, sans combattre, abandonna la place" [My Reason, without resisting, abandoned the field] (I, 13, 12). From *Rime* 2 cited above Ronsard derives the scenario:

> Je souspire la nuict, je me complains le jour
> Contre toy, ma Raison, qui mon fort abandonnes,
> Et pleine de discours, confuse, tu t'estonnes
> Dés le premier assaut, sans defendre ma tour. (I, 47, 5–8).[55]

I sigh at night, by day I complain against you, my Reason, who abandon my stronghold, and full of speech, confused, you are stunned from the first assault, without defending my tower.

The following poem combines this image with that found in *Rime* 3 of the lady's eyes as the fatal agents:

> Bienheureux fut le jour, où mon ame sujette
> Rendit obeyssance à ta douce rigueur,
> Quand d'un traict de ton oeil tu me perças le coeur,
> Qui ne veult endurer qu'un autre luy en jette.
> La Raison pour neant au chef fit sa retraite,
> Et se mit au dongeon, comme au lieu le plus seur:
> D'esperance assaillie, & prise de douceur,
> Rendit ma liberté, qu'en vain je re-souhaite. (I, 48, 1–8)

Most happy was the day when my subjected soul gave its obeisance to your sweet severity, when a shaft from your eye pierced my heart that would tolerate it from no other. Reason made its retreat to my head to no avail, and hid in the dungeon as the place of greatest safety: assailed by hope, and overcome by sweetness, it yielded up my liberty, that I wish for now in vain.

And again in a poem late in the Premier Livre:

Vous avez telle peste en mon coeur respandue,
Que mon sang s'est gasté, & douloir il me faut
Que ma foible Raison dés le premier assaut,
Pour craindre trop vos yeux, ne s'est point defendue.
Je n'en blasme qu'Amour, seul autheur de mon mal,
Qui me voyant tout nud, comme archer desloyal,
De mainte & mainte playe a mon ame entamee. (I, 54, 5–11)

You have spread such a plague throughout my heart that my blood is tainted, and I must lament that my feeble Reason, from the first assault, from fearing your eyes too much, mounted no defense at all. For that I blame only Love, the only author of my pain, who like a treacherous archer, seeing me quite naked, penetrated my soul with countless wounds.

The conclusion of the poem, as noted by Ronsard's editors, is then drawn directly from the version of the innamoramento in *Rime* 3. There Petrarch's poet laments that Amor, finding him "completely disarmed," wronged him by wounding him in that state while failing even to show his weapons to the well-defended lady, "a voi armata non mostrar pur l'arco," and Ronsard follows closely: "Et à vous, qui estiez contre nous deux armee, / N'a monstré seulement la poincte de son traict" [and to you, who were armed against both of us, he did not even show the point of his shaft] (13–14).

The two representations, that of deliberate choice confirmed in a contractual engagement and that of fated innamoramento affecting the poet alone, set forth alternative explanations of the nature of the relation between poet and lady: between the Ronsard who proclaims, "je suis de mon fortune autheur," and the Ronsard who inculpates Amour as "seul autheur de mon mal."[56] The discrepancy remains characteristic, despite an apparent attempt in a few poems to reconcile the two versions:

L'Amour & la Raison, comme deux combatans,
Se sont escarmouchez l'espace de quatre ans:
A la fin j'ay perdu, veincu par destinee. (I, 23, 6–8)

Love and Reason, as two combatants, skirmished for some four
years; in the end I lost, vanquished by fate.

In at least one biographical reading of the *Sonets* the change has been
explained as a progression from the former interpretation to the latter, an
evolution in the poet's attitude reflecting Ronsard's response to Hélène's
early acquiescence and then her withdrawal—his early enthusiasm fol-
lowed by his disillusionment.[57] In fact, however, the attitudes do not occur
in sequence; on the contrary, they alternate throughout the collection and
even, on occasion, in the same poem. Evoking the lady's cruelty and dis-
dain, for example, Ronsard introduces—if only to reject it as impossible of
realization—the thought of *not* loving Hélène: "Si je changeois d'amour,
de douleur je mourrois. / Seulement quand je pense au changement, je
tremble" [If I were to change loves, I would die of sorrow. I tremble when
I merely think of changing] (I, 38); but in the opening verse of the same
poem he has rejected the possibility of other loves—"Pour voir d'autres
beautez mon desir ne s'appaise" [My desire is not assuaged by the sight of
other beauties]—for which the reason given is that "Tant du premier
assaut vos yeux m'ont surmonté" [So much did your eyes overcome me
from the first assault]. The verse, as Weber notes, recalls the "primiero
assalto" of *Rime* 2, 9 and 29, 21—an idea in contradiction with the resis-
tance that Ronsard claims he had at first mounted to the possibility of
loving Hélène.[58]

Petrarch's example, which had well served the Italian poets of the pre-
ceding century during which the *Rime* imposed itself as dominant model
for the production of love lyrics, had proven extraordinarily flexible.
Those poets had demonstrated that the repertory of Petrarchan "situa-
tions" afforded elements that could be readily assembled according to the
love story to be recounted, susceptible to introduction and recombination
in a variety of contexts. The major paradox of this "petrarchismo corti-
giano," Marco Santagata observes, lies in its having succeeded in making
of a lyric experience openly opposed to the social use of poetry the most
pliant vehicle for the representation of the gallant adventures of an entire
society.[59] In the case of the French courtly society of the early 1570s that
Ronsard determined to regain as his audience, one in which courtier-
poets overtly postured as postulants for the attention of ladies who were
no less well versed in the currents of poetic fashion,[60] the writing of poetry
itself was a part of the *aventure galante.*

Love poetry as well as love is, of course, thematically prominent in all
of Ronsard's earlier collections of *Amours.* Now in his self-representation
in the *Sonets pour Helene,* where he offers both a Petrarchan and an alterna-
tive version of his choice of love object, he offers too a doubled vision of

his choice of poetic subject. Here again we are confronted with an initial contrast, for though Ronsard's opening poem lacks any reference to poetry—his oath to Cassandre concerns exclusively his amorous fidelity, "Qu'autre part je ne veux chercher autre avanture"—the poem of the *Rime* generally alleged as its model is much concerned with the lady as poetic subject:

> Parrà forse ad alcun che 'n lodar quella
> ch'i' adoro in terra, errante sia 'l mio stile
> faccendo lei sovr'ogni altra gentile,
> santa, saggia, leggiadra, onesta e bella.
> A me par il contrario, e temo ch'ella
> non abbia a schifo il mio dir troppo umile,
> degna d'assai più alto et più sottile;
> et chi nol crede venga egli a vedella . . . (R 247, 1–8)

It will perhaps seem to someone that, in my praise of her whom I adore on earth, my style errs in making her noble beyond all others, holy, wise, charming, chaste, and beautiful. I believe the opposite, and I am afraid that she is offended by my too humble words, since she is worthy of much higher and finer ones: and who does not believe me, let him come to see her . . .

Petrarch's poet has not chosen to celebrate Laura in verse; it is his destiny to do so (vv. 12–14); and Ronsard will proclaim his autonomous and deliberate choice of Hélène as poetic subject, creating a scenario perfectly consonant with the voluntary choice of love object of which he boasts in the opening sonnet of the *Sonets*.

The willful nature of the choice is confirmed in poems throughout the collection, perhaps most directly here late in the second book, where it is claimed as a consequence of his need for poetic inspiration:

> Il me faut donc aimer pour avoir bon esprit,
> Afin de concevoir des enfans par escrit,
> Pour allonger mon nom aux depens de ma peine.
>   Quel sujet plus fertil sçauroy-je mieux choisir
> Que le sujet qui fut d'Homere le plaisir,
> Ceste toute divine & vertueuse Heleine? (II, 46, 9–14)

I am obliged then to love in order to have a good wit, if I wish to conceive children through my writing, to perpetuate my name at the expense of my pain. What more fertile subject could I choose than the subject that was Homer's pleasure, this all divine and virtuous Helen?

More than ten years earlier, Ronsard had penned a less bold but equally explicit scenario as justification for an earlier phase of his amorous engagement, the youthful amours for which he had been reproached by "Predicans & Ministres de Geneve":

> Aussi tost que la Muse eut emflé mon courage
> M'agitant brusquement d'une gentille rage,
> Je senti dans mon cueur un sang plus genereux,
> Plus chaut & plus gaillard, qui me fist amoureux:
> A vint ans je choisi une belle maistresse . . . [61]

> Just as soon as the Muse had inflated my courage, agitating me suddenly with a noble rage, I felt in my heart a blood more generous, warmer and more hearty, that rendered me amorous: at the age of twenty, I chose a beautiful Mistress . . .

These elements in the necessary union of love and poetic creation are affirmed elsewhere in terms of a physiology and psychology appropriate to the young, a poetic *fureur* that "n'a poinct de vigueur / Sy le sang jeune & chault n'escume en nostre cueur" [totally lacks vigor if young and warm blood does not foam up in the heart]. [62] Not surprisingly, what is represented in this poem as the "sang . . . genereux & chault" in the young "poëte gaillard" is attributed, in the "Response," to the Muse, prompting him to choose an object for both love and poetry, and he insists that it was "pour hausser ma langue maternelle" [to raise my mother tongue] that he had composed poems in her honor, claiming the laurel crown as a consequence. In the *Sonets*, the contrast of his self-representation as aging with his portrayals of the inevitable impulses of youth serves further to underline the willed nature of his choice.

And yet . . . the coincidence of the innamoramento and the fated song—whether fated by the lady's name itself or dictated by Amour—is also fundamental in the collection. As early as sonnet 3 of Book I, Ronsard identifies the name—"ma douce Helene"—as object of his love: "Heureux celuy qui souffre une amoureuse peine / Pour un nom si fatal" [Happy he who suffers an amorous pain for such a fatal name]. Not only Hélène but Surgères: it is not without interest that the first mention of poetry in the collection occurs in the first poem to represent the innamoramento according to the Petrarchan model, for here Amour inflicts a wound that, however conventional, is redefined as an ardor, not to love but to "chanter":

> Et me mostrant son arc, comme Dieu, me tança,
> Que j'oubliois, ingrat, ses loix & ses mysteres.

Il me frappa trois fois de ses ailes legeres:
Un traict le plus aigu dans les yeuz m'eslança.
La playe vint au coeur, qui chaude me laissa
Une ardeur de chanter les honneurs de Surgeres. (I, 8, 3–8)

And showing me his bow, as a God, he reproached me that I was ungratefully forgetting his laws and his mysteries. He struck me three times with his light wings: he hurled the sharpest of shafts into my eyes. The wound continued on to my heart and it, warmed, left me with a desire to sing the honors of Surgeres.

Early in Book II, in a poem "Anagramme," which reconstructs Elene de Surgeres as "LE RE DES GENEREUX" and explicitly invokes the dialogue of Plato in which the natural affinity of words and the things they name is affirmed, he attributes to her name the origin of his love:

Les noms (ce dit Platon) ont tresgrande vertu:
Je le sens par le tien, lequel m'a combatu
Par armes, qui ne sont communes ny legeres.
Sa Deité causa mon amoureux soucy. (II, 6, 9–12)

Names (so Plato says) have very great power: I feel it through yours, which has fought me with arms that are neither common nor light. Its Deity was the cause of my amorous care.

In fact, as Nathalie Dauvois points out, the scenes of poetic innamoramento in the *Sonets* lead back constantly from the name to the myth, in that it is the image not of the name but of the myth that is reborn, as in this often-cited celebration:

Nom tant de fois par Homere chanté,
Seul tout le sang vous m'avez enchanté.
O beau visage engendré d'un beau Cygne . . . (II, 16, 9–11)[63]

Name sung by Homer so many times, you alone have enchanted all my blood. O lovely face engendered by a lovely Swan . . .

As Dauvois notes, moreover, in a number of his expansions of name/poetry/myth Ronsard adds new dimensions to a Petrarchan model in which the Italian poet frequently avows his incapacity to sing adequately of the lady; particularly deft is his evocation of the background of the Trojan conflict.[64] But as in so many other instances illustrative of his deviations from the Petrarchan model, other resonances remind us of its continued presence. Not least among these are the famous opening verses of *SH*

I, 3, the poem cited above for Hélène's name as object of the poet's devotion. Here that name, as it occurs for the first time in the collection, is identified through paronomasia: "Ma douce Helene, non, mais bien ma douce haleine, / Qui froide rafraischis la chaleur de mon coeur" [My sweet Hélène, no, rather my sweet breath that with its coolness tempers the heat of my heart]. The sweetness of the lady's breath and its suggestiveness of the kiss that vivifies the lover are, as Rigolot reminds us, among the familiar topoi of amorous poetry, and Ronsard had made use of them in his poems for Cassandre and for Marie.[65] For readers familiar with the *Rime*, however, it would now at once recall also Petrarch's repeated celebratory punning on Laura's name as the breeze, "l'aura."

There are other elements suggestive of close attention to the Petrarchan prototype in Ronsard's representation of his new poetic subject. In that first poem to recall the *innamoramento* and simultaneously initiate the theme of poetry, he recalls Love's admonition on that occasion:

> Chante (me dist Amour) sa grace & sa beauté,
> Sa bouche, ses beaux yeux, sa douceur, sa bonté:
> Je la garde pour toy le sujet de ta plume.
> —Un sujet si divin ma Muse ne poursuit.—
> Je te feray l'esprit meilleur que de coustume:
> L'homme ne peut faillir, quand un Dieu le conduit. (I, 8, 9–14)

Sing (Love tells me) her grace and her beauty, her mouth, her lovely eyes, her sweetness, her goodness: I keep her for you as the subject of your verses.—My Muse does not pursue such a divine subject.—I shall make your wit better than usual: a man cannot fail when a God leads him.

The scene is typical of Ronsard's artful blending of related sources. Love's gesture of striking the poet with his wings that precedes this command has its origin, as indicated in Weber's notes to the sonnet, in an ode of the Greek Anthology, and whereas in that poem the god orders the poet to follow him, the command to write inevitably recalls the opening of *Rime* 93: "Più volte Amor m'avea già detto: 'Scrivi'" [Many times had Love already said to me: "Write"]. And if that voice in turn merely urges the poet to testify to his experience of love—"quel che vedesti" [that which you saw]—and does not engage the imposition of the lady as the subject of his verses, the latter too has its place in Ronsard's dialogue with Petrarch. It recalls a poem from the *Rime* in which the question is central, the last canzone of Petrarch's collection (*R* 360), in which Amor, accused by the poet of having acted as "tiranno," advances in his defense his own account of his gift of the lady. Here Amor at the outset counters the accusations of the lover-as-plaintiff by a reminder of what he has achieved as poet—"salito in qualche fama / solo per me, che 'l suo intelletto alzai / ov'alzato per sé non fora mai" [risen to some fame only through me, who have raised up his intellect to where it could never have raised itself] (88–90)—and continues by underlining the magnitude of the privilege thus accorded: "a costui di mille / donne elette eccellenti n'elessi una, / qual non si vedrà mai sotto la luna / benché Lucrezia ritornasse a Roma" [for this fellow, from among a thousand worthy, excellent ladies I chose one such that her like will never be seen under the moon even though Lucrezia were to return to Rome] (98–100).

What are the implications of these two versions for the lady's poetic destiny? "Nostre contract" of *SH* I, 5 appears, as we have seen, to presuppose reciprocity, and late in a poem in Book I he urges her, in her interest as well as his own, not to discourage his poetic endeavor by dampening his ardor:

> Dés le premier berceau n'estoufe point ton nom.
> Pour bien le faire croistre, il ne le faut sinon
> Nourrir d'un doux espoir pour toute sa pasture:
> Tu le verras au Ciel de petit s'eslever.
> Courage, ma Maistresse, il n'est chose si dure,
> Que par longueur de temps on ne puisse achever. (I, 56, 9–14)[66]

Do not smother your renown from its very cradle. To make it grow well, you only need nourish it with a sweet hope for all its food: you will see it, from a small thing, rise up to Heaven. Courage, my Mistress, there is nothing so hard that it cannot be achieved in time.

The explicit record of Hélène's acceptance of the pact, however, is deferred until late in Book II, where it is formalized in her award to the poet of a crown of myrtle and laurel. Once again the notion of reciprocity is figured by the presence of an Amour who, effecting the *innamoramento*, at the same time ordains Ronsard as Hélène's "Chantre"; as Evelyn Birge Vitz points out, "while Ronsard is becoming *her* subject (in one sense of the word), she is becoming *his* (in another)."[67] In fact, this poem near the end of Book II offers a particularly suggestive rewriting of the scenario, for here it is Hélène's initiative in offering Ronsard a "couronne" and designating him as her poet that *causes* Love's intervention:

> De Myrte & de Laurier fueille à fueille enserrez
> Helene entrelassant une belle Couronne,
> M'appella par mon nom: Voyla que je vous donne,

De moy seule, Ronsard, l'escrivain vous serez.
Amour qui l'escoutoit, de ses traicts acerez
Me pousse Helene au coeur, & son Chantre m'ordonne:
Qu'un sujet si fertil vostre plume n'estonne:
Plus l'argument est grand, plus Cygne vous mourrez.
    Ainsi me dist Amour, me frappant de ses ailes:
Son arc fist un grant bruit, les fueilles eternelles
De Myrthe je senty sur mon chef tressaillir.
    Adieu, Muses, adieu, vostre faveur me laisse:
Helene est mon Parnasse: ayant telle Maistresse,
Le Laurier est à moy, je ne sçaurois faillir. (II, 39)

Weaving a lovely Crown of myrtle and laurel intertwined leaf by leaf, Hélène addressed me by my name. "Here is what I give you, Ronsard, you shall be the poet of me alone." Love, who was listening, with his steely shafts thrusts Hélène into my heart and ordains me her poet. Let not such a fertile subject intimidate your pen: the greater the subject, the more you will die a Swan. Thus Love spoke to me, striking me with his wings: his bow made a great sound, I felt the eternal leaves of Myrtle quivering on my brow. Farewell, Muses, farewell, your favor leaves me: Hélène is my Parnassus: with such a Mistress the Laurel is mine, I cannot fail.

While the innamoramento is once again, as in I, 8 above, effected by an Amour who strikes the poet with his wings, that gesture results now from the words that Hélène bestows upon Ronsard. Here, then, the exclusive nature of the choice is attributed, not to Ronsard or to Amour, who merely consecrates it, but to Hélène herself, whose "de moy seule . . . l'escrivain vous serez" contrasts sharply with the versions of the choice of subject— "vous seule me plaisez," "seule je te choisy"—he had advanced in earlier poems.[68]

    Ronsard's part of the bargain, he reminds Hélène repeatedly, is kept through his verses. When, on a rare occasion, he questions his ability to raise her to Laura's exalted status in the annals of poetry, his protestation of unworthiness has multiple Petrarchan subtexts:

    Si pour sujet fertil Homere t'a choisie,
Je puis, suivant son train qui va sans compagnon,
Te chantant, m'honorer, & non pas toy, sinon
Qu'il te plaise estimer ma rude Poësie . . .
    Laure ne te veincroit de renom ny d'honneur
Sans le Ciel qui luy donne un plus digne sonneur,
Et le mauvais destin te fait present du pire. (II, 37, 5–8, 12–14)

If Homer chose you as fertile subject, I can, following his peerless example, honor myself in singing you, and not you, unless it should please you to value my rough Poetry . . . Laura would not vanquish you in renown nor in honor except that Heaven gives her a more worthy trumpeter, and unlucky destiny makes you a present of a worse one.

Here the mention of Homer, anticipated by its appearance in Ronsard's earlier praise of Cassandre (*A* 84, 1–4) and now obviously appropriate to the celebration of Hélène's "fatal" name, is introduced to sound out, as it does in the *Rime sparse*, the new poet's unworthiness—to protest his awareness, as Petrarch had done, of "quanto mia laude è 'ngiuriosa a voi" [how much my praise injures you] (*R* 71, 17).[69] But the movement of the poem, which opens with the speaker's suggestion—in a past tense—that "Je te voulois nommer pour Helene, Ortygie" [Instead of Hélène, I wanted to name you Ortygie] and thereby signals at the outset a rivalry with the Desportes who had himself celebrated Hélène under that name, leads through the evocation of Homer's own depiction of Helen of Troy and Petrarch's poems for Laura to a focus not on the ladies but on their poets.[70] And more frequently, he assures Hélène of the success of his enterprise, even though she may have failed in her response to his devotion: "Vous aurez en mes vers un immortel renom," he tells her; "Pour n'avoir rien de vous la recompense est grande" [you will have immortal renown in my verses . . . the reward is great for having nothing from you] (I, 51, 13–14). Thus, he boasts to Hélène, his art will assure her a poetic longevity and an ever-increasing acclaim equal to that of Laura: "Vous vivrez (croyez-moy) comme Laure en grandeur, / Au moins tant que vivront les plumes & le livre" [You shall live (believe me) like Laura in grandeur, at least as long as pens and books shall live] (II, 2).

In addition to the fundamental contrast with Petrarch—the return to the Petrarchan posture *a contrario*—in Ronsard's proclamation of his independence of choice in the *Sonets pour Helene*, critics have discerned other "new" attitudes, new notes that sound out an emphasis on the poetic persona himself in ways that go well beyond his amorous predicament. To put it in the general terms of Robert Garapon, it is a principle of such a lyric collection that the personality of the poet not appear, or not appear too much, and Ronsard has notably broken this rule in the *Sonets*."[71] The more "personal" Ronsard discerned by many readers of the collection corresponds to the new profile of its dedicatee, a beloved notably more defined, more "individual" than the ladies of earlier amorous recueils; Mary Morrison comments that "the way in which Hélène's personality, character and tastes are revealed in the sonnets . . . was Ronsard's great originality, and in this respect he seems to be unique in the sixteenth century."[72] But Morrison has demonstrated too that a number of the poems that establish the "individuality" of Hélène contain clear Petrarchan echoes: "There are enough hostile sonnets echoing phrases from Petrarch," she concludes, "to enable us to consider that the parody of Petrarch is one of Ronsard's methods of revealing the flaws in Hélène's character."[73] And a closer look at some of the most salient "individual" traits of Ronsard's *self*-representation in the collection is equally in order. If the poet-lover of the *Rime*, confronted with his lady's absence or—more fundamentally— her inaccessibility, is subject to illusions of her presence or her response, Ronsard's poet as lover both willfully embraces the delights of self-delusion and acknowledges them with ironic lucidity; and much of his frustration is experienced in terms of the perceived incongruity of his adopting the suppliant lover's role in his advancing age. Closer scrutiny discloses that, despite repeated critical assertions to the contrary, these representations of a more "personal" Ronsard invoked as evidence of his departure from or subversion of the Petrarchan vein frequently reflect aspects of the experience of Petrarch's own poetic persona in ways that, though they have largely escaped the critical attention devoted to other aspects of the collection sanctioned by time and convention, did not escape the attention of Ronsard himself.

Let us take an often-cited pair of poems: *SH* I, 19, "Je fuy les pas frayez du meschant populaire" [I flee the steps of the popular mob] and the sonnet it can hardly fail to recall, "Solo e pensoso" (*R* 35). "Though readers of Horace and Petrarch will easily recognize Ronsard's debt to favorite authors," K. R. Jones comments, "they will also notice the new note of self-mockery which adds another dimension to the poem. The flight from the *vulgus profanus*, the lover brooding alone, Love as keeper of secrets are all made personal and believable aspects of Ronsard's own inner life by the revelation of his self-deception and his own awareness of it."[74] In the opening of a sonnet in the *Septiesme Livre des Poemes* (1569), the poet had put the question of reciprocity in terms of the lady's thoughts that might correspond to his own: "Que dittes vous, que faites vous mignonne? / Que songez vous? Pensez vous point en moy? / Avez vous point soucy de mon esmoy / Comme de vous le soucy m'espoinçonne?" [What are you saying, what are you doing, my sweet? What do you dream of? Do you ever think about me? Are you ever concerned about my emotion like my concern for you spurs me?][75] Now in the *Sonets*, as he seeks consolation through a retreat into nature, he addresses the question to himself:

Je m'arreste, & je dy: Se pourroit-il bien faire
Qu'elle pensast, parlast, ou se souvint de moy?
  Qu'à sa pitié mon mal commençast à desplaire? (I, 19, 10–12)

I pause, and I say: could it really be that she thinks or speaks of me,
or remembers me? That my pain begins to displease her?

Kennedy probes the nature of this imagining as a process of invention in
response to the lover's own conflicting feelings. In this striking gesture of
self-conscious rhetoric, "the speaker now represents Hélène as speaking
to herself just as he is speaking to himself. He projects his own inner dis-
course upon her, but in so doing he fabricates new reality. Although it
might falsify Hélène's response to him, it nonetheless has the power to
restore the lover's tranquility."[76]

This move on the part of the solitary lover is indeed not in evidence in
"Solo e pensoso," the poem of the *Rime* frequently cited as its Petrarchan
source. But it is present (as Weber notes) in *R* 295:

Soleano i miei penser soavemente
Di lor oggetto ragionare inseme:
"Pietà s'appressa et del tardar si pente;
forse or parla di noi, o spera o teme." (1–4)

My thoughts used to converse together gently about their object:
"She will soon feel pity and be sorry for the delay; perhaps she now
speaks of us, or hopes, or fears."

And it is in many respects identical to that of the poet in Petrarch's well-
known canzone "Di pensier in pensier":

ch'i' dico: "Forse anco ti serva Amore
ad un tempo migliore;
forse a te stesso vile, altrui se' caro";
et in questa trapasso sospirando:
"Or porrebbe esser ver? or come? or quando?" (*R* 129, 22–26)

for I say: "Perhaps Love keeps you for a better time; perhaps, though
vile to yourself, you are dear to someone else." And I go over to this
thought, sighing: "Now could it be true? But how? But when?"

And again, in the same poem:

Poscia fra me pian piano:
"Che sai tu, lasso? forse in quella parte

or di tua lontananza si sospira."
Et in questo penser l'alma respira. (62–65)

Then to myself softly: "What do you know, wretch? perhaps off there someone is sighing now because of your absence." And in this thought my soul breathes more easily.

And though the often-cited conclusion to Ronsard's poem, with its declaration of self-awareness, would seem to set it in contrast to these wishful thoughts, these pleasant fantasies beyond the lover's conscious control— "Encor je me trompe, abusé du contraire" [I deceive myself again, abused by the contrary] writes Ronsard; "Pour me faire plaisir, Helene, je le croy" [To please myself, Hélène, I believe it]—this voluntary embracing of illusion is in fact the defining characteristic of the lover's experience in *R* 129:

sento Amor sì da presso
che del suo proprio error l'alma s'appaga;
in tante parti e sì bella la veggio
che se l'error durasse, altro non cheggio. (36–39)

I feel Love so close by that my soul is satisfied by its own deception, in so many places and so beautiful I see her, that, if the deception should last, I ask for no more.

In fact, this "new" attitude of Ronsard's poet contrasts sharply, not with the Petrarch of the *Rime*, but with the Ronsard of the earlier *Amours*. Now, as Castor notes, the pleasure afforded by illusion in the 1552–53 collection, whether sensual or affective, is replaced by self-deception, and with it "the acknowledgement, insistence even, that illusion and self-deception are inevitably present in the love-relationship."[77] But Ronsard does not lament their presence. In his long poem on the well-worked theme of the "Cyclope amoureux," published in the first collective edition of the *Oeuvres* in 1560, he had advised the lovesick subject that

. . . feindre d'estre aymé (puis que mieux on ne peut)
Allege bien souvent l'amoureux qui se veult
Soymesmes se tromper, se garissant la playe
Aussi bien par le faux que par la chose vraye.[78]

. . . to pretend to be loved (since one can do no better) very often soothes the lover who wishes to deceive himself, healing his wound as well through the false as through the true thing.

Now, when the poet imagines holding in his arms during "ces longues nuicts d'hyver" [these long winter nights] a Hélène whose form "toute nue" "vient par une feinte alleger mon amour," [completely naked . . . comes through a pretense to give relief to my love] the feint is not hers but his own, activated deep within him as he sleeps:

> Rien ne m'est refusé. Le bon sommeil ainsi
> Abuse par le faux mon amoureux souci. (II, 23, 13–14)

> Nothing is refused me. Thus does the good sleep deceive, through the false image, my amorous care.

And this simulacrum is welcomed in contrast to the "vraye" by the waking lover, who even boasts to Hélène of an intimacy with her "forme doutouse" that she is unable to deny him: "Vraye tu es farouche, & fiere en cruauté; / De toy fausse on juoyst en toute privauté" [When true you are fierce, and proud in your cruelty; with the false you one can take pleasure in all familiarity] (9–10). In another poem, "J'attachay des bouquets de cent mille couleurs" [I attached bouquets of a hundred thousand colors], he leaves flowers whose petals are wet with his tears over Hélène's door, but with them this notice:

> Je reviendray demain. Mais si la nuict, qui ronge
> Mon coeur, me la donnoit par songe entre mes bras,
> Embrassant pour le vray l'idole du mensonge,
> Soulé d'un faux plaisir je ne reviendrois pas. (I, 57)[79]

> I shall come back tomorrow. But if night, that gnaws at my heart, should give her to me within my arms in a dream, embracing the idol of the lie instead of the true and sated with a false pleasure I would not return.

In II, 23 he will acknowledge that what he enjoys is only "une joye menteuse" [a lying joy], but it is not at all sure that the famous closing of the poem, "S'abuser en amour n'est pas mauvaise chose" [to deceive oneself in love is not a bad thing] achieves, as Weber proposes, the movement from frustrated desire to melancholy resignation.[80] In any case, while the suggestiveness of the *songe amoureux* to which these poems pay grateful tribute had ready models in the *Anthologie grecque*,[81] and with all due regard for the erotic finesse with which Ronsard shapes these scenes, they too have Petrarchan precedent, as we have seen in examining poems with similar content in the early *Amours*.

This "new" clarity of insight on the part of Ronsard's poet in the *Sonets* has other consequences than a certain irony in acknowledging the pleasure his illusions afford him. It is also a source of irritation:

> Je suis seul, me noyant, de ma vie homicide,
> Choisissant un enfant, un aveugle pour guide,
> Dont il me faut de honte & pleurer & rougir.
> Je ne crains point la mort . . .
> . . . seulement je me fasche
> De voir un si beau port, & n'y pouvoir surgir. (I, 6, 9–14)

I am, in drowning myself, the sole destroyer of my life, choosing a blind child as my guide, which makes me both weep and blush for shame. I have no fear of death . . . I am only angry to see such a fine port, and be unable to attain it.

Ronsard's mariner, despite his dramatic announcement that "Naufrage je mourray" [I shall die shipwrecked], is an adventurer who glimpses a "beau port" and finds himself unable to make harbor. Comparison with the two poems of the *Rime* often noted as models for the imagery in this poem, sestina 80, "Chi è fermato di menar sua vita" [He who has decided to lead his life], and sonnet 189, "Passa la nave mia colma d'oblio" [My ship laden with forgetfulness passes] discloses more difference than similarity: Petrarch's sestina closes with a prayer to God—"Signor de la mia fine et de la vita" [Lord of my death and of my life]—for assistance in reaching a "buon porto" [a good port] that is clearly of a spiritual nature; Amor who holds the helm of the mariner's buffeted craft in *R* 189 is identified as "'l signore anzi 'l nimico mio" [my lord, rather my enemy], and the final verses—"morta fra l'onde è la ragion et l'arte / tal ch' i' 'ncomincio a desperar del porto" [dead among the waves are reason and skill; so that I begin to despair of the port]—have a solemnity that is totally lacking in Ronsard's version of imminent shipwreck. Ronsard's poet's reaction to his plight is not experienced as a moral or spiritual weakness, nor does he draw from it a moral or spiritual lesson. The farewell poem near the end of the *Sonets* that opens with "Adieu, cruelle, adieu" concludes with the reflection that "il se faut resoudre, & tenir pour certain / Que l'homme est malheureux, qui se repaist d'un songe" [one must be resolved, and hold as sure that the man is unhappy who feeds on a dream].[82] But this bit of worldly wisdom inevitably recalls, in its very contrast, the equally resigned and weary "lesson" of the entire *Rime sparse* set out at the end of Petrarch's proemial poem: "'l conoscer chiaramente / che quanto piace al mondo è breve sogno" [the clear knowledge that whatever pleases in the world is a brief dream].

It is a sad bit of worldly wisdom, painfully won and wearily proposed. While some readers have found a "belle sérénité" in some of Ronsard's many poems acknowledging his advancing age, even among those of the *Sonets*, others emphasize instead "the discouragement and despair that the years bring . . . the theme of despondent old age."[83] But across much of its tonal range, the theme of the aging of the poet-lover frequently serves as the context for his development of the theme of self-illusion. It is the convergence of the two themes, Mariann Regan proposes, that marks the end of an evolution in Ronsard's three major lyric collections read as an ensemble": All this shedding of illusions climaxes in the last few poems of the sequence, where the accusations of Helene are perhaps his most virulent, the meditations on death his most sombre. . . . Love and Death alike hold only disappointment, only 'rigueur' and 'tristesse,' when the Lover has been freed of all pleasant deceptions about them."[84]

Like the theme of self-illusion, the figure of the aging poet-lover in the *Sonets pour Helene* has elicited considerable critical response, and many readers have concluded that Ronsard's introduction of the theme figures among the principal indices of a new, highly personal self-representation in this late recueil. Of course, it is a considerably older Ronsard who represents himself as Hélène's suitor in the 1570s; and certainly, as Garapon remarks, whatever the correspondence of the image to "reality," it corresponds precisely to the image that he sought to project of himself in the 1580s, as evident elsewhere in his work of this period.[85] But it is all the more important to put the question because, as Bellenger also observes, poets on occasion speak of their own age as a hyperbolic gesture—Ronsard in particular depicted himself as old at the age of thirty, for example in the *Odes* of 1555: "Ma douce jouvance est passée, / Ma premiere force est cassée, / J'ai la dent noire, & le chef blanc" [my sweet youth has passed, my early strength is broken, I have blackened teeth and white hair].[86]

What is the poetic effect, and what the supposed motivation, of such an avowal? In one ode, a young girl's mockery of his white hair and aging body affords a new occasion for a plea for her complaisant acquiescence to his desire;[87] in other poems, it prompts replies that are yet more explicit evidence of Ronsard's perennial *gauloiserie*, affirming not only his desire but his capacity for lovemaking:

> Pour cela, cruelle, il ne faut
> Fuir ainsi ma teste blanche:

Si j'ay la teste blanche en haut,
J'ay en bas la queüe bien franche. (*L* VI, p. 255)[88]

On that account, cruel one, you should not thus avoid my white head: if I have a white head above, I have a quite virile tail below.

This particular variety of boasting is excluded from Ronsard's self-representation as aging lover in the *Sonets pour Helene,* but here too we may discern a note of pride as well as apology. If he appears, in a poem cited above, to lament the perseverance of his amorous nature in the autumn of his age (II, 10, 9–11), his explanation of his susceptibility to all the effects of Amour is, if not a boast, nonetheless not an excuse, one that, like the erotic suggestiveness of a number of his *songes amoureux* in the *Sonets,* he may well have found in the *Greek Anthology:*[89]

Mon sang chaut en est cause. Or comme on voit souvent
L'Esté moins bouillonner que l'Automne suivant,
Mon Septembre est plus chaut que mon Juin de fortune.
(II,15, 9–11)

My hot blood is the cause of it. Just as one often sees the summer boil with heat less than the autumn that follows, my September is by chance hotter than my June.

In the *Sonets,* however, the limitations imposed by advancing age are not only acknowledged but occasionally detailed by Ronsard, and it is obvious in some poems that he is fully aware of the rather ridiculous figure cut by his poet-lover, as when he describes his arduous climb up the palace stairs—"Je perds à chaque marche & le pouls & l'haleine: / J'ay la sueur au front, j'ay l'estomac penthois" [With each step I lose my pulse and my breath: I have sweat on my forehead, I am suffocating]—only to be greeted by Hélène's cold disdain (II, 43, 5–6). Hermann Lindner in fact proposes that the lover of the *Sonets,* whose passion is inappropriate to his advancing age according to sixteenth-century norms, is a comic figure *per definitionem,* one readily related to a stereotypical figure with a long theatrical history and much present in the French comedy of the period.[90] To limit the interest of this aspect of Ronsard's self-representation to its comic potential, however, would be to give too little credit to its innovative energy. In other poems he appears intent to counter the implication that his love is "unnatural" and, on that account, not to be seriously regarded. When he alleges that Hélène's gaze has made him young again but questions the value of the reversal—

Quand tu as reverdy mon escorce ridee
De l'esclair de tes yeux, ainsi que fit Medee
Par herbes & par jus le pere de Jason,
    Je n'ay contre ton charme opposé ma defense:
Toutefois je me deuls de r'entrer en enfance,
Pour perdre tant de fois l'esprit & la raison—(II, 21, 9–14)

When you restored youth to my wrinkled bark with the sparkle of
your eyes, just as Medea did for Jason's father with herbs and juices,
I did not defend myself against your charm: and yet I am distressed
to reenter childhood, losing my wit and my reason so many times—

there is indeed irony in the comparison, just as there is irony in his compli-
ment to the Hélène who resides high up in the palace that "tu es vrayment
Deesse, assise en si haut lieu. / Or pour monter si haut, je ne suis pas un
Dieu" [you really are a Goddess, resident in such a high place. But to
climb so high, I am not a God] (II, 43, 9–10); but the lucidity of its self-
mockery does not invite ready laughter.

In fact, it is ironic that Ronsard's introduction of the theme of the poet's
aging in the *Sonets* was to be judged severely, on account of this "autobio-
graphical" note, by a reader who preferred his presumably more imitative
vein: "He would do better not to stray from his *discipline d'école*," writes
Glauser; "When he offers reflections on his age, on his greying hair, the
poem loses its mystery."[91] It is ironic because this "new" note, however
intimate in appearance, is not without literary precedent; however closely
it may have conformed to the experience of Ronsard himself, it is fre-
quently patterned in the *Sonets* on that of the lyric protagonist of the *Rime
sparse*. In the *Rime* the theme of aging is central to the acknowledgment of
mortality and the meditation on the fragility of human hope, as in the
well-known sonnet "Quanto più m'avvicino al giorno estremo / che
l'umana miseria suol far breve" [The more I approach that day that makes
all human misery brief] (*R* 32, 1–2). And when Glauser further remarks
that Ronsard must have considered his old age as yet another metamor-
phosis, one he could not believe,[92] his insight may well unwittingly paral-
lel Ronsard's own concerning Petrarch's self-representation in the *Rime
sparse*, one made explicit in the Italian poet's *Seniles* (3.1) in the definition
of the process of aging, with its inevitable and irreversible changes, as
"insueta metamorphosis."

The note of aging, while attenuated, was already sounded by Ronsard
in the *Amours* of 1552–53, in the opening of Cassandre's prophecy for the
poet that foretells his premature graying (*A* 19). And there, we have seen,
her formula "avant le temps" is derived from the *Rime sparse*, a clear echo

of Petrarch's complaint that Laura's indifference may be read in her apparent ignoring of his premature graying: "o s'infinge o non cura o non s'accorge / del fiorir queste inanzi tempo tempie" [she does not know or she does not care how these temples are blossoming white before their time] (*R* 210, 13–14). The progressive graying of his temples is recorded repeatedly by Petrarch as he meditates on his continued vulnerability to Love's attack—

Se bianche non son prima ambe le tempie
ch'a poco a poco par che 'l tempo mischi,
securo non sarò ben ch'io m'arrischi
talor ov' Amor l'arco tira et empie—(*R* 83, 1–4)

As long as both my temples are not white, which now time variegates little by little, I shall not be fully secure in risking myself where Love draws and loads his bow—

and later it figures his uncertainty about the hope Love seems sometimes to extend:

In questa passa 'l tempo, et ne lo specchio ·
mi veggio andar ver la stagion contraria
a sua impromessa et a la mia speranza.
Or sia che po: già sol io non invecchio,
già per etate il mio desir non varia . . . (*R* 168, 9–13)

In the meanwhile time passes, and in the mirror I see myself nearing the season that is contrary to his promise and to my hope. Now come what will: I am not the only one who is growing old, and my desire does not vary at all with age; but I do fear that what remains of my life may be short . . .

As Wido Hempel has pointed out, it was Petrarch who, well before Goethe, offered serious reflection on the theme of the "old man in love."[93] In the *Rime* the Italian poet anticipates Ronsard in the insistence that his perdurable passion, however it might be perceived by some witnesses and however much lamented by himself, is not incongruous. While the self-identification of the speaker of the proemial poem as one who reflects upon a "primo giovenile errore" experienced "quand'era in parte altr'uom da quel ch'i'sono" appears to acknowledge the traditional assumption that passionate love is appropriately associated only with youth, he finds instead in his personal experience confirmation of the verity of a proverb:[94]

Vero è 'l proverbio ch'altri cangia il pelo
anzi che 'l vezzo, et per lentar i sensi
gli umani affetti non sono meno intensi;
ciò ne fa l'ombra ria del grave velo. (*R* 122, 5–8)

True is the proverb, one's hair will change before one's habits, and human passions are no less intense because of the slackening of sense; the bitter shadow of the heavy veil does that to us.

And Ronsard will offer his own defense in the opening poem of Book II of the *Sonets* by citing a natural fact that has the ring of a proverbial verity:

Soit qu'un sage amoureux, ou soit qu'un sot me lise,
Il ne doit s'esbahir, voyant mon chef grison,
Si je chante d'amour: volontiers le tison
Cache un germe de feu sous une cendre grise. (II, 1, 1–4)

Whether a wise lover or a fool reads me, he must not be startled, seeing my gray hair, if I sing of love: the half-burned log readily hides a bit of fire beneath a gray cinder.

These examples not only demonstrate that the occasional note of moral philosophy sounded in the *Sonets* resonates with the reflection character-istic of Petrarch's meditation on the experience of human love;[95] they demonstrate too that for his theme of the aging lover Ronsard was once again responsive to the "story" of the poet of the *Rime sparse*. For his col-lection dedicated to Hélène that concerns the production of love poetry as well as the experience of love, moreover, he may well have been aware of a potential advantage of that stance, one anticipated by a Petrarch who had imagined a greater affective range for a love poet whose style had matured with his age. That possibility, according to the fiction of the *Rime*, was denied him, like that of sharing with Laura the story of his amorous suffering, by her death:

Quel foco è morto e 'l copre un picciol marmo
che se col tempo fossi ito avanzando
(come già in altri) infino a la vecchiezza,
di rime armato ond'oggi mi disarmo,
con stil canuto, avrei fatto parlando
romper le pietre et pianger di dolcezza. (*R* 304, 9–14)[96]

That fire is dead and a little marble covers it: if it had gone on grow-ing with time, as it does in others, into old age, armed with the rhymes of which today I am disarmed, with a mature style I would speaking have made the very stones break and weep with sweetness.

It remained very much present, however, for a Ronsard who set out to demonstrate his supremacy in the face of a challenge from a much younger rival for the laurel crown.

In a variety of ways, once again, recognition of the presence of the Petrarchan model also allows us to sound out Ronsard's originality. While retaining the Petrarchan resonances in many poems, he is capable also of exploiting a much broader range of its thematic possibilities. One of these is grounded in a fundamental difference between the presuppositions of his poet's circumstances and those of the protagonist of the *Rime sparse*, for the Laura of the *Rime* may be assumed to be Petrarch's contemporary, and among the poems *in vita* he represents the lady to whom he would at last *convenablement* confide his love in a "tempo . . . contrario ai be'desiri" [time . . . hostile to my sweet desires] (*R* 12, 12) as elderly like himself. And following the death of Laura, there are poems *in morte* based on a *futurum optativum* that fantasize a phase of love in later life now definitively foreclosed for him:[97]

> Pur vivendo veniasi ove deposto
> in quelle caste orecchie avrai, parlando,
> de' miei dolci pensier l'antica soma,
> et elle avrebbe a me forse resposto
> qualche santa parola sospirando,
> cangiati i volti et l'una et l'altra coma. (*R* 317, 9–14)

> If only she had lived, we would have come to where, speaking, I could have put down in those chaste ears the ancient burden of my sweet thoughts, and she would perhaps have answered me with some holy word, sighing, though our faces were changed, and the hair of both.

Hélène, in contrast, is presented throughout the *Sonets* in her relation to a much older lover, and Ronsard will play on the consequences of the discrepancy. Already in a poem of the *Continuation* of 1555 he had hinted at a way in which that difference could be turned to the lover's advantage, in invoking his maturity as warrant of the sincerity of the love he professes:

> Non, vous ne me povés reprocher que je sois
> Un effronté menteur, car mon teint, & ma voix,
> Et mon chef ja grison vous servent d'asseurance. (57, 9–11)

> No, you cannot reproach me that I am a brazen liar, for my complexion, and my voice, and my already gray hair serve you as assurance.

Yet once again there is paradox, for Ronsard, like Petrarch, will confess to a sense of shame inspired by the inability to reject an amorous state that causes the lover, in varying measure, both pain and embarrassment. The proemial sonnet of the *Rime* identifies that shame as a principal result of the love in which the speaker of the poem was long bound:

> Ma ben veggio or sì come al popol tutto
> favola fui gran tempo, onde sovente
> di me medesmo meco mi vergogno;
> et del mio vaneggiar vergogna è il frutto . . . (R 1, 9–14)

> But now I see well how for a long time I was the talk of the crowd, for which often I am ashamed of myself within . . .

In Ronsard's *Sonets* there is no ambivalence or ambiguity to equal that of this retrospective judgment, but there are repeated avowals of a sense of shame. Then, with the incontrovertible evidence of his advancing age, it is that shame itself that prompts a renunciation:

> J'ay honte de ma honte, il est temps de me taire,
> Sans faire l'amoureux en un chef si grison . . . [98]

> I am ashamed of my shame, it is time to fall silent, without playing the lover with such a gray head . . .

But yet again, in the nature of this shame—and, as we shall see, of its consequences—the contrast to the poet's experience in the *Rime sparse* is highly suggestive. The sentiment of Petrarch's poet is strongly put by one of his own thoughts in the canzone "I' vo pensando," the great poem that opens the second part of the *Rime sparse,* in the reproach "non intendi / con quanto tuo disnore il tempo passa?" [do you not understand with how much dishonor for you time is passing?] (R 264, 21–22). And he continues to lament his inability to effect a change, very near the end of the collection: "ché vo cangiando 'l pelo, / né cangiar posso l'ostinata voglia" [for my hair is turning, but I cannot turn from my obstinate will] (360, 41–42). We find Ronsard's poet putting to a quite different use a reference to the "lesson" of his own gray hair early in the Premier Livre of the *Sonets pour Helene:*

> Je ne suis pas marry de me voir en servage:
> Seulement je me deuls des ailes de mon âge,
> Qui me laissent le chef semé de cheveux gris. (I, 15, 2–4)

> I am not grieved to see myself in bondage; I am distressed merely by the wings of my age, that leave my hair sown with gray.

Whereas Petrarch almost invariably evokes his aging as a sign of mortality and of his own moral failure to abandon earthly ties, Ronsard regrets the limitations that it imposes upon him as suitor or as lover. His elaboration of the theme is often in terms of an "effet du réel" that enhances the difference from the Petrarchan model: his emphasis on the symptoms of an aging body—his shortness of breath, his slowness in climbing the palace stairs—that not only contrasts to the perdurable nature of his ardor but affords an impediment to his proclaimed efforts to win a response from Hélène. Much of his irritation at his inability to abandon that pursuit, as Castor observes, is occasioned by the perception of a ridiculous incongruity, that "of an old man trying to play a young man's game"; indeed, he summarizes, the *Sonets* are not only a collection of love lyrics: "In a very important sense they are also about the pain, the impatient irritation of growing old—or at least, of growing irrevocably middle-aged."[99]

In the elaboration of the theme of the aging poet-lover, then, we find once again confirmation of Kennedy's observation that Ronsard's revisions of the Petrarchan model "shift its focus from Petrarch's austere moral world to Ronsard's transitory, provisional, and often ironic one."[100] While Ronsard's poet shares the irritation and weariness of the poet of the *Rime sparse*, the latter's perception of his advancing age involves a very different experience. His unsuccessful striving to change is repeatedly recorded:

> Di dì in dì vo cangiando il viso e 'l pelo,
> né però smorso i dolci inescati ami
> né sbranco i verdi et invescati rami
> de l'arbor che né sol cura né gelo. (R 195, 1–4)

From day to day my face and hair are changing, but not for that do I give up the sweetly baited hook or unhand the green enlimed branches of the tree that regards neither sun nor frost.

In the great canzone that stages his debate with Love before the bar of Reason, the incapacity of his will to effect a change is central in his case against his adversary:

> ché vo cangiando 'l pelo,
> né cangiar posso l'ostinata voglia.
> Così in tutto mi spoglia
> di libertà questo crudel ch'i accuso. (R 360, 41–44)

For my hair is turning, but I cannot turn from my obstinate will: thus this cruel one whom I accuse despoils me of all liberty and has turned bitter living into sweet habit.

It is only in the following poem, very near the end of the collection, that he yields to the urging of Reason and the evidence of Nature, registering his submission to that universal law as an awakening: "Subito allor, com'acqua 'l foco amorza, / d'un lungo et grave sonno mi risveglio . . . " [Quickly then, as water puts out fire, I awake from a long and heavy sleep . . .] (*R* 361, 7–8). Only now, at last, is he able to confront his mirror's confirmation of the evidence:

> Dicemi spesso il mio fidato speglio,
> l'animo stanco, et la cangiata scorza
> et la scemata mia destrezza et forza:
> "Non ti nasconder più, tu se' pur veglio;
> obedir a Natura in tutto è il meglio,
> ch'a contender con lei 'l tempo ne sforza." (361, 1–6)

My faithful mirror, my weary spirit, and my changing skin and diminished agility and strength often say to me: "Do not pretend anymore, you are old; to obey Nature in all is best, for time takes from us the power to oppose her."

Ronsard's readers will recognize in this general conclusion the lesson afforded him in turn, that "la loi de la Raison" is one with "la loi de la Nature":

> Ja dix lustres passez, & ja mon poil grison
> M'appellent au logis, & sonnent la retraite . . .
> J'obeïs à la loy, que la Nature a faite. (II, 54, 3–4, 8)

Now the ten times five years I have passed, and now my gray hair calls me home, and sounds the retreat . . . I obey the law that Nature has made.

For this message addressed to Hélène, Castor suggests the paraphrase that it is "time to acknowledge defeat and go home; it is not that I am being unfaithful to you—merely that old age has caught up with me."[101] The admission is rich in implications; indeed, its consequence is fundamental in that, with this return of the poet to a state more appropriate to his age, at the end of the *Sonets* love disappears.[102]

While in both collections the acknowledgment of advancing age is cast in terms that project a change of course, the contrast between their consequences is radical indeed. Through the increasing sense of weariness and alienation that marks the final poems of the *Rime sparse* is felt also the poet's loneliness, the intolerable loss of Laura sustained for many years after her death:

. . . Non è chi faccia et paventosi et baldi
i miei penser, né chi li agghiacci et scaldi,
né chi gl'empia di speme et di duol colmi.
Fuor di man di colui che punge et molce,
che già fece di me sì lungo strazio
mi trovo in libertate amara et dolce;
et al Signor ch'io adoro et ch'i' ringrazio,
che pur col ciglio il ciel governa et folce,
torno stanco di viver, non che sazio. (*R* 363, 6–14)

. . . There is no one to make my thoughts fearful and bold, nor to
freeze and scorch them, no one to fill them with hope and overflow
them with sorrow. Out of the hands of him who pierces and heals,
who once made of me such a long torture, I find myself in bitter and
sweet liberty; and to the Lord whom I adore and whom I thank, who
governs and sustains the heavens with His brow, I return, weary of
life, not merely satiated.

In the last poems of the collection, the note of weariness is conjoined and
dominated by the fear of death as he reviews his past:

Omai son stanco, et mia vita reprendo
di tanto error che di vertute il seme
à quasi spento; et le mie parti estreme,
alto Dio, a te devotamente rendo
pentito et tristo de' miei sì spesi anni,
che spender si deveano in miglior uso,
in cercar pace et in fuggir affanni. (*R* 364, 5–11)

Now I am weary and I reproach my life for so much error, which has
almost extinguished the seed of virtue; and I devoutly render my
last parts, high God, to You, repentant and sorrowing for my years
spent thus, which ought to have been better used, in seeking peace
and fleeing troubles.

And finally, in the penultimate poem, addressed to God:

A quel poco di viver che m'avanza
et al morir degni esser tua man presta:
tu sai ben che 'n altrui non ò speranza. (*R* 365, 12–14)

To what little life remains to me and to my dying deign to be present:
You know well that I have no hope in anyone else.

Even this acknowledgment of his "error" remains ambiguous, however, a
renunciation less of Laura than of the belief in the possibility—fundamen-

tal to the *Rime*—of the transformation of *eros* into *caritas*. In the canzone addressed to the Virgin that concludes the collection, he acknowledges to the heavenly Lady that the love of Laura has distracted him from his thoughts of eternal things, and his aging is insistently evoked in terms of his nearness to the "final screams," to his "final year." And it is with that urgency of need that he prays that the Virgin offer her aid "ch'almen l'ultimo pianto sia devoto" [let at least my last weeping be devout] and that Christ "accolga 'l mio spirto ultimo in pace" [receive my last breath in peace].

The sentiment was not unknown to the Ronsard who, very near the end of his life, penned the moving sonnet "Il faut laisser maisons & vergers & jardins":

> Heureux qui ne fut onc, plus heureux qui retourne
> En rien comme il estoit, plus heureux qui sejourne
> D'homme fait nouvel ange aupres de Jesuchrist.[103]

> Happy he who never existed, happier he who returns to the nothing that he once was, happier still he who dwells, man made a new angel, near Jesus Christ.

Even in this poem, however, there remains an element of pride and worldliness, "attitudes [that] may well appear conflicting ones,"[104] and in the *Sonets pour Helene* his protestations and complaints of aging lack the urgency of Petrarch's "final things." And when he decides that it is "time to fall silent," he, unlike Petrarch's poet writing under Love's absolute compulsion, does not doubt his ability to do so. When he declares, in the poem that opens with "I am ashamed of my shame" cited above, that "Il vaut mieux obeyr aux loix de la Raison, / Qu'estre plus desormais en l'amour volontaire" [It is better to obey Reason's laws than to continue any longer as headstrong in love], the importance of the phrasing is singularly heightened by its apparent response to the opening sonnet of the collection, in which Ronsard defined himself, as so many readers have remarked, as "en amour volontaire," implicitly subject to no law but his own. Formerly *volontaire* in love, he remains so in his renunciation of love. Thus, when Reason calls him, he is able to respond:

> La Raison maintenant me r'appelle, & me tense:
> Je ne veux si long temps devenir furieux.
> Il ne faut plus nourrir cest Enfant qui me ronge,
> Qui les credules prend comme un poisson à l'hain,
> Une plaisante farce, une belle mensonge . . . (II, 53, 7–11)

Now Reason calls me back, and reproaches me: I do not want to be mad for such a long time. I must no longer nourish this Child who gnaws me, who catches the credulous like fish on the hook, a pleasing farce, a pretty lie . . .

It is as if throughout, from the inception of his willed love for Hélène in *SH* I, 1, he has reserved the ultimate veto over his continued participation in it; he can retreat just as he had attacked, abandon the field just as he had so confidently sallied forth upon it. His consequent declaration in the following poem that he renounces his love in obedience to the universal law of Nature—"Je m'enfuy du combat, ma bataille est desfaite: / J'ay perdu contre Amour la force & la raison" [I flee from the fray, my battle is lost: I have lost against Love my strength and my reason] (II, 54, 1–2)—is in one sense of course the acknowledgment of defeat in which he casts it: he is no longer physically able to carry on the "battle" of the suppliant lover. But as he now abandons his love for—along with the pursuit of—Hélène, his regret is phrased not in terms of a prolonged inability to renounce a love whose status he cannot help but question but in terms of what he had himself chosen, what he had willed. Even if Hélène's glory, achieved through his celebration of her, is not all he might have wished, Love has nonetheless polished his verses, and he adds as his own retrospective evaluation of the long process: "Je ne me plains du mal, du temps ny du labeur, / Je me plains de moymesme et de ton fier courage" [I do not complain of the pain, of the time or the labor, I complain of myself and of your proud attitude] (11–12). Term for term, his declaration in refusing to regret the years and the torments sounds the contrast to that of Petrarch's "sì spesi anni" in *R* 364. Instead, it resolutely sustains the emphasis on the willful subject that was established in the opening poem: the subject as victim, the subject as obedient to Nature, but always the subject as agent.

The closing poem of the *Sonets pour Helene* relocates that subject within a larger frame. "Je chantois ces Sonets, amoureux d'une Heleine, / En ce funeste mois que mon Prince mourut," the sonnet begins [I was singing these Sonnets, in love with a Hélène, in that fatal month when my Prince died] (II, 55, 1–2). This is a "turn outside the plot," as Alan Nagel observes, and as such it "resembles Petrarch's turn, in the final canzone, to the Virgin Mary—from love to charity and from private obsession to the public and institutionalized transcendence that is religion." But the moral allegory of the *Rime sparse* is alien to the spirit of the *Sonets,* and the spiritual imperatives that progressively assume an obsessive nature in the *Rime* are absent from the French collection. Hence no possibility of transcendence is opened for Ronsard's persona by the loss of both lady and king; that loss leads only, at the end of the poem, to the realization that "l'Amour & la Mort n'est qu'une mesme chose" [Love and Death are but a single thing].[105]

Nonetheless, as we have seen, the frequent designation of the *Sonets pour Helene* as essentially "antipetrarchan" tends to occult the complex relations woven here by Ronsard between his poet's "story" and that of the protagonist of the *Rime sparse*. As he once again positions himself with regard to Petrarch, "difference" is again often brought into focus through similarity, and the measure of his self-distancing may in a number of instances better be taken in his new uses of the model—uses that contribute to the new thematic complexity of his final lyric collection.

In the final analysis, we may be tempted to conclude that the uniqueness of the aging poet-lover of the *Sonets* lies neither in the confident pride of his willful choice, so frequently invoked to distinguish him from his Italian precursor, nor in the fated innamoramento that compels him in the alternative version to reenact the time-honored conventions of love and its lament. The stakes were high for Hélène, as Ronsard did not hesitate to remind her, rather ungallantly, near the collection's end:

> Les Dames de ce temps n'envient ta beauté,
> Mais ton nom tant de fois par les Muses chanté,
> Qui languiroit d'oubly, si je ne t'eusse aimee. (II, 49, 12–14)

> The Ladies of this age do not envy your beauty, but rather your name sung so many times by the Muses, that would languish forgotten if I had not loved you.

But the stakes were high for Ronsard as well. His return to court and to courtly lyric signals his ultimate defense of his poetic laurels.[106] And at stake was not only the judgment of the court, in whose light both his "story" and that that he fashioned for Hélène took shape, but also his own poetic posterity. If love was a game, poetry was another, but ultimately more serious; and in reentering the game with yet another amorous recueil late in life, he was aware of the gamble:

> Soit que je sois hay de toy, ma Pasithee,
> Soit que j'en sois aimé, je veux suivre mon cours:
> J'ay joué comme aux detz mon coeur & mes amours;
> Arrive bien ou mal, la chance en est jettee. (I, 14, 1–4)

Whether I be hated by you, my Pasithea, or whether I be loved, I shall pursue my course: I have played as in gaming my heart and my loves; whether good or ill comes of it, the die have been cast.

For himself as for Hélène, Ronsard counted above all on readers yet to come;[107] and for both Ronsard and Hélène, as for the Italian Petrarch and his Laura, posterity has amply rewarded them.

4

Lyric Appropriation

In morte di Laura, "Sur la mort de Marie"

In the opening poem of the second book of the *Sonets pour Helene*, Ronsard introduced a disclaimer concerning the disparity between real and fictional virtues strikingly similar to that with which he had two decades earlier inculpated Petrarch in "A son Livre": "Lecteur, je ne veux estre escolier de Platon, / Qui la vertu nous presche, & ne fait pas de mesme" [Reader, I do not want to be a student of Plato, who preaches virtue to us and does not practice it himself] (*SH* II, 1, 9–10). And despite the fact that the publication of this new recueil was at least in part an attempt to recapture his aristocratic public by entering into competition with Desportes, his challenges to both the neo-Petrarchism and the neoplatonism whose mode other court poets had recently renewed are evident, as we have seen, throughout that collection and particularly at its end. But we have seen too that in the *Sonets pour Helene* he was sounding out new resonances from the *Rime sparse*, ample testimony to his renewed response to the Petrarchan model near the end of his long poetic career. Definitive confirmation of both the complexity and the fruitfulness of that late response is found in the almost contemporaneous appearance of the compilation "Sur la mort de Marie," added to the *Second livre des Amours* in Ronsard's fifth collective edition of his *Oeuvres* in 1578; and that confirmation is the more striking because here we find a Ronsard engaged in a return not only to the Petrarchan vein but to the Petrarchan "law" as well.

Both sets of poems first appeared in print in 1578, but both were probably composed before the middle of the decade. In any case, it is not insignificant that Ronsard connected his *Sonets pour Helene* in opening the final poem of the collection with the death in 1574 of Charles IX, "in that fatal month in which my Prince died" (II, 55, 2). During this period, Bensimon points out, funereal verse was in fashion, and Ronsard inscribed his love poems under the sign of mourning: Love and Death, concludes the poem, are but a single thing.[1] The new poems for Marie, composed during the same general period, were prompted both by death and by the circumstances of royal patronage: while a few components of this small new collection contain elements reminiscent of the young Marie celebrated by Ronsard in the *Second livre des Amours,* who died prematurely, others are evidently *pièces de commande* commemorating the death of another Marie, the beloved of the future Henri III, Marie de Cleves.[2] Given the new king's extravagant display of grief at the death that occurred during his absence in Poland, as Desonay observes, the extent to which it is commemorated in circumstantial poetry is hardly surprising, and Ronsard was not alone in rising to the occasion; the poetic contest that ensued forms one of the episodes in his rivalry with Desportes.[3]

Whatever the proportion of such autobiographical or circumstantial motivation, however, for Ronsard's collection of love poems *in morte* the recall of Petrarch's poems for Laura in the second part of the *Rime sparse* was inevitable; it afforded the perfect model.[4] And no doubt Ronsard welcomed the occasion to compose a sequence *in morte* because of the opportunity to enter once again into rivalry with the Italian master.[5] The nature of that rivalry, however, remains to be fully explored. Critical pronouncements frequently delimit both the extent and the import of the Petrarchan presence: Ronsard, we are told, "retains only the most universal themes: beauty menaced, death unpitying, love powerless to protect from death, mortals unwitting of their destiny"; from Petrarch's poems he borrows "a number of themes, sometimes certain movements, but never does he paraphrase or follow a poem from beginning to end."[6]

Yet the Petrarchan presence is in fact massive in this collection. If neither the opening of the "tombeau," whose liminal Latin inscription "Trajicit et fati littora magnus amor" is drawn from and explicitly attributed to Propertius, nor the dramatic image of a pale and frightened Death that opens the first sonnet suggests a return to the Petrarchan mode,[7] that first sonnet closes with verses that resonate with Petrarch's celebration of Laura *in morte*—

Pren courage, mon ame, il fault suivre sa fin:
Je l'entens dans le ciel comme elle nous appelle:
Mes pieds avec les siens ont fait mesme chemin (1, 12–14)[8]

Take courage, my soul, one must follow one's fate: I hear her from Heaven calling to us: my feet have followed the same path as hers

—and echoes of the *Rime sparse* are present thereafter in almost every poem of the sequence: only two among them—the Dialogue "Le Passant et le Génie," a brief composition filled with mythological allusions which is imitated from the "Epitaphium Quinterii" of the neo-Latin poet J. Cotta, and the celebrated sonnet "Comme on voit sur la branche au mois de May la rose" [As one sees the rose on the branch in the month of May]—lack the evident imprint of Ronsard's reading of Petrarch.[9] The range of the source poems, moreover, is remarkably extensive: almost half of Petrarch's poems *in morte di Laura*—by my count some forty-four poems— are present in direct verbal recalls in Ronsard's collection, along with thematic echoes of numerous others; nor is it insignificant that the poems in question begin with the announcement of Laura's death in *R* 267 and continue to the last sonnets preceding the explicitly penitential pieces that close Petrarch's volume.

What, then, is the nature of this recall, this renewal, this return? A preliminary observation is that the borrowings are once again not only massive but composite, frequently to an even greater extent than in the most imitative poems of the early *Amours*. The practice is readily illustrated in the "Stances" which immediately follow the opening sonnet, in which at least twenty recalls are drawn from fifteen different poems of the *Rime*. Many are Petrarchan topoi: the reproach to an Amor found powerless to prevent the loss of his, and the poet's, greatest treasure (vv. 10–12; *R* 270 and 333); the disillusionment with earthly beauty and worldly hope (vv. 25–27; *R* 294, 319, and 350); and the emphasis on the transience of mortal beauty (vv. 65–66; *R* 248, 311, and 323). There is the same amazement on the part of the poet that he still lives despite such a loss (v. 70; *R* 343), and the complaint to Amor that "Tous deux contre un mesme rocher / Avons froissé nostre navire" [We have both destroyed our ship on the same rock] (vv. 17–18); "ad uno scoglio / avem rotto la nave" [we have wrecked our ship on the same rock] (*R* 268, 15–16). There are the painful images of an extraordinary earthly beauty that is no longer, that is now subject to decay, indeed now mere earth (vv. 50ff, cf. 82–84; *R* 311 and 292); there is the rhetorical lament, echoing Petrarch's versions, of the *ubi sunt* topos in which the enumeration of losses to time and death includes the many attributes beloved in the lady (vv. 55–56; *R* 267 and 299) and the identification of these same qualities: "Ce ris qui me faisoit apprendre / Que c'est qu'aimer" [that laugh that taught me what it is to love] (vv. 57–58), echoing ". . . col suon de le parole / ne le quali io imparai che cosa è amore" [. . . with the sound of those words in which I learned what love is] (*R* 270, 52–53), and the affirmation that his love has rendered everything in the world displeasing with the single exception of this lady (vv. 136–38; *R* 116,

7–8).[10] There is the same self-reproach for the failure to anticipate the possibility of her death (vv. 28–30; *R* 311). Now the lover remains miserable and alone while she, liberated from her mortal state, is happy in Heaven (vv. 115–26 and VIII, 12–14; *R* 321 et al.), and he calls on the death that has caused his grief to come now to his rescue (vv. 163–64; *R* 327). Both bereaved poets would draw pity from the very rocks (vv. 77–78; *R* 294). Petrarch would, like Orpheus, draw his lady back from death (*R* 323), Ronsard would be a new Orpheus whose song would move Death to pity (vv. 21–24), and his challenge to Love is closely patterned on that of Petrarch:

> . . . Amor, se vuo' ch'i' torni al giogo antico . . .
> il mio amato tesoro in terra trova . . .
> ritogli a morte quel ch'ella n'a tolto . . . (*R* 270, 1, 5, 14)

> . . . Love, if you wish me to return to the old yoke . . . find my beloved treasure in the earth . . . take back from Death what she has taken from us . . .

> Si tu veux, Amour, que je sois
> Encore un coup dessous tes lois,
> M'ordonnant un nouveau service,
> Il te faut sous la terre aller
> Flatter Pluton, & r'appeller
> En lumiere mon Eurydice. (139–44)

> Love, if you want me to continue for a time under your law, ordaining for me a new service, you must go beneath the earth to flatter Pluto and call my Eurydice back to the light.

These and other topical themes are treated in other poems: the accusation that Death has enriched heaven while impoverishing the lover (*MM* 8, 2; *R* 338); the complaint of injustice, that the lady is happy and at peace while the lover remains miserable and in strife (*MM* 8, 11–14, and "Elegie," 125; *R* 268); the affirmation that sorrow, however intense, does not occasion death (*MM* 10, 1; *R* 271); the sad proclamation of his newfound liberty from Love (*MM* 15, 11–12; *R* 363).

While the massive presence of Petrarchan echoes bears its own witness to Ronsard's engagement with the Italian master in this late collection, closer examination of the sequence leads us rapidly to challenge the conclusion that "their resemblances with Petrarch remain quite superficial,"[11] as well as the overtly unfavorable judgment that the influence of Petrarch in this collection is not only "invasive" but "indiscrete."[12] For those resemblances are not limited to the topical echoes of the *Rime sparse* that appear

routinely in footnotes to Ronsard's poems or to the broad thematic ana-
logies routinely suggested by commentators. Not only does this small
recueil afford "ample evidence of Ronsard's mature and individualistic
use of Petrarch's poetry," as Donald Stone affirms.[13] That use is in this case
particularly ambitious, for it is informed by an overarching strategy that
grounds the coherence of the poems as sequence—a strategy through
which Ronsard challenges Petrarch's sequence *in morte* by appropriation.

"Appropriation" is not intended here merely to suggest the adoption
in individual poems of the stance of the bereaved poet-lover, which
Ronsard now assumed as readily as he, like so many others, had adopted
the stance of the Petrarchan lover *in vita di madonna*. It suggests rather the
adoption of a number of elements of the "story" of Petrarch and Laura to
rewrite that of the poet-lover and Marie, whether fictive or authentic, as
previously inscribed in the lyrics of the *Second Livre des Amours*. The strat-
egy is particularly significant in "Sur la mort de Marie" because in this
recueil, compiled at least in part to commemorate a loss experienced by a
royal patron but included in Ronsard's *Oeuvres* as the second part of his
Amours de Marie, the autobiographical presumption central to Petrarchan
lyric collections is doubly complicated. The fact that the king's young
mistress was named Marie, like the young Angevine depicted in the *Con-
tinuations* of 1555–56, afforded a ready pretext for constituting the collec-
tion as an addition to the *Second Livre des Amours*. Yet it also opened the
possibility of striking incongruities. For example, it could hardly have
escaped the attention of Ronsard's contemporary readers that many of the
poems of the *Second Livre* had been composed, not for Marie but for other
ladies.[14] Hence there was in fact no collection unambiguously devoted to
the celebration of Marie *in vita* that would stand now as the precursor of
the poems commemorating Marie *in morte*—poems to which Ronsard
nonetheless affixes the explicit title "Sur la mort de Marie." His awareness
of the potential dissonance is suggested by the fact that in 1578, the collec-
tion to which he now appended the small new recueil *in morte* was re-
vised, largely by the suppression of poems overtly addressed to or recall-
ing other objects of his desire, to reserve the *Second Livre* for Marie alone.[15]

Even if we take Ronsard's cue, however, and read the newly purged
Second Livre retrospectively to recall only those poems addressed to or
evidently associated with Marie, there is a yet more serious incongruity to
be confronted. Whatever Ronsard's relations with one or more young
women bearing that name, the Marie celebrated in his earlier poems was
a charming country girl, and his verses for her had been appropriate to
her state. "Of all the young women glimpsed in the *Continuation des
Amours*," Dassonville observes, "the most chaste, the most rebellious, the

most cruel of them is never a goddess," and the love that each stirs in the lyric protagonist, similarly less disembodied, is reflected in a style now more charming than sublime.[16]

And now, for the solemn tribute of the poems *in morte*, this Marie becomes a problematic figure. Ronsard's professed scorn for the Petrarch who had exalted Laura's chastity, the Petrarch to whom he had in "A son Livre" at the opening of the *Second Livre des Amours* accorded the unflattering label of "un grand fat d'aymer sans avoir rien" [a great fool to have loved while having nothing] stands in marked contrast to the repeated exaltation of Marie's chastity and virtue in the poems "Sur la mort de Marie," which in turn represent a radical departure from his characterization of Marie *in vita*. Such encomia are not absent from the poems that Ronsard had penned much earlier for Cassandre, but they are radically different from his characterization of the teasing, flirtatious Marie, object of his desire in the *Continuations*. We need only recall the *chanson* "Petite pucelle Angevine" (*Nouvelle Continuation*, 3) in which the beloved, "fille trop sotte & trop nice" [a girl too stupid and too naive], had left the poet for "nouvelle amitié" with "je ne scay quel Seigneur" [new friendship with I know not what lord] and compare it now with the recollection of Marie *in vita* by the poet of the compilation *in morte*:

> De ceste belle, douce, honneste chasteté
> Naissoit un froid glaçon, ains une chaude flame,
> Qu'encores aujourd'huy esteinte sous la lame
> Me reschauffe, en pensant quelle fut sa clarté . . . (*MM* 13, 1–4)

> From this lovely, sweet, honest chastity was born a cold block of ice, or rather a hot flame, that still today beneath the tombstone warms me again as I recall its clarity . . .

a bit of preciosity that is indebted, as Weber notes, to Petrarch:

> D'un bel chiaro polito e vivo ghiaccio
> Move la fiamma che m'incende e strugge. (*R* 202, 1–2)

> From beautiful, clear, shining ice comes the flame that kindles and melts me.

A cynical reading—and one that Ronsard might well have endorsed—could of course argue that the relation of the new collection for Marie to its precursor exemplifies the practice recommended by Ronsard in "A son livre" cited in the preceding chapter, that the sensible lover should imitate the conduct that he there attributes to Petrarch: to take his pleasure of the lady and then present her as admirable, chaste, divine, holy, as "every lover should do." On the other hand, we might entertain the possibility that the disparity between the attitudes toward chastity in the two sets of poems associated with the name of Marie is yet another indication that Ronsard's love poems collectively reflect the opposing views of woman central to the *Querelle des Femmes*.[17] Closer reading, however, suggests a radically different explanation: that it is Ronsard's return to the *Rime sparse* that is reflected in his rewriting of Marie.[18]

In fact, it is very infrequently that we recognize the insouciant Marie in the poems *in morte*. And it was demonstrably in his reading of the *Rime sparse* that Ronsard found a means of resolving, or at the least attenuating, the incongruities between the Marie depicted in the *Second Livre des Amours* and the Marie celebrated in its sequel appended much later. We may readily imagine, as Desonay emphasizes, that the obligation of the "Prince of poets" to participate in the royal mourning of the death of Marie de Clèves prompted Ronsard to recur to the second part of the *Rime*, the *Sonetti e Canzoni in morte di Madonna Laura*.[19] But this insight is only partial, and it occults the full import of Ronsard's return to the Italian collection; for while the majority of his poems for Marie *in morte* owe their pronounced intertextual resonance not to the Marie long ago celebrated *in vita* but to Petrarch's Laura, it is to a Laura who was herself depicted not only *in morte* but also *in vita*.[20]

The traces of this filiation are found repeatedly in the sporadic idealization of the lost lady. In the *Amours* of 1552–53 the Platonic resonance was strongly, if only intermittently, heard:

> Par ce doux mal j'adorai la beaulté,
> Qui me liant d'une humble cruaulté
> Me desnoua les liens d'ignorance.
> Par luy me vint ce vertueux penser,
> Qui jusqu'au ciel fit mon cuoeur eslancer,
> Aillé de foy, d'amour & d'esperance. (174, 9–14)

> Through this sweet pain I adored the beauty that, binding me with a humble cruelty, freed me from the bonds of ignorance. Through it came to me that virtuous thought that made my heart soar to the heavens, on wings of faith, of love, and of hope.

In the *Second Livre des Amours*, however, an obviously Petrarchan verse describing Marie as one "dont la vertu me monstre un droit chemin aux cieux" [whose virtue shows me a straight path to heaven] ("Elegie a Marie," added to the *Second Livre* in 1560) stands out as an apparently isolated Platonic accent.[21] Now in the new collection these accents proliferate: the declaration in the "Elegie" that "Vous m'ostastes du coeur tout vulgaire penser, / Et l'esprit jusqu'au ciel vous me fistes hausser" [You removed from my heart all base thoughts, and made me raise my spirit up to heaven] (*MM* 12, 75–76) echoes Petrarch's praise of Laura's beauty that "ogni basso penser del cor m'avulse" [uprooted from my heart every low thought] (*R* 351, 8); the proclamation in the "Epitaph de Marie" (*MM* 16) that "En ta tombe repose honneur & courtoisie" [honor and courtesy rest in your tomb] echoes the binomial recurrent in the *Rime sparse*, for example in *R* 37, 338, and 352. "Quand je pense à ce jour, où je la vey si belle / Toute flamber d'amour, d'honneur et de vertu" [When I think of the day, when I saw her so lovely all aflame with love, with honor and virtue] (*MM* 9, 1–2) echoes Petrarch's "Tornami a mente . . . qual io la vidi in su l'età fiorita / tutta accesa de' raggi di sua stella; / sì nel mio primo occorso onesta e bella" [She comes to mind . . . just as I saw her in her flowering, all burning with the rays of her star; I see her in the first encounter so chaste and beautiful] (*R* 336, 1, 3–5).

This Marie, moreover, is now affirmed as a creature of Heaven, one descended from Heaven. The Petrarchan commonplace had been deployed by Ronsard, although infrequently, to praise Cassandre, but not to represent Marie.[22] Now, like Petrarch, Ronsard repeatedly imagines the lost lady among the angels, "assis au rang des Anges precieux" [seated in the ranks of the precious angels] ("Elegie," 124),[23] and some of these mentions occur in passages closely tied to his praise of her soul and of her virtue: "La terre aime le corps, & de l'ame parfaite / Les Anges de là sus se vantent bien-heureux" [The earth loves her body, and the blessed angels on high boast of her soul] (*MM* 11, 10–11). The poet's expression of jealousy with regard to those angels who now enjoy the company of the lady that he has lost closely follows Petrarch, here as in the "Epitaphe": "Tu es belle Marie un bel astre des cieux: / Les Anges tous ravis se paissent de tes yeux" [You are, beautiful Marie, a beautiful star in the heavens: the angels, ecstatic, delight in your eyes] (16, 9–10); cf. *Rime* 300, 332, 348).[24] Or he avows his error in having imagined his beloved invulnerable to death:

Je me suis tout seul offensé,
Comme celuy qui n'eust pensé
Que morte fust une Deesse. ("Stances," 2, 28–30)

I alone deceived myself, as one who had not thought that a Goddess could die.

Although a recent reader finds in these verses evidence that Ronsard's Petrarchan metaphor is inane,[25] here again Ronsard directly translates

Petrarch: ". . . ch'altri che me non ò di chi mi lagne, / che 'n dee non credev'io regnasse Morte" [. . . for I have no one to complain of save myself, who did not believe that Death reigns over goddesses] (*R* 311, 7–8).

Thus as Ronsard now adopts the posture of the bereaved Petrarch, at the same time he adopts Petrarch's characterization of Laura to define the character of the Marie commemorated in the new, small recueil. And it is highly significant, although it has largely escaped critical comment, that to do so he repeatedly revisits the poems of the *Rime* celebrating Laura *in vita* as well as those following her death. The practice is readily illustrated by the "Elegie," a long poem which, like the "Stances" near the beginning of the sequence, is on the whole a mosaic of Petrarchan echoes but with a high concentration of recollections of poems *in vita*. After the impact of the lady's unique beauty, all else is a source of displeasure (14–16; *R* 37, 39–40), but it is his destiny to have known it (49; *R* 307). Her image, graven in the lover's heart on the occasion of the innamoramento, is projected onto all of nature and occupies the poet's thoughts to the exclusion of all else (17–22; cf. *R* 96, 5–6; 129, 40–43). Another passage (41–44) takes up Petrarch's famous metaphor, most fully developed in *R* 189, of the storm-driven ship. Or those who saw the lady *in vita* are called upon to witness her miraculous nature (67–70; *R* 309, 13–14). Death has robbed the kingdom of Love of its greatest beauty (108–10; cf. *Rime* 326, 1–3); now the poet would wander like a wild man because of his grief, in a particularly interesting instance of Ronsard's adoption of the persona of the *Rime sparse* (132–4; *R* 306, 5).[26]

And there are more significant, more suggestive indications that Ronsard patterned his Marie *in morte* on Petrarch's Laura *in vita*, whether rendered in the poems of the *Rime in vita* or recalled in those *in morte*:

> Des presens de Nature elle vint si pourveuë,
> Et sa belle jeunesse avoit tant de pouvoir,
> Qu'elle eust peu d'un regard les rochers esmouvoir,
> Tant elle avoit d'attraits et d'amours en la veuë. (*MM* 15, 5–8)

> She came so endowed with Nature's gifts, and her lovely young age had so much power, that she could have moved stones with a glance, so much allure and love she had in her eyes.

Compare this to the "miraculous" young Laura of a long passage of *Rime* 325. Or Ronsard recalls Marie's marvelous qualities in the "Elegie":

> Son divin se vestoit d'une mortelle nue,
> Qui mesprisoit le monde, et personne n'osoit
> Luy regarder les yeux, tant leur flame luisoit.

Son ris, & son regard, & sa parole pleine
De merveilles, n'estoient d'une nature humaine:
Son front ny ses cheveux, son aller ny sa main.
C'estoit une Deesse en un habit humain,
Qui visitoit la terre, aussi tost enlevée
Au ciel, comme elle fut en ce monde arrivée. (*MM* 12, 50–58)

Her divinity was clothed in a mortal cloud that scorned the world, and no one dared look into her eyes, so bright was their flame. Her laugh, her glance, and her speech full of marvels, were not of a mortal nature: her brow nor her hair, her carriage nor her hand. She was a Goddess in a human guise who visited the earth, very soon taken up to the heavens as she had arrived in this world.

These various praises locally echo Petrarchan formulations, in poems both *in vita* and *in morte,* very closely: eyes so bright that mortals could not look upon them, a speech itself full of marvels—the latter especially unsuited, be it noted, to the charming but simple Marie formerly depicted by Ronsard *in vita.*

The result toward which these various poems collectively tend is no less than a rewriting of Marie in the collection *in morte.* Even the emphasis on her name, which in Ronsard's poems for Marie *in vita* had given rise to a literary play fertile in variants such as "Marie, qui voudroit vostre beau nom tourner, / Il trouveroit Aimer . . ." [Marie, he who would rearrange your lovely name would find To Love . . .],[27] is adapted now to the recall of Petrarch's celebration of Laura: ". . . & je n'ay sinon / Pour reconfort que son beau nom, / Qui si doux me sonne en la bouche" [. . . and I have nothing to comfort me except her fair name that sounds so sweetly in my mouth] ("Stances," 70–72) echoes Petrarch's formulation of "'l suo chiaro nome / che sona nel mio cor sì dolcemente" [her bright name, which sounds so sweetly in my heart] (*R* 268, 49–50). The rapt attention to the name, moveover, discloses yet more direct indicators of his indebtedness. When Petrarch protests following Laura's death that "nè di sé m'a lasciato altro che 'l nome" [she left me nothing of herself but her name] (*R* 291, 14), that name itself, in its homophonic near-identity with "lauro" fundamental to the theme of poetic celebration *in vita di Laura,* now affords a new emblem of sublimation, in Laura's declaration to the grieving poet that "il lauro segna / trionfo, ond'io son degna / mercé di quel Signor che mi diè forza" [the laurel means triumph, of which I am worthy, thanks to that Lord who gave me strength] (*R* 359, 50–52).

If there were no other clues to Ronsard's assimilation of the Petrarchan model in Ronsard's collection, we need only read *MM* 11, in which he combines the image of the "Laurier triomphant" with the retrospective summation in another of Petrarch's poems. First Petrarch:

Due gran nemiche inseme erano agiunte,
Bellezza et Onestà . . .
Et or per Morte son sparse e disgiunte:
l'una è nel Ciel che se ne gloria et vanta,
l'altra sotterra che' begli occhi amanta
onde uscir già tant'amorose punte. (*R* 297, 1–2, 5–8)

Two great enemies were united, Beauty and Chastity . . . And now Death has scattered and separated them: one is in Heaven, which glories and vaunts of it; the other in the earth, which mantles the lovely eyes from which so many amorous darts used to come forth.

And now Ronsard:

Deux puissans ennemis me combattoient alors
Que ma dame vivoit: l'un dans le ciel se serre,
De Laurier triomphant: l'autre dessous la terre . . .
C'estoit la chasteté . . . / Et la douce beauté . . . (1–3, 5, 6)

Two powerful enemies fought against me while my lady lived: one is held close in heaven, the triumphant Laurel: the other beneath the earth . . . was chastity . . . and the sweet beauty . . .

But the Petrarchan sonnet is, of course, a retrospective tribute, found among the poems *in morte di Laura* that have often been cited as Ronsard's obvious model for his own collection *in morte*. For the shaping imprint of the *Rime* as a whole on that collection, the most compelling, indeed decisive, evidence is found in his most detailed characterization of the status of the lost Marie, found again in the "Elegie":

Bien qu'elle eust pris naissance en petite bourgade,
Non de riches parens, ny d'honneurs, ny de grade,
Il ne l'en fault blasmer; la mesme Deité
Ne desdaigna de naistre en trespauvre cité:
Et souvent sous l'habit d'une simple personne
Se cache tout le mieux que le destin nous donne. (61–66)

Although she was born in a small village, not of rich parents or of honors or rank, she is not to be blamed for that; the Deity itself did not disdain to be born in a very poor city: and often, beneath the garb of a simple person, is hidden the very best that destiny gives us.

This affirmation of the lady's humble birth is strikingly inappropriate to characterize the status of Marie de Clèves, princess of Condé, and commentaries on the collection have done little to explain its presence.

Ronsard makes a similar claim for himself, notes the recent Pléiade edition with reference to his boast that in centuries to come a reader, revisiting his Loir "Et voyant mon pays, à peine pourra croire / Que d'un si petit lieu tel Poëte soit né" [and seeing my country, will scarcely be able to believe that such a Poet was born in so humble a place].[28] And it may of course be argued that the inapposite reference concerning Marie's origins affords evidence that Ronsard's poems *in morte* celebrate not only the Marie of whose company death had deprived the king but also that other, "humble" Marie whom the poet had years ago celebrated *in vita*, she whose setting was repeatedly "bourg" or "village"; it is possible, Roger Sorg suggests, that the "Elegie" was written somewhat later than most of the poems "sur la mort de Marie," just before the publication of the collection, and that the allusion to the Marie beloved by the poet was intended to contribute to the desired illusion.[29] But how then are we to explain that a poem from the *Nouvelle Continuation* (1556) in which Ronsard was explicit about the humble origin of the beloved—"Si vous n'estes d'un lieu si noble que Cassandre" [if you are not from as noble a place as Cassandre] (16)—is finally eliminated from the *Second Livre des Amours* in the 1578 edition in which the "Elegie" first appears? And any illusion of reference to Marie-*paysanne* is to be definitively eliminated from the "Elégie" in the 1587 edition, where verse 66 is corrected to read "Le ciel cache les biens qu'aux Princes il ne donne" [Heaven hides the good that it gives to Princes]. In any case the various biographical hypotheses are not necessary, for the verses in question testify to the status of neither of the putative Maries in question but to the presence of an infrequently cited poem from the *Rime sparse:*

[Dio] di sé nascendo a Roma non fe' grazia,
a Giudea sì, tanto sovr' ogni stato
umiltate esaltar sempre gli piacque.
Ed or di picciol borgo un sol n'à dato,
tal che natura o 'l luogo si ringrazia
onde sì bella donna al mondo nacque. (*R* 4, 9–14)[30]

He, when He was born, did not bestow Himself on Rome, but rather on Judea, so beyond all other states it pleased him always to exalt humility. And now from a small village He has given us a sun, such that Nature is thanked and the place where so beautiful a lady was born to the world.

Yet another fundamental aspect of Ronsard's assimilation of the Petrarchan model must be noted. Strikingly evident in his rewriting of Marie, it is not limited to that rewriting: at the same time, Ronsard effectively creates a new past for the bereaved speaker of the poems as well, by rewriting the chapter of *his* own story that emerges from the *Second Livre des Amours*. The attentiveness to the elements that help to define a "story" in Petrarch's collection of "scattered rhymes," much in evidence, as we have seen, in Ronsard's earliest collection of his *Amours*, is in this regard yet more decisive for the sequence "Sur la mort de Marie." Consider the extended passage in the "Elegie" that depicts the fateful occasion of the *innamoramento*:

> J'avois au-paravant, veincu de la jeunesse,
> Autres dames aimé (ma faute je confesse):
> Mais la playe n'avoit profondement saigné,
> Et le cuir seulement n'estoit qu'esgratigné,
> Quand Amour, qui les Dieux & les hommes menace,
> Voyant que son brandon n'eschauffoit point ma glace,
> Comme rusé guerrier ne me voulant faillir,
> La print pour son escorte, & me vint assaillir. (25–32)

I had before that time, overcome by youth, loved other ladies (I confess my fault): but the wound had not bled deeply, and the skin was but scratched, when Love, who menaces Gods and men, seeing that his firebrand did nothing to warm my ice, like a crafty warrior not wishing to miss me took her as his escort, and came to assail me.

The principal development of this passage is closely patterned on the account, on which Ronsard draws also for the innamoramento in the *Sonets pour Helene* (*SH* 27), in Petrarch's "metamorphosis canzone":

> . . . che sentendo il crudel di ch'io ragiono
> infin allor percossa di suo strale
> non essermi passato oltra la gonna,
> prese in sua scorta una possente Donna
> ver cui poco giamai mi valse o vale
> ingegno o forza o dimandar perdono . . . (*R* 23, 32–37)

For that cruel one of whom I speak, seeing that as yet no blow of his arrows had gone beyond my garment, took as his patroness a powerful Lady, against whom wit or force or asking pardon has helped or helps me little . . .

The closeness of Ronsard's poem to the Petrarchan original is transparent in "son escorte" translating "sua scorta" for the lady herself whose participation is essential to an offended Amour's design of conquest, and it is reinforced by borrowings from other poems early in the *Rime:* the depiction of Amour as a "rusé guerrier" recalls the initial innamoramento poem (*R* 2) in which a conventionally stealthy Amor lies in wait for his victim "come uom ch'a nocer luogo e tempo aspetta" [like a man who waits for the time and place to do harm]. Ronsard had demonstrated his early interest in the narrative thrust of *R* 23 in sonnet 216 of the 1552–53 *Amours,* "Depuis le jour que mal sain je soupire" [Since the day that I sigh for ill at ease] and in the *Sonets pour Helene,* we have seen that a rewriting of the innamoramento enabled him to reconcile his protestations of having succumbed to Hélène's fatal charm with the declarations of love generously distributed in collections past. Here the account serves precisely the same function of accommodation: Ronsard confesses to his earlier affections but declares them superficial in nature; those early wounds—in fact mere scratches—were insufficient to constitute an innamoramento in the sense revealed to him at last by the new passion. Again the detailing of the fatal moment is particularly significant, for the adaptation of the Petrarchan version affords him an occasion to qualify the self-proclaimed past of the lyric protagonist as that of one who had not previously seriously loved—a posture difficult to reconcile with the protestations of the earlier collections of his *Amours,* to which he was now adding the *Sonets pour Helene.*

Intensified in this new small collection, however, is Ronsard's recourse to passages of the *Rime* that are exceptional in providing or appearing to provide markers of autobiographical authentification while promoting the perception of an implicit narrative. In the "Elegie a Marie" *in vita* he had recorded leaving his "Loir et Gastine" for Anjou, where he met and fell in love with Marie. When a similar indication opens the "Epitaphe de Marie"—"Cy reposent les oz de toy, belle Marie, / Qui me fis pour Anjou quitter le Vandomois" [Here rest your bones, fair Marie, who made me leave the Vendomois for Anjou] (1–2)—its formulation is very closely modeled on a verse from the *Rime sparse* that identifies Laura as "Quella per cui con Sorga ò cangiato Arno" [she for whom I exchanged Arno for Sorgue] (*R* 308, 1).

Or consider the scene, set in an imagined future, when the lyric protagonist would have recounted to a newly receptive beloved the pains of love suffered long ago. Death has deprived him of even this deferred solace:

Già traluceva à' begli occhi il mio core . . .
Ahi, Morte ria, come a schiantar se' presta
il frutto di molt'anni in sì poche ore! (*R* 317, 5, 7–8)

My heart [and my high faithfulness] were now visible to her lovely
eyes. . . Ah, cruel Death, how quick you are to shatter in so few hours
the fruit of many years!

Esperant luy conter un jour
L'impatience de l'Amour
Qui m'a fait des peines sans nombre,
La mort soudaine m'a deceu . . . ("Stances," 43–46)

Hoping to tell her one day the impatience of Love that has given me
pains beyond counting, death suddenly deceived me . . .

Amor, quando fioria
mia speme e 'l guidardon di tanta fede,
tolta m'è quella ond'attendea mercede. (*R* 324, 1–3)

Love, when my hope, the guerdon of so much faithfulness, was flow-
ering, she was taken away from me from whom I expected mercy.

Alors que plus Amour nourrissoit mon ardeur,
M'asseurant de jouyr de ma longue esperance:
A l'heure que j'avois en luy plus d'asseurance,
La Mort a moissonné mon bien en sa verdeur. (*MM* 4, 1–4)

When Love was most nourishing my ardor, assuring me that I
would profit from my long hope: at the hour when I felt most sure of
him, Death harvested my treasure before its time.

Or he recalls their last meeting. First Petrarch, in two consecutive poems:

Quel vago, dolce, caro, onesto sguardo
dir parea: 'To' di me quel che tu poi,
ché mai più qui non mi vedrai . . .
[Laura's eyes] taciti, sfavillando oltra lor modo,
dicean . . . (*R* 330, 1–3, 9–10)

That sweet, dear, virtuous, yearning glance seemed to say: "Take
what you can from me, for you will never see me here again" . . .
Silently, sparkling beyond their wont, they were saying . . .

Se stato fusse il mio poco intelletto
meco al bisogno, e non altra vaghezza
l'avesse disviando altrove vòlto,
ne la fronte a Madonna avrei ben letto . . . (R 331, 49–52)

If my little intellect had been with me at need, and another hunger
had not driven it elsewhere and made it stray, on my lady's brow I
might have read . . .

Then Ronsard in the "Stances," combining the two into a single lament:

Si je n'eusse eu l'esprit chargé
De vaine erreur, prenant congé
De sa belle et vive figure,
Oyant sa voix, qui sonnoit mieux
Que de coustume, & ses beaux yeux
Qui reluisoient outre mesure,
   Et son soupir qui m'embrasoit,
J'eusse bien veu qu'ell' me disoit:
Or soule toy de mon visage,
Si jamais tu en euz soucy:
Tu ne me voirras plus icy,
Je m'en vay faire un long voyage. (91–102)

If my spirit had not been weighted down with grave error, on taking
leave of her beautiful, vibrant person, hearing her voice that
sounded forth more lovely than ever, and her beautiful eyes that
sparkled beyond measure, and her sigh that fired me, I would have
seen well that she was saying to me: Now take your fill of my face,
if ever you have cared for it: you will no longer see me here, I am
going to make a long journey.

It is evident that if, as Alexandre Micha suggests, Ronsard creates his af-
fective life with a view to its poetic expression,[31] here he goes further, to
recreate his *vie sentimentale* as that of Petrarch himself.

It is the "histoire vraye" of Ronsard that the Passant is invited to hear in
the "Elégie" dedicated to Marie *in morte*. The story is destined, the poet-
narrator affirms, as an epitaph, for inscription on the tomb that he pro-
poses to share with Marie. Ronsard's predilection for the genre of the
epitaph, which also figured frequently in the lyric collections of his imme-
diate precursors, was well established;[32] he had composed other epitaphs
for himself, some, like the one that figures at the close of the "Elegie" for

Marie, invoking his experience as lover. Already he had made frequent use of the "device for declaring his martyrdom" that he found in the Roman elegists, who had composed their own epitaphs as victims of the fatal wound inflicted by Cupid;[33] a poem from the *Bocage* of 1554 added to the *Amours* in 1578, for example, lightly reproaches Marie for provoking his death by taking possession of his heart while not offering hers in exchange:

> Et veus que sur ma lame Amour aille ecrivant:
> Celui qui gît ici sans coeur estoit vivant,
> Et trespassa sans coeur, & sans coeur il repose. (2, 12–14)

> And I want this to be written by Love on my tombstone: He who lies here without a heart was once alive, and he died without a heart, and without a heart he reposes.

However conventional, the epitaph offered considerable potential as vehicle for biographical content and, in the case of the self-composed epitaph, for ostensibly autobiographical declaration. The opening sonnet of the *Sonets et Madrigals pour Astree* posits the commemorative inscription on the poet's eventual tomb: "Ronsard, voulant aux astres s'élever, / Fut foudroyé par une belle Astrée" [Ronsard, wishing to raise himself to the stars, was struck down by a beautiful Astrée].[34] In a poem added to the *Second Livre des Amours* in 1560, in a lengthy inscription whose execution is entrusted to Ronsard's friend Buttet, Cassandre is inculpated along with Marie for his death:

> Celuy qui gist sous cette tombe icy
>   Aima premiere une belle Cassandre,
>   Aima seconde une Marie aussy,
>   Tant en amour il fut facile a prendre.
> De la premiere il eut le coeur transy
>   De la seconde il eut le coeur en cendre,
>   Et si des deux il n'eut onques mercy. (II, 9–15)

> He who lies here beneath this tomb loved first a beautiful Cassandre, second a Marie too, so easily was he taken in love. By the first he had his heart broken, by the second he had his heart reduced to ashes, and from the two of them he never had mercy.

The playful tone of this inscription implicating Cassandre and Marie *in vita* is replaced by one more serious in the collection *in morte*. While the tomb on which it is to be inscribed is the one that the poet proposes to share with Marie—once again he expresses the desire "que mes oz pour toute couverture / Reposent pres des siens sous mesme sepulture" [that my bones for their only shelter rest near hers within the same grave] (149–50)—its "true story" is that of Ronsard himself:

Passant, de cest amant enten l'histoire vraye.
De deux traicts differents il receut double playe:
L'une que feit l'Amour, ne versa qu'amitié;
L'autre que feit la Mort, ne versa que pitié.
Ainsi mourut navré d'une double tristesse,
Et tout pour aimer trop une jeune maistresse. (12, 153–58)

Passerby, hear the true story of this lover. From two different arrows he received a double wound: the one made by Love poured forth only affection; the other, made by Death, poured forth only pity. Thus he died heartbroken of a double sadness, and all for loving a young mistress too much.

This address to the anonymous "Passant" is a *mise en abyme* of the fiction of the collection as a whole, for the figure has already been assigned a role: in the introductory sonnet, the poet's premonitory dream of an open tomb inscribed with the name of Marie ends when "un Passant, adeulé de souci" [a passerby, fraught with care] brings the news of her death, and in the "Dialogue," whose form is borrowed from poems in the Greek Anthology, it is the comment of a "Passant" familiar with Marie's now-destroyed beauty that elicits Genie's affirmation of the creative potential of Ronsard's tears to raise a flower from her ashes.[35] Now the "Passant" whose attention is drawn to the verses carved on the tomb is invoked, not to read but to listen to Ronsard's story. And the text of that story, proclaimed as his "histoire vraye," is adapted from Petrarch's description of the two wounds inflicted by Amor:

et, ben che 'l primo colpo aspro et mortale
fossi da sé, per avanzar sua impresa
una saetta di pietate à presa . . .
L'una piaga arde et versa foco et fiamma,
lagrime l'altra, che 'l dolor distilla
per li occhi mei . . . (R 241, 5–7, 9–11)

and, although the first blow was bitter and mortal in itself, to advance his undertaking he took a dart of pity . . . One wound burns and pours forth smoke and flame; the other, tears, which sorrow distills through my eyes on account of your suffering state . . .

Interestingly, the complex textual web that joins Ronsard's poems "Sur la mort de Marie" with the *Rime sparse* also affords us insight into the function of the poems that seem most resistant to that influence. Take first the recontextualization of the image of the labyrinth, which in the 1552–53 *Amours* had figured the "captivity" of Ronsard's love for Cassandre, with full emphasis on the classical allusion, on the casting of the poet as Theseus:

> Puis que je n'ay pour faire ma retraitte
> Du Labyrinth qui me va seduysant,
> Comme Thesée, un fil conduysant
> Mes paz doubteux dans les erreurs de Crete . . . (163, 1–4)

Since I do not have, like Theseus, to effect my retreat from the Labyrinth that draws me in a thread to guide my doubting steps through the circuitous ways of Crete . . .

In "Sur la mort de Marie," however, the tone is very different:

> Comme elle je devrois reposer à mon tour:
> Toutesfois je ne voy par quel chemin je sorte,
> Tant la Mort me r'empaistre au labyrinth d'Amour. (4, 12–14)

Like her I should rest in my turn: and yet I do not see by what path I can exit, so much does Death detain me in the labyrinth of Love.

Micha measures with these latter verses the distance that separates Ronsard from Petrarch, in that in the case of the former, death has not transfigured his love.[36] But it is surely worthy of note that Ronsard's lament, in opposing the image of the labyrinth to the unattainable repose desired by the bereaved lover, is derived directly from Petrarch, and it is only fully intelligible with reference to the *Rime sparse*. For not only does Petrarch define his love experience as "un lungo errore in cieco laberinto" [a long wandering in a blind labyrinth] (*R* 224, 4). In a poem full of unrest, that opens "Voglia mi sprona, Amor mi guida e scorge, / Piacer mi tira, Usanza mi trasporta" [Desire spurs me, Love guides and escorts me, Pleasure draws me, Habit carries me away] it is with the image of the labyrinth that he recapitulates his anxiety, in the single poem of the collection to record the date and the time of the *innamoramento*:

> Mille trecento ventisette, a punto
> su l'ora prima, il dì sesto d'aprile,
> nel laberinto entrai, né veggio ond'esca.(*R* 211, 12–14)[37]

One thousand three hundred twenty-seven, exactly at the first hour of the sixth day of April, I entered the labyrinth, nor do I see where I may get out of it.

Or consider the inextricable blending of images of the lady. Petrarch sets the formula: "mal per noi quella beltà si vide / se viva e morte ne devea tor pace" [ill did we see that beauty if living and dead it was to rob us of peace] (*R* 273, 13–14), closely echoed by Ronsard in the poem cited above: "Je suis bien malheureux, puis qu'elle vive & morte/ Ne me donne repos . . . " [I am unhappy indeed, since she alive and dead gives me no rest . . .] (*MM* 4, 9–10). The binomial immediately recurs in the famous closing verse of the best-known poem of the small recueil: "Afin que vif, & mort, ton corps ne soit que roses" (*MM* 5, 14) [So that, living and dead, your body be but roses]. This verse, which follows upon others recording the classical offering of milk and flowers at Marie's tomb, redirects the energy of the abstract "viva e morte" of the Petrarchan formula as an unexpectedly sensuous recall of Marie's body *in vita*.

"Comme on voit sur la branche au mois de May la rose" [As we see the rose on the branch in the month of May] is also, of course, the poem that links the sequence most closely with the characterization of Marie *in vita*, the Marie of the *Second Livre des Amours* to which the new collection is now appended as "seconde partie": it is the only poem now that mentions either the month of May or the rose, both so prominently associated elsewhere in Ronsard's amorous verse with the young Marie.[38] The sonnet passes gracefully along its nostalgic course to arrive at the final image of the presentation of milk and flowers. And it is the image of flowers that links it to the immediately following "Dialogue: Le Passant et le Genie" (*MM* 6), where the "Passant," recalling the beauty of the body now enclosed in the tomb, declares, "Je suis esmerveillé qu'une fleur n'est sortie, / Comme elle feit d'Ajax, du creux de ce tombeau" [I marvel that a flower has not emerged, as was the case for Ajax, from the depths of this tomb] to be told by Genie that "L'ardeur qui reste encore, & vit en ce flambeau, / Ard la terre d'amour" [the heat that still remains, and lives in this torch, burns the earth with love].

Unlike "Comme on voit sur la branche," the "Dialogue" has received minimal comment. The two commemorative poems, however, are closely linked in highly suggestive ways. They are related, first, as scenes enacted at Marie's tomb. The first is identified as such only at its close, where, following the famous meditation comparing Marie to the rose destroyed in its "premiere fleur," the poem offers her "*ce* vase plein de laict, *ce* panier plein de fleurs" [this vase full of milk, this basket full of flowers]; the second opens with the Passant's indication of *"ce* marbre." The poems are related too in their emphasis on the beauty of Marie's body, as the Passant in the "Dialogue" recalls "un corps qui fut plus beau / Que celuy de Narcise, ou celuy de Clitie" [a body that was more beautiful than that of Narcissus or of Clitia] and takes her very ashes as evidence:

> A la cendre on cognoist combien vive estoit forte
> La beauté de ce corps, quand mesmes estant morte
> Elle enflame la terre, & sa tombe d'amour. (12–14)

> From the ashes we know how intense was the beauty of this body when alive, when even in death it inflames the earth and her tomb with love.

The most fundamental connection between the two poems, however, is that suggested by the juxtaposition in each of images of ashes—"La Parque t'a tuée, & cendre tu reposes"; "l'humide cendre . . . A la cendre" [The Fate has killed you, and you rest as ashes . . . the damp ash . . . by the ashes]—with images of flowers.[39] And in the latter poem a new promise is offered: while Marie's ashes, dry, can produce nothing new, "rien . . . de nouveau," if watered by Ronsard's tears "soudain l'humide cendre / Une fleur du sepulchre enfanteroit au jour" [suddenly the damp ashes would give birth to a flower from the grave].

This secular redirection of the Petrarchan lament is found again in another passage anticipated by Genie's observation, now in the "Elegie" in which the familiar binomial recurs:

> Puis Amour que je sens par mes veines s'espandre,
> Passe dessous la terre, & r'attize la cendre
> Qui froide languissoit dessous vostre tombeau,
> Pour r'allumer plus vif en mon coeur son flambeau,
> Afin que vous soyez ma flame morte & vive. (12, 89–93).

> Then Love, that I feel coursing through my veins, passes beneath the earth and rekindles the ashes that are languishing cold beneath your tomb, to relight his torch more intensely in my heart, so that you be my flame both dead and alive.

Here a Petrarchan note is heard, if only distantly, for Petrarch too had implicated Love in the contrast between life and death, fire and ashes:

> O' servito a signor crudele et scarso:
> ch'arsi quanto 'l mio foco ebbi davante,
> or vo piangendo il suo cenere sparso. (*R* 320, 12–14)

I have served a cruel and niggardly lord: I burned as long as my fire was before me, now I go bewailing the scattering of its ashes.

In Petrarch's poem, however, the falling emphasis of the final word closes the poem with a sense of finality and at the same time relates it to the entire poetic enterprise of the *Rime sparse:* the ashes that were once Laura's body are scattered like the poet's rhymes. In Ronsard's poem, the funereal tone is not only absent but defied: his lord Amour, here neither "crudele" nor "scarso," will first rekindle the cold ashes in Marie's tomb, then re-kindle his torch, "son flambeau," in the poet's heart. From Marie's ashes, not now a flower but a flame: once again the poem affirms not only the promise of a poetic immortality conferred upon the earthly creature but the creative, generative energy of Ronsard's response to her death. It was to this energy that later poets were to pay tribute, as, here, Heredia:

> Tout meurt. Marie, Hélène, et toi, fière Cassandre,
> Vos beaux corps ne seraient qu'une insensible cendre,
> —Les roses et les lys n'ont pas de lendemain—
> Si Ronsard, sur la Seine ou sur la blonde Loire,
> N'eût tressé pour vos fronts, d'une immortelle main,
> Aux myrtes de l'Amour le laurier de la Gloire.[40]

> Everything dies. Marie, Hélène, and you, proud Cassandre, your fair bodies would be only an unfeeling ash—roses and lilies have no tomorrow—if Ronsard, near the Seine or the pale Loire, had not woven for your foreheads, with an immortal hand, the laurel of Glory into the myrtles of Love.

Another prominent set of recalls invites us to take the measure of the distance that separates Ronsard's collection *in morte* from that of Petrarch. The oneiric returns of a consolatory and solicitous Laura are among Petrarch's principal innovations in the second part of the *Rime sparse*,[41] and while a sensual suggestiveness is not absent from his report of these encounters, their edifying presupposition is maintained by the words attributed to the lady—"ma pur per nostro ben dura ti fui" [still for our good I was cruel to you] (R 341, 13) is but one example—even as she exhorts him to leave off his weeping: "ch'or fostu vivo com'io non son morta!" [would that you were as much alive as I am not dead!] (R 342, 14). Ronsard's adaptation of the motif is unquestionably more vivid and more erotic, and therefore not incongruous with aspects of his portrayal of Marie in the *Second Livre des Amours*. Both poets render the lady's nocturnal returns as hallucinatory presence—

. . . quando torni, te conosco e 'ntendo
a l'andar, a la voce, al volto, a' panni . . . (*R* 282, 13–14)

. . . when you return I know you, by your walk, by your voice, by
your face, by your dress . . .

Dormant ne me deçoit: car je la recognoy
A la main, à la bouche, aux yeux, à la parole . . . *MM* 10, 13–14)

Asleep she does not disappoint me: for I recognize her by her hand,
her mouth, her eyes, her speech . . .

and both record her consolatory gestures:

Ben torna a consolar tanto dolore
Madonna (*R* 283, 9–10)

My lady does indeed come back to console so much sorrow;

. . . al letto in ch'io languisco . . .
et pietosa s'asside in su la sponda.
Con quella man che tanto desiai
m'asciuga li occhi . . . (*R* 342, 6, 8–10)

. . . to the bed where I lie sick . . . and full of pity sits on the edge. With
that hand which I so much desired she dries my eyes . . .

Elle se sou-riant du regret qui m'affole,
En vision la nuict sur mon lict je la voy,
Qui mes larmes essuye, & ma peine console. (*MM* 10, 9–11)

She, smiling at the regret that drives me mad, appears to me in a
vision above my bed at night, drying my tears and consoling my
pain.

But Ronsard adds characteristically that she allows him "le voir, le parler,
/ Et luy baiser ses mains de roses: / Torche mes larmes de sa main, / Et
presse mon coeur en son sein" [to see, and speak, and kiss her hands of
roses: She dries my tears with her hand, and presses my heart to her
breast" ("Chanson," 86–89) and in that same poem laments that while
other lovers "ont le toucher & l'ouyr, / Avant-courriers de la victoire . . . je
ne puis jamais jouyr / Sinon d'une triste memoire" [have touch and hear-
ing, precursors of victory . . . I can never take pleasure except in a sad
memory] (49–52).

Or both poets repeatedly express the desire to rejoin the lost lady in
death:

—et volendol seguire,
interromper conven quest'anni rei,
perché mai veder lei
di qua non spero, e l'aspettar m'è noia. (*R* 268, 5–8)

—and if I wish to follow [my heart, departed with my lady] I must
break off these cruel years, for I never hope to see her on this side,
and waiting is painful to me.

Le traict qui la tua, devoit faire descendre
Mon corps aupres du sien pour finir mon esmoy:
Aussi bien, veu le mal qu'en sa mort je reçoy,
Je ne sçaurois plus vivre, & me fasche d'attendre. (*MM* 3, 5–8)

The blow that killed her should have made my body descend next to
hers to put an end to my distress: so much that, given the pain I
receive from her death, I can no longer imagine living, and am an-
gered to wait.

For Petrarch's poet, the desire for his life's end is one with the desire to see
Laura again, and the prayers to Death intensify with the passing of the
years:

Noia m'è 'l viver sì gravosa et lunga
ch'i' chiamo il fine per lo gran desire
di riveder cui non veder fu 'l meglio (*R* 312, 12–14)

Living is such heavy and long pain, that I call out for the end in my
great desire to see her again whom it would have been better not to
have seen at all

and he reproaches the "dispietata Morte" who will not allow him to rejoin
her:

. . . mi ten qua giù contra mia voglia,
et lei che se n'è gita
seguir non posso, ch'ella no 'l consente. (*R* 324, 7–9)

. . . [Life] keeps me down here against my will, and I cannot follow
her who has gone, for Death does not permit it.

He has lost the light of his life, protesting that "a seguitarlo / lecito fusse
è 'l mi' sommo desio" [my highest desire is to be permitted to follow her]
(*R* 331, 29–30) and praying again to Death to end his suffering: "ripre-
gando te, pallida Morte, / che mi sottragghi a sì penose notti" [begging

you often, pale Death, to rescue me from such painful nights] (*R* 332, 29–
30). In this famous sestina, "Morte" assumes an obsessive force as one of
the six rhyme-words of each stanza: "mi son mosso a pregar Morte / che
mi tolla di qui per farme lieto / ove è colei che i' canto et piango in rime"
[I have turned to beg Death to take me from here, to make me glad where
she is whom I sing and bewail in rhymes] (58–60), and he urges his privi-
leged audience of those who respond to the poetry of love to second his
prayer:

> O voi che sospirate a miglior notti,
> ch'ascoltate d'Amore o dite in rime,
> pregate non mi sia più sorda Morte, (67–69)

> O you who sigh for better nights, who listen about Love or write in
> rhymes, pray that Death be no longer deaf to me,

closing the poem with a final prayer of his own: "prego che 'l pianto mio
finisca Morte" [I pray that my weeping may be ended by Death].

Thus the prospect of rejoining Laura in Heaven at least tentatively as-
suages the grief of Petrarch's bereaved poet in a number of the poems *in
morte*. Ronsard's professed desire for death, in stark contrast, does not
accommodate this positive vein. He does indeed declare himself ready to
"follow" Marie: "Si quelcun trepassoit d'une extreme tristesse, / Je fusse
desja mort pour suivre ma maistresse" [if one died from extreme sadness,
I would be already dead to follow my mistress] (*MM* 10, 2–3), and like
Petrarch's poet, he fantasizes the lady's desire that he follow her, or that
she waits for him. Petrarch's yearning verses "et parte ad or ad or si volge
a tergo, / mirando s'io la seguo, e par ch'aspetti" [and still from time to
time she turns back, looking to see if I am following her, and seems to
wait] (*R* 346, 11–12) correspond to Ronsard's:

> Se faschant de me voir si long temps la survivre,
> Me tire, & fait semblant que de mon voile humain
> Veult rompre le fardeau pour estre plus delivre. (*MM* 14, 10–12)

> Annoyed to see me survive her for so long, she draws me, and indi-
> cates that she wants to break the burden of my human veil to make
> me more free.

But while these images of the bodily veil and its burden are elements of
the unmistakably Petrarchan rhetoric adopted by Ronsard in this collec-
tion—see, for example, *R* 349—they are detached here from their mooring
within a religious register in which earthly existence is contrasted to the

spiritual. Such a mooring was not unfamiliar to Ronsard; the poet who had in the early *Amours* repeatedly exploited the erotic potential of the "mort amoureuse" and imagined himself, succumbing as Love's victim, wandering "bienheureus . . . là-bas sous le bois amoureus" [happy in the forest of love][42] could also express the most orthodox Christian consolation, as in the opening of his epitaph for Charles IX:

> Si le grain de forment ne se pourrist en terre
> Il ne sçauroit porter ny feuille ny bon fruit:
> De la corruption la naissance se suit,
> Et comme deux anneaux l'une en l'autre s'enserre.[43]

If the wheat seed did not decay in the earth it could bear neither leaf nor good fruit: birth follows upon decay, and like two rings one is linked to the other.

In the invocation of death in the poems "Sur la mort de Marie," however, the earth is a refuge for one who awaits deliverance from a life grown weary, as in his wish, expressed early in the collection, to be buried with Marie: "ô terre, cache moy / Sous mesme sepulture avec sa belle cendre" [O earth, conceal me within a single grave with her fair ashes] (*MM* 3, 3–4). The anticipation of a rebirth to a Christian eternity is lacking in these poems, and with it the anticipation of a joyful reunion with the lady in Heaven.

This contrast in the lover's response to the death of the beloved signals a more fundamental difference. Petrarch's poem cited above, in which the bereaved lover invokes Amor's counsel, affirms at the outset his desire to follow Laura in death: "Tempo è ben di morire, / ed ò tardato più ch'i' non vorrei" [It is surely time to die, and I have delayed more than I would wish] (*R* 268, 2–3). But Amor will not endorse that judgment and responds with a caution on religious grounds: "Pon freno al gran dolor che ti trasporta," his partner in bereavement counsels the lover; "ché per soverchie voglie / si perde 'l Cielo ove 'l tuo core aspira" [Rein in the great sorrow that transports you; for excessive desire will lose the Heaven to which your heart aspires] (67–69). Fearful for the state of his soul, the lover accepts the prohibition against ending his own life, even as he desires its ending; his fantasies of Laura's unvoiced concern and compassion in the poems *in vita* are matched now by imagining her eyes declaring, on their last encounter, that he must endure growing old (*R* 330, 14). Powerfully conjoined with the desire for death in these poems is the desire for salvation. As he endures the years of waiting, as he continues the imagined communion with Laura begun in the poems *in vita*, the sensuous recalls that continue to people his fantasy and his dreams alternate with a new reverence: "Vinca 'l cor vostro in sua tanta vittoria, / angel novo, lassù di me pietate, / come vinse qui il mio vostra beltate" [In such a victory, O new angel, let pity for me vanquish your heart up there as your beauty vanquished mine here] (*R* 326, 12–14). The Laura who now appears in his dreams to console him will, he hopes, welcome him to Heaven:

> et spero ch'al por giù di questa spoglia
> venga per me con quella gente nostra,
> vera amica di Cristo et d'onestate (*R* 334, 12–14)

> and I hope that when I put off these remains she will come for me with our people, the true friend of Christ and of virtue

and the vision expands to include that of Christ and the heavenly Host, as Laura's image is progressively positioned within a larger vision of celestial beauty:

> ché più bella che mai con l'occhio interno
> con li angeli la veggio alzata a volo
> a pie' del suo et mio Signore eterno. (*R* 345, 12–14)

> for more beautiful than ever I see her with my internal eye, risen in flight with the angels to the feet of her and my eternal Lord.

And he imagines her, as she awaits his presence in Heaven, admonishing him to attend to the fate of his soul so he can join her there: "Prega ch'i' venga tosto a star con voi," he implores her [Pray that I may soon come to be with you] (*R* 347, 14).

The contrast between this fundamental current in Petrarch's poems *in morte di Laura* and Ronsard's response to the lady's death is delineated clearly in his version of Petrarch's lament that God had chosen to draw her from mortal life prematurely. Petrarch's poet cries out to Laura in Heaven that "Dio, che sì tosto al mondo ti ritolse, / ne mostrò tanta et sì alta virtute / solo per infiammar nostro desio" [God, who so soon took you away from the world, showed us so much high virtue only to inflame our desire] (*R* 270, 99–101). This tribute, which echoes the intimations of the lady's divine agency in Dante's youthful *Vita Nuova*,[44] returns near the end of the *Rime* in the dramatic exchange in which the lover indicts Amor; here, to the latter's defense that Laura had been given to this privileged mortal "per colonna / de la sua frale vita" [as the support of his frail life] erupts the anguished protest:

. . . A questo un strido
lagrimoso alzo, et grido:
"Ben me la die,' ma tosto la ritolse!"

. . . At this I raise a tearful cry, and shout: "He gave her to me indeed,
but he soon took her back!"

to which Amor in turn responds: "'Io non, ma chi per sé la volse'" ["Not
I, but One who desired her for himself"] (*R* 360, 147–50). Of his loss of
Marie Ronsard frames an apparently similar reproach: "Et toy Ciel, qui te
dis le pere des humains, / Tu ne devois tracer un tel corps de tes mains /
Pour si tost le reprendre" [And you Heaven, who call yourself the father
of mortals, you should not have formed such a body with your hands only
to take it back so soon] ("Elegie," 115–17). But not only does his protest
cancel the force of Petrarch's protestation that attempts but fails to find
consolation for his loss in the divine plan; it further deflects its impact by
the nominative substitution of "Ciel" for "Dio." And a poem that opens
with verses much like Petrarch's celebration of Laura—"Je voy tousjours
le traict de ceste belle face / Dont le corps est en terre, et l'esprit est aux
cieux" [I still see the form of that lovely face whose body is in the earth,
and whose soul is in Heaven]—and resonates with Petrarch's evocation of
the Laura who visits him in sleep, nonetheless identifies the happy status
of Marie postmortem in terms clearly more classical than Christian:

> Elle qui n'a soucy de ceste terre basse,
> Et qui boit du Nectar assise entre les Dieux,
> Daigne pourtant revoir mon estat soucieux,
> Et en songe appaiser la Mort qui me menace. (*MM* 14, 5–8)

She who has no care for this lowly earth, and who drinks divine
Nectar seated amid the Gods, nonetheless deigns to look again
upon my care-filled state, and in dreams to calm the Death that
threatens me.

In his *Odes* Ronsard had frequently made such references to a classical
paradise and to the Elysian fields;[45] the topos is found, for example, in his
"Epitaphe d'Anthoine Chasteigner de La Roche-de-Pose," as he ad-
dresses the soul of his friend:

> Soit que l'oubli te serre en son milieu
> Dans les champs Elysez, ou soit que sur la nüe
> Tu sois heureuse entre les Dieux venüe,
> Souvienne toy de moy . . . [46]

Whether forgetfulness holds you in its clasp in the Elysian fields, or whether above the clouds you are happy among the Gods, remember me . . .

In the occasional piece that is his "Epitaphe de Artuse de Vernon," moreover, he set this conception in explicit juxtaposition with that of the Christian Heaven:

Adieu, belle Arethuze, ou soit que tu demeures
Dedans le Ciel là haut franche de nos liens,
Soit que tu sois la bas aux plaintes demeures
Des vergers fleurissant es champs Elysiens . . . (25–28)[47]

Farewell, fair Arethusa, whether you dwell in the Heaven above freed from our bonds, or whether you be there below in the plaintive dwellings of the orchards flowering in the Elysian Fields . . .

In the "Discours amoureux de Genevre," as Gendre points out, the hesitation concerning conceptions of death is marked again and again, as in evoking a soul's fate "soit qu'elle aille aux enfers, soit qu'elle aille là haut" [whether it go to Hell, or whether it go there above].[48] The juxtaposition is recast in simple terms for his farewell to Marie at the close of the "Stances":

Soit que tu vives pres de Dieu,
Ou aux champs Elisez, adieu,
Adieu cent fois, adieu Marie . . . (169–71)

Whether you dwell near God or in the Elysian Fields, farewell, a hundred farewells, farewell Marie . . .

a postulation of two alternative versions of the afterlife that contrasts sharply to Petrarch's vision of Laura among the angels in Paradise, seated at the feet of Christ.

These observations collectively support the often-repeated judgment that Ronsard's secularization of Petrarch's meditation on death affords a major contrast between the two collections *in morte*.[49] But that difference has as its result not the occulting of the Petrarchan model but rather its return to serve Ronsard's affirmation of originality. While his rewriting of Marie *in vita* on the model of Laura *in vita* guarantees the recognition of Petrarch's "story" as subtext for the collection of poems "Sur la mort de Marie," his appropriations of essential elements of the poet's record of experience "in morte di Laura" in the *Rime sparse* form a counterpoint that sets his own response into sharp relief.

The final note of this counterpoint is sounded in the closing verses of the final poem. In the penultimate poem of the *Rime* Petrarch has acknowledged not only the evidence of his advancing age but the judgment, urged upon him by a number of voices in the course of his gathering together of his "scattered rhymes," that in loving Laura he has not attended to his own soul:

I' vo piangendo i miei passati tempi
i quai posi in amar cosa mortale
senza levarmi a volo, abbiendi'io l'ale
per dar forse di me non bassi esempi. (*R* 365, 1–4)

I go weeping for my past time, which I spent in loving a mortal thing without lifting myself in flight, though I had wings to make of myself perhaps not a base example.

To God he confides at the poem's close that "tu sai ben che 'n altrui non ò speranza" [You know well that I have no hope in anyone else] and the final poem of the *Rime* is the great canzone addressed to the "Vergine bella . . . di sol vestita, coronata di stelle" [Beautiful Virgin . . . clothed with the sun and crowned with stars]. As the Heavenly Lady now replaces the mortal lady as his addressee, to her he rededicates the praise and devotion long offered to a Laura who is evoked only in the sad and weary phrase "tale è terra" [one is now dust]. Ronsard's final tribute to Marie, for all its evident Petrarchan imagery, sounds a very different note:

Tu es belle Marie un bel astre des cieux:
Les Anges tous ravis se paissent de tes yeux,
La terre te regrette. O beauté sans seconde! (9–11)

You are beautiful Marie a beautiful star in the heavens. The angels, enchanted, delight in your eyes, earth regrets you. Oh beauty beyond compare!

But this is not the final note. For the closing of his final poem Ronsard turns again to Petrarch, not—significantly—to the final canzone but to the close of the proemial sonnet of the *Rime sparse*. The lesson anticipated by that well-known verse was one Ronsard declared that he too had learned well and that he often repeated, as in a poem having to do not with love but with "Philosophie," where he protests the destruction of the forest of Gastine. There is nothing stable, nothing enduring, he affirms: "Que l'homme est malheureux qui au monde se fie!" [Unfortunate is the man who trusts in the world!].[50] Petrarch's anticipatory summation of the pervasive "lesson" of the *Rime* as a whole—"'l conoscer chiaramente / che quanto piace al mondo è breve sogno" [the clear knowledge that whatever pleases in the world is a brief dream]—has also informed numerous passages of the "tombeau" for Marie: "Monde, tu es trompeur, pipeur & mensonger" [World, you are a deceiver, a flatterer, and a liar] (*MM* 9, 10) echoes "misero mondo, instabile e protervo" [Wretched world, unstable and obstinate!] (*R* 319, 5), or again in the "Elegie," enriched with images of "polvere et ombra" from, for example, *R* 294:

> Maintenant à mon dam je cognois pour certain,
> Que tout cela qui vit sous ce globe mondain,
> N'est que songe & fumée, & qu'une vaine pompe,
> Qui doucement nous rit, & doucement nous trompe. (119–22)

Now to my harm I know for sure that all that lives beneath this worldly globe is nothing but dream and smoke, and a vain display that sweetly laughs to us and sweetly deceives us.

Now, without the transcendent hope of the closing of the *Rime sparse*, it closes the "Epitaphe de Marie," and with it Ronsard's entire cycle *in morte*:

> Ha, siecle malheureux! malheureux est celuy
> Qui s'abuse d'Amour, & qui se fie au Monde.

Ah, wretched world! unfortunate is he who deludes himself about Love, and who trusts in the World.

Afterword
Rewriting and Reconnection

In a poem published in 1569 and known as "Elegie ou Amour Oyseau,"
Ronsard writes of a new love that once again commands his pen: "La
langue il me deslie, & luy-mesmes invente / En ma bouche caché, tous
les vers que je chante" (23–24) [It looses my tongue, and of itself invents,
hidden in my mouth, all the verses I sing].[1] In this incidental poem, the
presentation of Amour as a richly plumed bird affords a wealth of ex-
travagant imagery, but the circumstances of its composition in the poet's
individual experience are repeatedly suggested. His advancing age is
acknowledged, anticipating its thematic importance in the *Sonets pour
Helene:*

> Et sans avoir esgard aux neiges de ma teste
> (Comme si ma desfaite estoit despouille preste)
> [Amour] Nourrist mon coeur en braise & au feu qui me perd,
> Qui brusle d'autant mieux que le bois n'est plus verd. (31–34)

> And having no regard for the snows of my head (as if my sad state
> were ready spoils) [Love] nourishes my heart in the coals and the
> fire that destroys me, that burns all the better since the wood is no
> longer green.

As for the lady who now occasions both his ardor and his verse, she ap-
pears first as a "foreigner" in the guise of the exotic bird:

> Je ne sçaurois par art, estude, ny coustume
> Cognoistre bien ce Dieu qui est vestu de plume:
> Estrange est son plumage, & je crains à loger
> (Pour n'estre point deceu) un si bel estranger. (43–46)

> I would not be able by art, study, or practice to know well this God
> garbed in plumes: strange is his plumage, and I fear (in order not to
> be deceived) to lodge such a handsome stranger.

And the myriad "petits amoureaux" that fill the poet's heart and his days, inspired no doubt by the pseudo-Anacréon that Ronsard had already imitated in a sonnet of the *Amours* of 1552–53, are also exotic; they are charming and gay, warm and tender, as if they had arrived from another lineage and another clime:

> Ils ne sont Touranjaux, mais bien de la contrée
> Où Laure jusqu'au coeur de son Petrarque entrée
> Fit pour elle si haut chanter ce Florentin,
> Que Cygne par ses vers surmonta le Destin:
> Si qu'aujourd'huy le Rosne & Sorgue & Valecluze,
> Murmurant son renom, sont connuz par sa Muse. (75–80)

> They are not from Touraine, but rather from the land where Laura, touching the heart of her Petrarch, made that Florentine sing so nobly for her that, Swan through his verses, he overcame Destiny: so that today the Rhone and the Sorgue and Vaucluse, murmuring his fame, are known through his Muse.

In this singularly indirect avowal, notes Desonay, we are to understand that the lady who captured the heart of Ronsard was also not from the region of the Vendôme but of Provençal origin.[2] But we also find here, with the echoes of a well-known tercet from a poem of the early *Amours* evoked in Chapter Two,[3] the encapsulation of a famous "story" whose setting, along with its two protagonists, was immortalized by Ronsard's most celebrated precursor in the vernacular poetry of love.

The poem offers a particularly interesting example of the insistence with which Ronsard returned to the "story" of the *Rime sparse* for his own self-definition as lover and as poet. In the course of his extraordinarily varied poetic production, that return affords a notable counterpoint to what Terence Cave suggestively terms "the recurrence of non-integration as a problem in Ronsard's writing." A fundamental characteristic of Ronsard's poetic practice, Cave observes, is his "insatiable desire to write and rewrite"; following the *Amours* of 1552–53, the publication of subsequent major collections, complemented by the proliferation of *Meslanges* and *Amours diverses* whose poems frequently become part of those collections, impose as inevitable result that "Petrarch's exemplary sequence, its unity consecrated by the intervening centuries, is broken open, beyond any possibility of integration."[4] It is also evident from the preceding chapters, however, that the narrative impulse that relates the experience of Ronsard's lyric protagonist to that of the poet-lover of the *Rime sparse* remains constant, in varying degree, from the early *Amours* to the *Sonets pour Helene* and the sequence "Sur la mort de Marie."

It is particularly noteworthy, then, that that impulse may be traced, not only through the initial appearance of the successive collections but through the successive editions of Ronsard's *oeuvre*. Although that project as a whole lies well beyond the scope of this study, with regard to the question addressed in the preceding chapters it merits our full attention because, as some of Ronsard's most assiduous readers have argued, each new edition represents not a tentative arrangement but a definitive state as Ronsard understood it in his search for the work's perfection;[5] as part of these editions, the successive versions of his lyric collections each represents, at its own date of publication, the contours that he chose to give to his poet's story.[6] In correcting himself more than any other French poet, notes Isidore Silver, Ronsard tirelessly sought the perfect expression of his thought and his emotion, not only revising the detail of his poems but seeking the meaning of his entire life as artist and as man; his major revisions through the series of the several collective editions are "autant de variantes architecturales d'une étude persévérante qui mènera enfin à la découverte de la 'maistresse forme' et de l'idée maîtresse de ses *Oeuvres*."[7]

Evidence of that restless endeavor is found already in the first collection of the *Amours*. While in Chapter 2 we considered the 1552–53 collection as a single volume, there are differences between the 1552 recueil and that published in 1553 that, however minor in appearance, mark not only an expansion but an evolution, and it is one that is already suggestive of Ronsard's attention to the relation between his collection and the *Rime*. Of the new order assumed by the *Amours* in 1553, Dassonville concludes that it results in giving "une importance indue au récit et finalement transformait une oeuvre lyrique en roman d'amour," a surreptitious sense of *durée*.[8] And the new order to which Ronsard commits himself with the addition of thirty-nine new poems, as attentive comparative readings have disclosed, both enhances the Petrarchan coloration of the early collection and brings it into a closer relation with the poet's story of the *Rime sparse*.[9]

As Ronsard prepared the editions of his works that were to follow, further revisions to the *Amours* were effected; new poems were added and others deleted, and yet more poems were redistributed from one volume to another. When the first collective edition was published in 1560, the intervening years had seen the appearance of the *Continuation des Amours* (1555) and the *Nouvelle Continuation des Amours* (1556), centering progressively on the figure of Marie.[10] The first collection was now seen to cohere around the figure of Cassandre, and Ronsard returned to its "story" in new poems: that addressed "A Cassandre" published in 1559 opens with "L'absence, ny l'obly, ny la course du jour" and goes on to recapitulate it in now-familiar terms.[11] But other interventions as well tended to intensify the affinities of the early collection with the poet's "story" of the *Rime sparse*: in the new collective edition, Ronsard removed from the poems now published under the title of *Premier Livre* a number of those from the 1552–53 collection that presented a Cassandre more immediate and accessible than the Laura of the *Rime*. With this revision, Gisèle Mathieu-Castellani suggests, Ronsard reveals "une conscience si nette de ces dissonances que la première édition collective les effacera, rendant ainsi le *Premier Livre* plus proche, par sa tonalité, du *Canzoniere*."[12]

In that same year, Ronsard penned a new closing for the *Premier Livre*. We have seen that the sonnet that closed the recueil of 1552–53, while explicitly inserting the collection within a historical moment—"Lors que HENRY loing des bornes de France, / Vangeoyt l'honneur de ses premiers ayeulx"—also returned the reader to the Petrarchan context of the lover's *contrari affetti*—"J'alloy roullant ces larmes de mes yeulx, / Or plein de doubte, ores plein d'esperance"—and to the memoralization of his sighs that recalls once again the proemial sonnet of the *Rime*. Now the new "Elegie," whose function as closure is made clear in its opening injunction to Cassandre to seek a new poet, not only foregrounds once again both Cassandre as subject and Ronsard as her poet but also challenges us to take the measure of the distance that it at once establishes between their "story" and that of Petrarch as the poet of Laura.[13]

The challenge to Cassandre in the new "Elegie," to find a new poet "Qui apres moy se rompe le cerveau / A te chanter" [who after me will tax his brain to sing of you], on the one hand measures the distance from the Petrarchan model in its affirmation of the freedom of both poet and lover to abandon the lady at will. But on the other, the poem also resonates with many poems in the 1552–53 *Amours* in its foregrounding of Ronsard's self-conscious engagement in poetic rivalry, beginning now with a boast: any new poet who might seek to celebrate Cassandre in verse would find himself challenged, were he even a Baïf, to do as well. We cannot but recall again the famous sonnet "Que n'ay-je, Dame, & la plume & la grace," its emphasis on what the poet would achieve for Cassandre and her name— an achievement to surpass the work of Pindar, of Horace, of Du Bellay, and last but not least of Petrarch himself—colored by the conditional tense in which it is repeatedly rendered; Cassandre's name, he has told her, would take flight on the wing of his rhyme. In the new poem the motif of self-disparagement disappears along with all pretense at modesty, for

Ronsard has shown himself the equal of Tibullus in his ability to celebrate the lady:

> Si nostre empire avoit jadis esté
> Par noz François aussi avant planté
> Que le Rommain, tu serois autant leüe
> Que si Tibull' t'avoit pour sienne esleüe (5–8)

> If our dominion had long ago been established as far afield by the French as was the Roman, you would be praised as much as if Tibullus had chosen you for his own

and while Cassandre cannot of course hope for that particular honor because of historical accident, she need nonetheless not resign herself to a much lesser fate:

> Et neantmoins tu te dois contenter
> De veoir ton nom par la France chanter,
> Autant que Laure en Tuscan anoblie
> Se voit chanter par la belle Italie. (9–12)

> And nonetheless you must content yourself with seeing your name sung throughout France, as much as Laura enobled in Tuscan finds herself sung throughout fair Italy.

No more apologies to a Cassandre worthy of the great love poets of antiquity but born too late, and no more protestations that "a single Tuscan" would be worthy to sing her praises; Ronsard, by his own proclamation, has won his wager for the favor of posterity, vindicating for himself the title of "the French Petrarch."

But the poem continues. What has Ronsard himself gained from his poetic prowess exercised on Cassandre's behalf? Only gray hair, a wrinkled forehead, a sad face, without having earned any response at all (14–16). Had Cassandre not prophesied as much, in the extraordinary poem (A 19) examined in Chapter 2? In a long strophe he now reproaches her for an inflexible cruelty "for which Nemesis must one day punish you." All of the ills of which he laments here had been protested repeatedly in the poems of the *Amours* of 1552–53. There had indeed been more auspicious, more promising auguries of his amorous and poetic destiny, as in his apostrophe to his Gastine and his Loir, witnesses to his plight, in recalling an encounter with Cassandre in another poem:

> Si dextrement l'augure j'ay receu,
>   Et si mon oeil ne fut hyer deceu

> Des doulx regardz de ma doulce Thalie,
> Dorenavant poëte me ferez,
> Et par la France appellez vous serez,
> L'un mon laurier, l'aultre ma Castalie . . . . (*A* 160, 9–14)

If I have received the augury correctly, and if my eye was not deceived yesterday by the sweet glances of my sweet Thalia, henceforth you will make me a poet, and you will be called throughout France, on the one hand my laurel, on the other my Castalie . . .

But the augury, he had admitted, was not sure; his reading of Cassandre's "doulx regardz" that would enable his poems may be inaccurate. Or he might imagine a more favorable augury from Cassandre herself:

> Mesmes la nuict, le somme qui vous mét
> Doulce en mon lict, augure, me promet
> Que je verray vos fiertez adoucies:
> Et que vous seule, oracle de l'amour,
> Vériferez dans mes bras quelque jour,
> L'arrest fatal de tant de propheties. (*A* 194, 9–14)

Even at night, the sleep that places you sweet in my bed, as augury promises me that I shall see your proudness softened: and that you alone, oracle of love, will one day verify in my arms the fatal decree of so many prophecies.

But this augury of Cassandre's yielding, like his possession of the lady, occurs in his dreams, and in the new ending that Ronsard devises for the collection in 1560 there has been no reprieve from the dark vision of Cassandre's prophecy, for the "Elegie a Cassandre" continues on to a rather unexpected end:

> Je voy ma faulte & la prens à mercy,
> Comme celuy qui sçait que nostre vie
> N'est rien que vent, que songe, & que folye. (34–36)

I see my fault and I pity it, like one who knows that our life is nothing but wind, but dream, and but folly.

This closing meditation on the ephemeral and illusory nature of human existence seems strangely out of tune with the characteristic preoccupations of Cassandre's poet. But its importance is evident: these verses are the conclusion, not only of this poem, but of the whole First Book of the *Amours* and of the "épisode Cassandre."[14] Its tone is that precisely of the conclusion of *Rime* 1, "'l conoscer chiaramente / che quanto piace al mondo è breve sogno" [the clear knowledge that whatever pleases in the world is a brief dream], and it leads us back to the opening poem of the *Rime sparse* in relation to which Ronsard had initiated his poetic rivalry with Petrarch in the opening sonnet of the 1552 *Amours*. There, we noted in the absence of any meditative note or trace of regret a striking contrast to Petrarch's proemial poem:

> del vario stile in ch'io piango e ragiono,
> fra le vane speranze e 'l van dolore,
> ove sia chi per prova intenda amore,
> spero trovar pietà, non che perdono. (*R* 1, 5–8)

> for the varied style in which I weep and speak between vain hopes and vain sorrow, where there is anyone who understands love through experience, I hope to find pity, not only pardon.

Nor was such a note sounded in the concluding sonnet of the 1552–53 collection which, as we have seen, recalled the weeping and the tension between hope and doubt found in these verses. Now in the "Elegie," as in *A* 1, an audience is again invoked, but no longer to assume the role of spectator to privilege the speaker's flamboyant posture as suffering lover:

> Ceux qui amour cognoissent par espreuve
> Lisant le mal dans lequel je me treuve,
> Ne pardon'ront à ma simple amytié
> Tant seulement, mais en auront pitié. (27–30)

> Those who know love through experience, reading the pain in which I find myself, will not only pardon my simple affection, but will pity it.

Now the evocation of youth and its passing comes to the fore, that youth of which the collection of *Amours* I is seen now in retrospect as a record.

While it is surely fair to point out in Ronsard's "Je voy ma faulte & la prens à mercy" the disappearance of the religious remorse of Petrarch's poem,[15] it has not disappeared without leaving a trace, and the trace once again points to Petrarch, rendering the affinity transparent. For if the declaration by Ronsard's speaker stands in marked contrast to the shame and regret voiced by the speaker of *Rime* 1, his affirmation leads us at last from *Rime* 1 to another poem of closure, *Rime* 364, in which on the threshold of the closing of his collection Petrarch recapitulates his amorous experience in spiritual terms: "mia vita reprendo / di tanto error" [I reproach my life for so much error], he affirms to God, and continues to describe his state:

pentito e tristo de' miei sì spesi anni:
che spender si deveano in miglior uso,
in cercar pace ed in fuggir affanni.
Signor che 'n questo carcer m'ài rinchiuso:
tramene salvo da li eterni danni,
ch'i' conosco 'l mio fallo e non lo scuso. (9–14)

repentant and sorrowing for my years spent thus, which ought to
have been better used, in seeking peace and fleeing troubles. Lord
who have enclosed me in this prison: draw me from it safe from
eternal harm, for I recognize my fault and I do not excuse it.

It is Petrarch's "sì spesi anni" that are echoed in Ronsard's lament to Cassandre, that

Or, quand à moy, je pense avoir perdue
En te servant ma jeunesse, espendue
Deçà, delà dedans ce livre icy. (31–33)

Now, as for myself, I deem that I have lost my youth in serving you,
spent here and there within this present book.

From the lucid affirmation of responsibility in Petrarch's "conosco 'l mio
fallo e non lo scuso" to the note of self-affirmation and self-pity in Ronsard's "Je voy ma faulte & la prens à mercy" the distance is long indeed,
and there is perhaps no better example of the often-noted secularization
effected by Ronsard than his adaptation of elements of both *Rime* 1 and
Rime 364 to encapsulate the "Elégie à Cassandre." If both poets close on a
note of renunciation, the two notes have a very different ring.[16] Petrarch's
collection closes with an appeal for divine assistance addressed to God;
Ronsard's closes with a farewell to Cassandre addressed to Cassandre.

Set now as final poem of his first collection of *Amours*, Ronsard's
"Elégie" reminds us once again that to be the "new" Petrarch means to
write both "as" Petrarch and against him. But it was under the sign of
Petrarch that he was finally to inscribe his first lyric collection, in a late
revision of its original closing sonnet (*A* 221) appearing for the first time in
the posthumous 1587 edition. That sonnet, after evoking the transience of
earthly life illustrated in the death of the king, appeals to the Muses, sources
of poetic immortality, to engrave his sighs forever in the Temple of Memory.
The first version appeals to these Muses who "desserrez voz doctes eaux à
ceulx qui les vont boyre" [pour out your learned waters to those who would
drink of them] and recalls that he himself had received their blessing: "si
quelque fois vous m'avez abreuvé" [if sometimes you have given me to

drink]. It was the phrasing of this appeal to the Muses that was to undergo revision, as in 1578 the nature of his inspiration is identified: "Si autrefois vous m'avez permis de boire / les eaux qui ont Hesiode abreuvé" [if formerly you allowed me to drink the waters that were furnished to Hesiod]. But in 1587, these verses become "Si autrefois vous m'avez permis de boire/ L'eau dont Amour a Petrarque abreuvé" [If formerly you allowed me to drink the water that Love gave Petrarch to drink].

As we follow Ronsard's intermittent revisions, we find more markers along the curve of that relationship, markers that further attest to both its continuity and its complexity. Additions of new poems to the *Premier Livre* of the *Amours* intensify the recalls of the poet's experience in the *Rime sparse*, notably with the transfer in 1571 of twenty-one sonnets from *Le septiesme Livre des Poëmes*, that results in the formation of new series that tend to create what Louis Terreaux terms homogeneous ensembles within the *roman d'amour*.[17] Yet more suggestive is the revision of the other liminal poem of the 1552–53 collection, its opening sonnet "Qui voudra voir comme un Dieu me surmonte." We recall the dramatic scenario of that poem: the attack by Love as archer, and the promise of what profit the invited witness will draw from the spectacle of the poet as Love's victim:

Il cognoistra combien la raison peult
    Contre son arc, quand une foys il veult
    Que nostre coeur son esclave demeure:
Et si voirra que je suis trop heureux,
    D'avoir au flanc l'aiguillon amoureux,
    Plein du venin dont il fault que je meure.

In 1567 the second of these tercets is revised, underlining the parallel construction with the substitution of "connoistra" for "voirra" to introduce now the image of the lamenting and dying swan:

Et connoistra, que je suis trop heureux
D'estre en mourant nouveau Cygne amoureux
Qui son obseque à soy mesme se chante.

And he will know that I am only too happy to be in dying a new amorous Swan who sings his own obsequies to himself.

This reduction of the emphasis on the act of witness that had permeated the entire poem in its early version anticipates an equally substantial revision, now of the first tercet, in 1578:

Il cognoistra que foible est la raison
Contre son trait quand sa douce poison
Corrompt le sang, tant le mal nous enchante.

He will recognize that reason is weak against his arrow when its sweet poison corrupts the blood, so much does the ill enchant us.

Here the drama of the scene is much attenuated: the "venin" of the closing verse in 1552 becomes now a "douce poison," and the speaker-as-martyr, only too happy to bear his exemplary wound, now represents himself as yielding gradually to an illness much like a spell, "tant le mal nous enchante," reinforcing his glad acquiescence. At the same time, the exhibitionism of the victim who had offered himself up to the potential witness as spectacle—"me vienne voir," v. 7—is attenuated in the invitation to "qui voudra voyr," not to see but to *read*, displacing the evidence of the lover's victimization from the spectacle to its poetic record: "me vienne lire."[18] Hence the subject returns in force, at the expense of the immediacy and physicality of the image. The flagrant "trop heureux" is transformed as it now serves to introduce, not the poisoned arrow, instrument of death, visible "au flanc"—a word that, as Rigolot has suggested, appears generally to have "un sens nettement sensuel" in the *Amours*[19]—but the more conventional image of the dying swan.[20]

But Ronsard had not finished with this poem. The 1584–87 text offers a yet more radical revision:

Qui voudra voir comme Amour me surmonte,
Comme il m'assaut, comme il se fait vainqueur,
Comme il r'enflamme & r'englace mon cueur,
Comme il reçoit un honneur de ma honte:
Qui voudra voir une jeunesse pronte
A suivre en vain l'objet de son malheur,
Me vienne lire: il voirra la douleur,
Dont ma Deesse & mon Dieu ne font conte.[21]

The replacement of "un Dieu me surmonte" with "Amour me surmonte" in the opening verse diminishes the inevitability of the aggressor's triumph, as does its reintroduction, "mon Dieu," with Love now forming an alliance with the lady designated as "ma Deesse" at the end of the second quatrain. The role of Amour is then further recast, first as metaphor—

Il cognoistra qu'Amour est sans raison,
Un doux abus, une belle prison,
Un vain espoir qui de vent nous vient paistre—

He will recognize that Love is without reason, a sweet abuse, a beautiful prison, a vain hope that comes to nourish us with wind—

then as a figure we are invited to envisage, not as an all-powerful aggressor who bears the responsibility for the speaker's plight, but as a blind child to whom the victim had voluntarily conceded dominion:

> Et cognoistra que l'homme se deçoit,
> Quand plein d'erreur, un aveugle il reçoit
> Pour sa conduite, un enfant pour son maistre.

And he will recognize that a man deceives himself when, full of error, he accepts a blind man to lead him, a child as his master.

What is reflected in these successive *rifacimenti*? For Desonay, they exemplify a "contre-courant du lyrisme" characteristic of Ronsard's revisions and illustrate the "phases affligeantes" of its deterioration.[22] Castor, on the other hand, finds in the 1584 revision a negative tone that recalls the poet's avowed intent to free himself from "cest Enfant qui me ronge, / Qui les credules prend comme un poisson à l'hain" at the end of the *Sonets pour Helene,* suggestive now of a "change . . . in the attitude with which Ronsard wishes the reader to approach the whole collection."[23] Other revisions to individual poems bring the first *Amours* yet closer to the emphases of the *Sonets pour Helene,* heightening the prominence of the themes of deception and deceit. This rewriting, Castor concludes, brings about "very clear modifications of emphasis at certain points, which serve, with the *Sonets pour Helene,* to underline the extent to which Ronsard's confidence in the full validity of the aesthetic and emotional experience of love has changed since the 1550s."[24]

But Ronsard's late revision of his initial poem is much more suggestive still for his self-positioning in relation to Petrarch, for the "vain espoir" now introduced to characterize Amour corresponds to the "vane speranze" of the proemial poem of the *Rime sparse.* Does the function of this "vain espoir," "qui de vent nous vient paistre," awaken too an echo of Petrarch's "quei sospiri ond'io nudriva 'l core"? That echo appears confirmed in the verses that follow: the poet's "jeunesse prompte a suivre en vain l'objet de son malheur," characterized as "plein d'erreur," resonates strongly with the "primo giovenile errore" identified as the time of the innamoramento in *Rime* 1. And so it is with the poem's closing, in a general statement that expands from a focus on the individual victim to the universal proposition: not "je" but "l'homme," "il," "sa conduite," and "son maistre." It has been proposed that this substitution of the generalized conception stands as example of the introduction of a counterpoint that "prevents the Petrarchan images from functioning in the way that the reader expects,"[25] but in this highly visible case it suggests precisely the contrary. For now *A* 1 closes, like *Rime* 1 with its quiet and reluctant affirmation of the acquired wisdom "che quanto piace al mondo è breve sogno," with the formula "conoscere" / "connaître" followed by a sententia. Taken together, these changes significantly heighten the sonnet's affinities with Petrarch's introductory poem.

In 1578 Ronsard had published another "Elegie," that dedicated to the lady lost to death in the collection "sur la mort de Marie." We have seen that that small recueil is marked both by a complex rewriting of the figure of Marie, bringing her image close to that of the Laura *in vita* of the *Rime sparse*, and by a secular recasting of Marie's death and the poet's loss that marks its distance from the Italian collection. Of the latter, a long passage in the "Elegie" is emblematic. Here Ronsard would honor Marie's "tombeau" with a great temple, where a hundred altars would be dedicated to her memory and *jeux funèbres* performed:

> Il vaut mieux d'un grand temple honorer son tombeau,
> Et dedans eslever d'artifice nouveau
> Cent autels dediez à la memoire d'elle,
> Esclairez jour & nuict d'une lampe eternelle,
> Et devant le portail, comme les anciens
> Celebroient les combats aux jeux Olympiens,
> Sacrer en son honneur au retour de l'année
> Une feste choumable à la jouste ordonnée. (135–42)

It would be better to honor her tomb with a great temple, and raise within it, in a new form, a hundred altars dedicated to her memory, lit day and night with an eternal lamp, and before the doorway, as the ancients celebrated the contests of the Olympic games, to consecrate to her honor at the turn of the new year a public holiday devoted to competitions.

These ordered festivities would preserve the renown, not only of Marie, but of Ronsard:

> Et seront appellez long temps apres ma vie,
> Les jeux que feist Ronsard pour sa belle Marie. (145–46)

They will be called long after my lifetime the games that Ronsard initiated for his beautiful Marie.

The "transformation du temps vécu en temps mythique" effected in this passage is characteristic of a number of Ronsard's epitaphs;[26] the assertion

of an enduring fame to be won through the poet's initiative, moreover, re-
calls the pretty fantasy of a "temple of Ronsard and of his Marion" where
the poet and his lady would be "invoked every day, like new Gods of faith-
ful loves," that had brought to an effective close the last of the poems ad-
dressed to Marie *in vita* ("Elegie à Marie," 67–70).[27] At the end of the se-
quence *in morte*, however, it produces an effect of dissonance:[28] much less
sombre than the earlier affirmation by Génie in the "Dialogue" in the same
collection, that Ronsard's tears shed over Marie's ashes would cause them
to bring forth "une fleur du sepulchre," this implied equivalence of his
poems celebrating Marie with "jeux" underlines the effect of doubling that
readers have noted in the collection as a whole, and distances it once again
from the *Rime sparse*.

Yet if we turn again to Ronsard's revisions, we find once again that this
is not to be the end of the story. The small recueil commemorating the death
of Marie, while it remained relatively stable through Ronsard's later revi-
sions of his *Oeuvres*, nonetheless discloses, in the 1584 version, one major
change in the sequence. It is a change easily overlooked by readers familiar
with the collection of 1578, as it entails nothing more than the replacement
of the relatively brief passage of the "Elegie" cited above. But in contrast to
sporadic minor alterations now effected in isolated verses of several other
poems, notably the "Epitaphe de Marie," the recasting of this segment of
the "Elegie" is striking and casts a quite remarkable light on Ronsard's con-
tinued appropriation of the poet's "story" in the *Rime sparse*.

The importance of this revision to the perceived coherence of the col-
lection as a whole is underlined by the manner of its implementation. The
last two verses of the passage cited above from the "Elegie à Marie" *in
morte* are now repositioned, almost word for word, as part of a four-line
interpolation into the "Elegie à Marie" *in vita* at the end of Livre II of the
Amours, where they blend effortlessly with that volume's celebration of
Marie:

Aux pieds de mon autel en ce temple nouveau
Luiroit le feu veillant d'un eternel flambeau,
Et seroient ces combats nommez apres ma vie
Les jeux que fit Ronsard pour sa belle Marie.

At the foot of my altar in this new temple the watchful flame of an
eternal torch would shine, and these games would be named after
my lifetime the games that Ronsard established for his beautiful
Marie.

The passage now substituted in the poems of "Sur la mort de Marie,"
however, is very different indeed. It consists fundamentally of two parts,

the first of them displaying clear Petrarchan attitudes as well as Petrarchan echoes:

> Il vaut mieux que je meure au pied de ce rocher,
> Nommant tousjours son nom qui me sonne si cher,
> Sans chercher par la peine apres elle de vivre
> Gaignant le bruit d'ingrat de ne la vouloir suivre.
> Aussi toute la terre, où j'ay perdu mon bien
> Apres son fascheux vol ne me semble plus rien
> Sinon qu'horreur, qu'effroy, qu'une obscure poussiere. (135–41)

It would be better that I die at the foot of this stone, naming still her name that resounds so dear to me, without seeking through pain to live on after her and earning the name of ungrateful from not seeking to follow her. Thus all the earth, where I have lost my treasure, after her sad flight seems no more to me than horror, than fright, than a dark dust.

While much more sombre than the passage that they replace, these verses nonetheless are not unlike others we have seen in other poems of this recueil that underline the lover's sense of loss and his desire to follow his beloved in death. The second movement of the passage, however, strikingly realigns the elements of his response:

> Au ciel est mon Soleil, au ciel est ma lumiere:
> Le monde ny ses laqs n'y ont plus de pouvoir:
> Il faut haster ma mort, si je la veux revoir:
> La mort en a la clef, & par sa seule porte
> Je revoiray le jour qui ma nuict reconforte. (142–46)

My Sun is in heaven, in heaven is my light: the world and its traps have no more power. I must hasten my death, if I wish to see her again: death has the key to it, and through its gate alone I shall see again the day that comforts my night.

Not only are the Petrarchan resonances once again plentiful and obvious.[29] Much more significant is that while the desire for reunion with the lady lost to death does not yield here, as it does in the final poem of the *Rime sparse*, to a full renunciation of earthly images along with earthly attachments, the anticipation of that reunion introduces into the sequence "Sur la mort de Marie" the element whose absence, as we have seen, distanced it from the "story" of the bereaved poet of the Italian collection. Here once again, as in the revisions of the opening and the closing of his early *Amours*, Ronsard returns to Petrarch, and here rewriting leads, not to further distancing, but to reconnection.

NOTES

Petrarch's poems and their English versions are cited from *Petrarch's Lyric Poems: The Rime sparse and Other Lyrics* (= R), translated and edited by Robert M. Durling (Cambridge: Harvard University Press, 1976). Translations from Ronsard and other French and Italian poets, unless attributed, are my own. Ronsard poems from *Les Amours*, unless otherwise indicated, are cited from Henri Weber and Catherine Weber, eds. (Paris: Dunod, 1993): *A* = *Amours* 1552–53, *MM* = "Sur la mort de Marie," *SH* = *Sonets pour Helene*. Other Ronsard citations are from *Pierre de Ronsard: Oeuvres complètes*, ed. Paul Laumonier, continued by Raymond Lebègue and Isidore Silver, 20 vols. (Paris: Société des Textes Français Modernes, 1914–75), cited as *L* with volume and page number. Unless otherwise indicated, Du Bellay's *Olive* (= *O*) is cited from the edition by E. Caldarini (Geneva: Droz, 1974).

Introduction

1. *Les Gayetez*, ed. A. R. Mackay (Geneva: Droz, 1968), p. 84; see Grahame Castor, "Petrarchism and the Quest for Beauty in the *Amours* of Cassandre and the *Sonetz pour Helene*," in Terence Cave, ed., *Ronsard the Poet* (London: Methuen, 1973), p. 80.

2. *Eclogue* III, 33–34; see Teodolinda Barolini, *Dante's Poets: Textuality and Truth in the Comedy* (Princeton: Princeton University Press, 1984), p. xiii.

3. For example, Ronsard's commentator Marc-Antoine de Muret identified Herberay Des Essars, author of the French version of *Amadis de Gaule*, as "l'Homere second, / Premiere gloire de la France," because of whom, "Tant le monde demourra, / Le los d'Amadis ne mourra." See Marian Rothstein, "Le genre du roman à la Renaissance," *Etudes françaises* 32 (1996), p. 45.

4. For Macrin, see Raymond Lebègue, "Horace en France pendant la Renaissance," *Humanisme et Renaissance* 3 (1936), p. 158. Gilbert Gadoffre notes among the several images of Ronsard that of the prince of poets "salué par les cours et les humanistes de toute l'Europe comme le Virgile des Temps modernes"; see *Ronsard* (Paris: Seuil, 1994), p. 7.

5. "Réponse à quelques Stances de Billard, par Minerve," v. 13, published from Bibliothèque Nationale fr. 25455 by Roger Sorg in *Cassandre, ou le secret de Ronsard* (Paris: Payot, 1925), pp. 235–36.

6. Pierre de l'Estoile, *Mémoires-journaux;* cited in R. A. Katz, *Ronsard's French Critics* (Geneva: Droz, 1966), p. 27.

7. *Recherches de la France,* cited in Enea Balmas, *Littérature française: La Renaissance,* II (Paris: Arthaud, 1974), p. 143.

8. *Art poëtique françois* II, 1116; see *Traités de poétique et de rhétorique de la Renaissance* (Paris: Le Livre de Poche, 1990), p. 108.

9. See Jean Balsamo, *Les Rencontres des Muses: Italianisme et anti-italianisme dans les Lettres françaises de la fin du XVIe siècle* (Geneva: Slatkine, 1992), who comments that the account of Petrarch's coronation as poet thus appears "comme le panégyrique de l'ancien et la préface aux oeuvres du nouveau poète lauréat, dont le libraire était le maître d'oeuvre et qu'il éditait en un même format et sous une même présentation" (pp. 223–24).

10. Maclou de la Haye, *Oeuvres poétiques,* cited in Fernand Desonay, *Ronsard poète de l'amour. Livre premier. Cassandre* (Brussels, 1952; repr. l965), p. 73. Marc-Antoine de Muret had in the preceding year addressed an ode "Ad P. Ronsardum Gallicorum facile principem"; see Pierre de Nolhac, *Ronsard et l'Humanisme* (Paris: Champion, 1921), pp. 147–48.

11. See, for example, Léonce Marmay, "L'Influence italienne au temps de Ronsard," *Bulletin historique et scientifique de l'Auvergne* 29 (1909): p. 425.

12. Leonard Forster, *The Icy Fire* (London: Cambridge University Press, 1969), p. 18.

13. Castor, "Petrarchism and the Quest for Beauty," pp. 80–81.

14. André Gendre, "Vade-mecum sur le pétrarquisme français," *Versants* 7 (1985): p. 82.

15. Joseph Vianey, *Le Pétrarquisme en France au XVIe siècle* (Geneva: Slatkine Reprints, 1969), p. 6.

16. Charles Dédéyan, "Ronsard et Bembo," in *Ronsard e l'Italia/Ronsard in Italia,* Atti del I° Convegno del Gruppo di Studio sul Cinquecento francese (Fasano di Puglia: Schena, 1988), p. 27; see also Gendre, "Vade-mecum sur le pétrarquisme français."

17. Michel Dassonville, *Ronsard: Etude historique et littéraire, III: Prince des Poètes ou Poète des Princes* (Geneva: Droz, 1976), p. 27; he cites as case in point the verses in which Ronsard laments that all his readings in Roman poets and in Petrarch are useless if the king does not allow him to pursue them, and that royal favor is essential to the success of his work: "les vers demeurent déprisés / Si d'un grand Roi ne sont favorisés."

18. Fernand Desonay categorizes it as the text "qu'il se met à feuilleter, comme il l'a fait régulièrement . . . chaque fois qu'il chante d'amour en service commandé." See *Ronsard poète de l'amour, III: Du poète de cour au chantre d'Hélène* (Brussels: Duculot, 1959), p. 265.

19. "Je ne fai point de doubt que ma Poësie tant varie ne semble facheuse aus oreilles de nos rimeurs, & principalement des courtizans, qui n'admirent qu'un petit sonnet petrarquizé, ou quelque mignardise d'amour qui continue tousjours en son propos." Preface, *Quatre Livres des Odes* (1550); see *L* I, p. 47.

20. For one inventory see Marmay, "L'Influence italienne au temps de Ronsard," *Bulletin historique et scientifique de l'Auvergne* 29 (1909): pp. 417–32, and 30 (1910): pp. 85–96.

21. For examples regarding one particular topic see Daniela Boccassini, "Figure di caccia nelle *Amours* de Ronsard," *Studi Francesi* 84 (1990): pp. 197–99.

22. James Wyatt Cook and Germaine Warkentin, "Toward Making a New English Verse *Canzoniere*," *Yale Italian Studies* 1 (1980): p. 25.

23. Richard Griffiths, "Some Uses of Petrarchan Imagery in Sixteenth-Century France," *French Studies* 18 (1964): pp. 311–12.

24. Terence Cave, *The Cornucopian Text: Problems of Writing in the French Renaissance* (Oxford: Clarendon, 1979), p. 77.

25. "Tu n'oubliras les comparaisons, les descriptions des lieux . . . te façonnant en cecy à l'imitation d'Homere, que tu observeras comme un divin exemple, sur lequel tu tirera au vif les plus parfaictz lineamens de ton tableau." *Abbrégé de l'art poëtique françois* (*L* 14, p. 15).

26. John Freccero, "The Fig Tree and the Laurel: Petrarch's Poetics," *Diacritics* 5 (spring 1975): p. 34.

27. Stephen Greenblatt, *Renaissance Self-Fashioning: From More to Shakespeare* (Chicago: University of Chicago Press, 1980), p. 2.

28. Ibid., p. 3.

29. The phrase is that of A. Micha, ed., *Le Second Livre des Amours* (Geneva: Droz, 1951), p. xvi.

30. Thomas Greene, "Imitative Insinuations in the *Amours* of Ronsard," in *The Light in Troy* (New Haven: Yale University Press, 1982), p. 201.

31. The Italian poet's powerful and prestigious discourse, Terence Cave observes, reaffirms itself insistently in each phase of the struggle, even in its defeat; see "La contamination des intertextes: Le sonnet 'Or que Juppin,'" in *Ronsard: Colloque de Neuchâtel*, ed. André Gendre (Geneva: Droz, 1987), p. 70.

Chapter 1. From "le Gaulois Apollon" to "le Pétrarque français"

1. Hélène's phrase, flattering for the poet, is less so for the lover, for it was her game as well, she having welcomed his attentions "pour avoir (ses) chansons." On the exchange between Hélène/"Minerve" and Ronsard/"Bilhard" see Fernand Desonay, *Ronsard poète de l'amour*, III (Brussels: Duculot, 1959), pp. 205–6 and 18.

2. As Homer, so Ronsard: ". . . pour sujet fertil Homere t'a choisie," he tells Hélène (*SH* II: 37, 5). For the importance of onomastics in the collection see Nathalie Dauvois, *Mnémosyne: Ronsard, une poétique de la mémoire* (Paris: Champion, 1992), pp. 198–215.

3. "La Lyre," *L* XV, p. 28.

4. The phrase is that of Terence Cave, *The Cornucopian Text: Problems of Writing in the French Renaissance* (Oxford: Clarendon, 1979), p. 262.

5. For detailed discussion see Guy Demerson, *La Mythologie classique dans l'oeuvre lyrique de la Pléiade* (Geneva: Droz, 1972), ch. 9, "Le Lyrisme de la Pléiade et l'essor de la poésie de cour," and Françoise Bardon, *Le Portrait mythologique*

à la cour de France sous Henri IV et Louis XIII (Paris: Picard, 1974), esp. pp. 276–79.

6. The range of pageantry and personae through which Elizabeth was cel-ebrated has been the object of considerable study; some telling examples are found in Stephen Greenblatt, *Renaissance Self-Fashioning: From More to Shakespeare* (Chi-cago: University of Chicago Press, 1980), pp. 165–69. For the political importance of such representations in the reign of Louis XIV see Virginia Scott, "The Fall of Phaeton: The Son of the Sun God in the Theatre of the Sun King," *French Studies* 48 (1994): pp. 141–54.

7. "François I en allégorie divine," c. 1545, Paris, Bibliothèque Nationale, repro-duced in *La cour de François Ier: Gouverner autrement* (Centre National de Documen-tation Pédagogique, 1996).

8. See Françoise Joukovsky, *La Gloire dans la poésie française et néolatine du XVIe siècle* (Geneva: Droz, 1969), who cites from *La chasse royale* Salel's description of Marie d'Autriche as a mounted Diana fully armed for the hunt (pp. 179–80). For Ronsard's role in the composition of spectacles from 1564 to 1570, see Daniel Ménager, *Ronsard: Le Roi, le poète et les hommes* (Geneva: Droz, 1979), pp. 323–32, and Michel Dassonville, *Ronsard: Etude historique et littéraire*, V (Geneva: Droz, 1990), pp. 89–98.

9. For Charles as new Mercury see Hymne V, "De Charles Cardinal de Lorraine" (*L* IX, p. 29); "les forts Guisians" are celebrated in the first ode of *Le Quatriesme Livre des Odes* (*L* VII, p. 90); in another poem Ronsard becomes Ennius to the Cardinal's brother's Scipio: "Je chante vos honneurs, qui seuls me pourront faire / Aussi bon Ennius en chantant vostre frere, / Comme en guerre il s'est fait Scipion des François" (*L* X, p. 82).

10. "A Monsieur de Belot," *L* VI, p. 27; *L* I, p. 48. For the memorial function of such appellations see Dauvois, *Mnémosyne*, esp. "le modèle et l'exemple," pp. 21–37.

11. As Philippe Desan observes, "Apollo, Jupiter, Hercules and Henri II became interchangeable"; see "The Tribulations of a Young Poet: Ronsard from 1547 to 1552" in *Renaissance Rereadings: Intertext and Context*, ed. Maryanne Cline Horo-witz et al. (Urbana: University of Illinois Press, 1988), p. 195. For the "Ode à la Reine" and the inscription for Marguerite de Savoie see *L* VII, p. 36; *L* IX, p. 197.

12. On the adoption by sixteenth-century poets of the neoplatonist theory of inspiration see Françoise Joukovsky-Micha, *Poésie et mythologie au XVIe siècle* (Paris: Nizet, 1969), pp. 123–41.

13. *L* XII, p. 35. On Apollo as poet-god as well as sun-god in the *Hyme de l'Esté* see Cave, *Cornucopian Text*, pp. 248–49, and for the association of fire with poetry here see André Gendre, "Aspects du feu dans l'imaginaire de Ronsard amoureux," in *Ronsard et les éléments*, ed. André Gendre (Geneva: Droz, 1992), p. 179.

14. Thomas Sébillet, *Art poétique françoys*, cited in Joukovsky-Micha, *Poésie et mythologie*, p. 133.

15. On this "dual seizure" see the examples in Robert J. Clements, "Ronsard and Ficino on the Four Furies," *Romanic Review* 45 (1954): pp. 161–69.

16. On Ronsard's transposition of the neoplatonist *fureur* from poetry to love in the 1552 *Amours* see Terence Cave, "Ronsard as Apollo: Myth, Poetry and Experience in a Renaissance Sonnet-Cycle," in *Image and Symbol in the Renaissance, Yale French Studies* 47 (1972): pp. 76–78.

17. As Fernand Desonay observes, "Moins qu'à des poèmes qui auront à être 'mesurés à la lyre,' c'est à Pindare, c'est à la réputation de Pindare que songe notre jeune autant qu'audacieux gentilhomme vendômois"; see *Ronsard poète de l'amour. Livre premier. Cassandre* (Brussels: Palais des Académies, 1952), pp. 72–73, 116, n. 29.

18. *Préface de Marc-Antoine de Muret sur ses "Commentaires"* (cf. L V, xxiv), cited by Desonay, *Ronsard poète de l'amour*, p. 72.

19. See Claude Faisant, "L'Herméneutique du sens caché dans les discours prefaciels de Ronsard," *Versants* 15 (1989): this "interlocuteur privilégié du poète-préfacier, joue en fait le rôle d'un médiateur: il permet à Ronsard non seulement de pressentir les résistances du public réel, mais d'en infléchir surtout les attentes et de modeler aussi peu à peu une opinion à son écoute" (p. 101). On this explicit reader "associé quelquefois à la reconnaissance de cette gloire" see also André Gendre, "Lecteur 'esthétique' et lecteur 'éthique' dans les liminaires de la poésie française de 1549 à la fin du siècle" (p. 127).

20. In his *Art poétique* of 1548, Thomas Sébillet had noted that the verses of the ode were necessarily short because they were to be played to a lute or similar instrument, and in his own preface Ronsard restricts the designation of "lyrique" to short verses meant to be accompanied by "un instrument à cordes pincées"; see Gilbert Gadoffre, *Ronsard par lui-même* (2nd ed. Paris: Seuil, 1994), pp. 89–90.

21. As Weber notes, the theme of the lady singing the poet's verses to the accompaniment of her lute is frequent among the Petrarchist poets; cf. Pontus de Tyard, *Erreurs Amoureuses*, I, 42, and Du Bellay, *Olive*, 94.

22. Addressing the beloved: "Quand j'aperçoy ton blond chef couronné/ D'un laurier verd, faire un Lut si bien pleindre . . ." (X, 1–2); and of herself, the famous "Lut, compagnon de ma calamité" (XII), and XIV: "Tant que ma main pourra les cordes tendre / Du mignart Lut, pour tes graces chanter" (5–6). *Louise Labé: Oeuvres complètes*, ed. François Rigolot (Paris: Flammarion, 1986).

23. Marcel Tetel, "Le luth et la lyre de l'école lyonnaise," in *Il Rinascimento a Lione*, ed. A. Possenti and G. Mastrangelo (Rome: Edizioni dell'Ateneo, 1988), p. 951.

24. See JoAnn DellaNeva, "Illustrating the *Deffence*: Imitation and Poetic Perfection in Du Bellay's *Olive*," *French Review* 61 (1987): pp. 45–47. This lyre does not refer to the *Amours*, which were yet to appear, but to the *Odes*; the reference is of particular interest because, as Caldarini notes of this poem, the expression "en lettres d'or" is a Petrarchan echo from R 93, 2 in which Amor tells the poet: "Scrivi quel che vedesti in lettre d'oro" (*Olive* ed., p. 116).

25. Du Bellay, *Oeuvres poétiques*, IV, ed. Henri Chamard (Paris: E. Cornely, 1908), vv. 17–20, 73–80; Du Bellay contrasts this lyre to the "luc vanteur" praising princes,

"ces faulx dieux." Ronsard will later depict Orpheus breaking his "luc payen" to follow the "chanson chrestienne" in his ode *Aux Soeurs Seymours;* see Michel Dassonville, *Ronsard: Etude historique et littéraire, III: Prince des Poètes ou Poète des Princes* (Geneva: Droz, 1976), pp. 19–20.

26. Cave, *Cornucopian Text,* p. 267; on the poem as a whole see pp. 256–68.

27. For discussion of the varied critical opinion on the question, see Isidore Silver, *Ronsard and the Hellenistic Renaissance in France,* Part II: *Ronsard and the Grecian Lyre* (Geneva: Droz, 1981), pp. 83–112.

28. In his *Art poétique,* Gadoffre observes, Peletier du Mans characterizes the poet as a hero who presents himself as "la plus spectable personne du théâtre, et ce théâtre est l'Univers'" (*Ronsard,* p. 20). Examples are abundant in Du Bellay's *Deffence,* in theatrical metaphors that drew the indignant objections of Barthélemy Aneau; see Margaret Ferguson, *Trials of Desire: Renaissance Defenses of Poetry* (New Haven: Yale University Press, 1983), p. 21. On the "motif héroïque" of the poet's enterprise see also Enea Balmas, *Littérature française: La Renaissance, II (1548–1570)* (Paris: Arthaud, 1974), pp. 74–75.

29. See Albert Py, *Imitation et Renaissance dans la poésie de Ronsard* (Geneva: Droz, 1984), who remarks that "la *Franciade* est présente dans des pièces bien antérieures à 1572" (p. 120).

30. "Ode à Michel de l'Hospital" (*L* III, pp. 148, 163); see Dassonville, *Prince des Poètes,* pp. 15–16. The text is dated by Laumonier as 1549.

31. Joachim Du Bellay, *Deffence et illustration de la langue françoyse,* ed. Henri Chamard (Paris: Didier, 1961).

32. Dassonville, *Prince des Poètes,* pp. 13–24. The crisis is reflected, he suggests, in the small number and the tenor of Ronsard's published pieces from fall 1550 until the publication of the early *Amours* in fall 1552.

33. See Dauvois, *Mnémosyne,* p. 103; these verses, she observes, are "déjà des 'avant-jeux' de l'oeuvre épique."

34. See Weber, ed., p. 605, note. The episode evidently caught Ronsard's imagination; he describes the Cardinal of Lorraine also playing the lute to evoke the heroic deeds of his family, "Comme Achille faisoit pour s'alleger un peu,/ Bien qu'en l'ost des Gregeois Hector ruast le feu, / Et que l'horrible effroy de la trompe entonnée / Criast contre le bruit de la Lyre sonnée" (Hymn V of Book I, "De Charles Cardinal de Lorraine").

35. See the comments of Dauvois, *Mnémosyne,* pp. 194–96.

36. In fact, Ronsard's allegiance to the name of Homer is not matched by that to Homer's text; he finds much of his Cassandre instead in Virgil (*Aeneid* II and III) and in Lycophron. See Jacques Pineaux, "Ronsard et Homère dans les 'Amours' de Cassandre," *RHLF* 86 (1986): pp. 650–58.

37. *Délie* 417. On Scève's imitative strategy in this poem see Lori Walters, "Un mythe fondamental de la *Délie*—Maurice Scève—Prométhée," *Romanic Review* 80 (1989): p. 183.

38. Etienne Jodelle, *L'Amour obscur,* ed. Robert Melançon (Paris: La Différence, 1991), p. 63 (poem XLI, vv. 5–8).

39. For a useful reappraisal of the reception of Petrarch in France see Jean Balsamo, *Les Rencontres des Muses: Italianisme et anti-italianisme dans les Lettres françaises de la fin du XVIe siècle* (Geneva: Slatkine, 1992), pp. 217–54.

40. See Paul Laumonier, "Ronsard poète pétrarquiste avant 1550," in *Mélanges Gustave Lanson* (Paris: Hachette, 1922), p. 109. Laumonier points out that in these poems for Cassandre Ronsard takes as his models poets such as Catullus, Ovid, and the Latin poet Jean Second and that he celebrates other ladies in equally sensuous accents borrowed from yet other poets. On the "veine gauloise" of Ronsard's poetry in this period see also Desonay, *Ronsard poète de l'amour. Livre premier. Cassandre*, p. 58.

41. For examples see Yvonne Bellenger, "Pétrarquisme et contr'amours chez quelques poètes français du XVIe siècle," in *Der Petrarkistische Diskurs*, ed. Klaus W. Hempfer and Gerhard Regn (Stuttgart: Franz Steiner Verlag, 1993), pp. 353–73, esp. pp. 359–60.

42. See Balmas, *Littérature française*, p. 73.

43. See André Gendre, ed., *Les Amours et les Folastries (1552–1560)* (Paris: Le Livre de Poche, 1993), p. 484: in this "sonnet étonnant, Ronsard supplie sa belle de mettre fin à son manège pétrarquiste et de dire clairement oui ou non," but only to reestablish "le *dissidio* pétrarquiste" in what follows.

44. See Marc Bensimon, "Introduction" to Ronsard, *Les Amours* (Paris: GF-Flammarion, 1981), p. 16.

45. See, for example, Pierre de Nolhac, *Ronsard et l'Humanisme* (Paris: Champion, 1921), p. 224; Charles Dédéyan, "Ronsard et Bembo," in *Ronsard e l'Italia/ Ronsard in Italia*, Atti del Iº Convegno del Gruppo di Studio sul Cinquecento francese (Fasano di Puglia: Schena, 1988), p. 32.

46. Laumonier, "Ronsard poète pétrarquiste," pp. 112–14. The poems appear among the "premières pièces" in *L* I, pp. 35–39.

47. On this poem see Fredi Chiappelli, *Studi sul linguaggio del Petrarca: La canzone delle visioni* (Florence: Olschki, 1971).

48. *Orlando Furioso*, VII, xiv (see *L* I, p. 38, n. 1; Laumonier, "Ronsard poète pétrarquiste," p. 114).

49. Dassonville, *Prince des Poètes*, p. 25.

50. Laumonier suggests both the first and the third canzoni of the *Rime* as Ronsard's inspiration and observes correlations with other poems by Petrarch as well (*L* I, pp. 35–39); in "Ronsard poète pétrarquiste" he notes that vv. 21–38 are from stanzas 3 and 6 of "Nel dolce tempo" (p. 112).

51. For Petrarch's versions of these Ovidian episodes, see Dennis Dutschke, *Francesco Petrarca: Canzone XXIII from First to Final Version* (Ravenna: Longo, 1977).

52. See Joukovsky, *La Gloire*, esp. p. 335.

53. Du Bellay here imitates an Italian sonnet by Hercole Bentivoglio; see Ernesta Caldarini, "Nuove fonti italiane dell'*Olive*," *BHR* 27 (1965): pp. 411–12.

54. This flight "par l'univers" is the same that Ronsard would wish to achieve for Cassandre's name to make its renown equal to that of Laura in the poem "Que n'ay-je, Dame, & la plume & la grace" cited above. For this "horizontal"—

earthly—concept of the poet's flight see David Cowling, "Ronsard, Du Bellay et Ennius: L'Image du vol dans une ode de Ronsard," *Nouvelle Revue du seizième siècle* 9 (1991): pp. 45–53.

55. Joukovsky cites as example Du Bellay's ode "De l'immortalité des poëtes" (*La Gloire*, pp. 335–38).

56. Calderini points out the translation of the final verse of Ariosto's sonnet X, "che morrei cigno, ove tacendo io moro," and that Barthélemy Aneau clearly regarded the motif as affectation, objecting that "swans die without singing, whatever the fables say" (*L'Olive*, ed., p. 63).

57. Desonay, *Ronsard poète de l'amour. Livre premier. Cassandre*, p. 75: "chez Pétrarque, au contraire, le poète ne se compare à un cygne que parce que, devenu chenu à la suite des refus de Laura, il n'a plus d'autre consolation que de pleurer, aux rives du fleuve, ses espérances mortes."

58. Here as elsewhere, Du Bellay combines the swan image with the story of Icarus; see Mark Eigeldinger, "Le mythe d'Icare dans la poésie française du XVIe siècle," *Cahiers de l'Association Internationale des Etudes françaises* 25 (1973): esp. pp. 265–66.

59. For Ronsard's various mentions of Petrarch see Rosa Maria Frigo, "Pétrarque devant le Tribunal de Ronsard," *Ronsard e l'Italia/Ronsard in Italia* (Fasano di Puglia: Schena, 1988), and on this poem, p. 174.

60. This flattering attribution, a response to Delbene, was not unambiguous: "Rabaissé par son interlocuteur au rang, même illustre, d' 'imitateur' de Pétrarque, Ronsard, en retour, [lui] accordait bien volontiers ce title." See Jean Balsamo, "Note sur l'*Elégie à Bartolomeo Delbene Florentin*," *Revue des Amis de Ronsard* 10 (1997): esp. pp. 154–55.

61. The latter examples are cited by Frigo, "Pétrarque devant le Tribunal de Ronsard," p. 168.

62. Yvonne Bellenger, "Ronsard imitateur infidèle de Pétrarque," in *Petrarca e la cultura europea*, ed. Luisa Rotondi Secchi Tarugi (Milan: Nuovi Orizzonti, 1997), p. 228.

63. Jodelle, *L'amour obscure*, pp. 65–66 (sonnet XLIV).

64. See Giovanni Parenti, "L'Infedeltà di Penelope e il Petrarchismo di Ronsard," *BHR* 49 (1987): pp. 558–60.

65. See L. Baldacci, *Il petrarchismo italiano nel Cinquecento* (Milan-Naples: Riccardo Ricciardi, 1957), ch. 1, "Il Petrarca specchio di vita"; Enrico Carrara, "La leggenda di Laura," in his *Studi Petrarcheschi e altri scritti* (Turin: Bottega d'Erasmo, 1959), pp. 79–111; François Lecercle, "La fabrique du texte: Les commentaires du *Canzoniere* de Pétrarque à la Renaissance," *Etudes de littérature ancienne* 3 (1987): pp. 167–80.

66. See William J. Kennedy, *Authorizing Petrarch* (Ithaca: Cornell University Press, 1994), pp. 45–52.

67. See Terence Cave, "Scève's *Délie:* Correcting Petrarch's Errors," in *Pre-Pléiade Poetry*, ed. Jerry C. Nash (Lexington, Ky.: French Forum, 1985), p. 113; for an astute discussion of the detail of these components see Kennedy, *Authorizing Petrarch*, pp. 45–52.

68. The fact distances the collection from its noted precursor, Dante's "libello" known as the *Vita Nuova*, in which the lyrics are inserted into a retrospective narrative that offers the reader both an account of personal experience and its "meaning." For Petrarch's response to the *Vita Nuova* see Sara Sturm-Maddox, *Petrarch's Metamorphoses: Text and Subtext in the Rime sparse* (Columbia: University of Missouri Press, 1985), ch. 3: "Dante and Beatrice: The Stilnovist Subtext."

69. See Marco Santagata, "Connessioni intertestuali nel *Canzoniere* del Petrarca," *Strumenti critici* 26 (1975): pp. 80–112, and Sturm-Maddox, *Petrarch's Metamorphoses*. See also Silvia Longhi, "Il tutto e le parti nel sistema di un canzoniere (Giovanni Della Casa)," *Strumenti critici* 13 (1979): pp. 265–300.

70. See Roberto Fedi, *La memoria della poesia: Canzonieri, lirici e libri di rime nel Rinascimento* (Rome: Salerno, 1990), pp. 74–75. Bembo, he suggests, marks the transition from a "weak" fifteenth-century Petrarchism to one that seeks to establish its own uncontested warranty of lyricism in part through the imposition of a *cornice,* or frame story.

71. In part through Bembo's attentions, both as editor (1501) and as author of the *Prose della volgar lingua* (1525), the vernacular Petrarch was "'revitalized' and put into circulation as textual example"; some 167 editions of the *Rime* were published in Italy during the sixteenth century. See Fedi, *La memoria della poesia*, pp. 35, 43–48.

72. Olivier Millet, "Le tombeau de la morte et la voix du poète: la mémoire de Pétrarque en France autour de 1533," in *Regards sur le passé dans l'Europe des XVIe-XVIIe siècles* (Bern: Lang, 1997), p. 189.

73. See Jean Balsamo, "Marot et les origines du pétrarquisme français (1530–1540)," in *Clément Marot, "Prince des poëtes françois" 1496–1996*, ed. Gérard Defaux and Michel Simonin (Paris: Champion, 1997), pp. 325–31; and J. E. Kane, "L'italianisme dans l'oeuvre poétique de François Ier," *Studi francesi* 84 (1984): pp. 485–94.

74. On Scève's "discovery" see Verdun L. Saulnier, *Maurice Scève* (Paris: Klincksieck, 1948–49), 1: pp. 38–48; Enzo Giudici, "Bilancio di un 'annosa questione': Maurice Scève e la 'scoperta' della 'tomba' di Laura," *Quaderni di filologia e lingue romanze. Ricerche svolte nell'Università di Maserata* (Rome: Ed. dell'Ateneo, 1980), 2: 7–70; Millet, "Le tombeau de la morte"; and Balsamo, "Marot et les origines du pétrarquisme français," in whose view the "discovery" was probably organized by Alamanni and promoted a connection between the king and Petrarch, "deux François," for political ends (pp. 529–30). Gérard Defaux cites further indications of the king's decisive role in the diffusion of Petrarchism in France in 1533–34 in "Des poèmes oubliés de Clément Marot: Le 'prince des Poetes Françoys' et *Les fleurs de Poesie* de 1534," *Travaux de Littérature* 5 (1992): pp. 37–65; see esp. p. 54.

75. The poems were to appear, under the same title, as the first book of Philieul's translation of *Toutes les Euvres vulgaires de Francoys Petrarque* in 1555; see Giovanna Bellati, "Il primo traduttore del *Canzoniere* petrarchesco nel Rinascimento francese: Vasquin Philieul," *Aevum* 59 (1985): 371–73.

76. Balsamo characterizes the collection as a "laboratory of forms" that in fact created the French sonnet (*Les Rencontres des Muses*, p. 222).

77. *Laure d'Avignon de Vasquin Philieul* (Paris: Actes Sud-Papiers, 1987), p. 27. Bellati notes that, again like Vellutello, Philieul frequently stresses the connections between groups of poems read as moments of a single episode (p. 379).

78. The six sonnets chosen by Marot for translation demonstrate his understanding of the structure of the *recueil* and that he accepted it as a coherent ensemble of texts ("Marot et les origines du pétrarquisme," p. 333). Enea Balmas suggests that both Marot and Peletier attempt to achieve a "thematic" suggestion of the Italian collection as a whole, in presenting their translations of a few poems in the order of the original and respecting the traditional selection "in vita" and "in morte." See "Prime traduzioni del *Canzoniere* nel Cinquecento francese," in *Traduzione e tradizione europea del Petrarca* (Padua: Antenore, 1975), pp. 47–50.

79. Balsamo, for whom Marot was the inventor of French "Petrarchism," comments that he seems to have had "a strange reticence with regard to his invention" ("Marot et les origines du pétrarquisme français," p. 336).

80. An account of the "discovery" was included in the preface to an Italian edition of the *Rime* that Jean de Tournes dedicated to the Lyonnais poet in 1545, one year after the appearance of the *Délie*. See the observations of JoAnn DellaNeva, *Song and Counter-Song: Scève's "Délie" and Petrarch's "Rime"* (Lexington, Ky.: French Forum, 1983), p. 19.

81. See François Rigolot, *Le texte de la Renaissance, des Rhétoriqueurs à Montaigne* (Geneva: Droz, 1982), pp. 176–77.

82. Doranne Fenoaltea, *"Si haulte Architecture": The Design of Scève's "Délie"* (Lexington, Ky.: French Forum, 1982), pp. 23–24; Cave, "Scève's *Délie*," pp. 112–14. The reader might also recognize the impact of the *Trionfi*, Petrarch's own re-writing in a different key of the story of his love for Laura, particularly significant in the closing poem of the *Délie*; see Cave, "Scève's *Délie*," pp. 114–16. The *Délie* is cited from *Maurice Scève: Délie*, ed. I. D. McFarlane (Cambridge, England: Cambridge University Press, 1966) (= *D*).

83. For the importance of this poem in defining Scève's broad imitative strategy, his "rewriting" of Petrarch, see DellaNeva, *Song and Counter-Song*, pp. 25–32; see also Doranne Fenoaltea, "Establishing Contrasts: An Aspect of Scève's Use of Petrarch's Poetry in the *Délie*," *Studi francesi* 55 (1975): pp. 18–19. Nancy Frelick calls attention also to Scève's other allusion to the bitterness of the laurel (*D* 310); see *Délie as Other: Toward a Poetics of Desire in Scève's Délie* (Lexington, Ky.: French Forum, 1994), pp. 77–78.

84. See JoAnn DellaNeva, "Poetry, Metamorphosis, and the Laurel: Ovid, Petrarch, and Scève," *French Forum* 7 (1982): pp. 197–209. Simone Perrier points out that in these poems—dizains 102, 175, 388, 407, and 417—is sketched "une démarche d'appropriation du laurier de Pétrarque-Apollon, ce laurier amoureux *et* poétique"; see "Inscription et écriture dans Délie," *Europe* nos. 691–92 (1986): 139–50; here p. 145.

85. See especially Hans Staub, "Rhodanus rodens: Métamorphoses d'un thème poétique de Pétrarque à Maurice Scève," *Studi di Letteratura Francese* 4 (1975): pp. 106–23; Fenoaltea, "Establishing Contrasts," pp. 19–20.

86. See DellaNeva, *Song and Counter-Song*, pp. 32–39; Walters, "Un mythe fondamental de la *Délie*," p. 183. For the *Rime* as the "negative intertext" of the *Délie* see Rigolot, *Le Texte de la Renaissance*, pp. 173–77.

87. Jerry C. Nash, "'Mont côtoyant le Fleuve et la Cité': Scève, Lyons, and Love," *French Review* 69 (1996): p. 944.

88. For the text of the 1559 preface "Au Lecteur" see Caldarini, ed., *L'Olive*, pp. 167–70.

89. Ibid., p. 13.

90. For Du Bellay's strategy in this poem see William J. Kennedy, "Ronsard's Petrarchan Textuality," *Romanic Review* 77 (1986): pp. 91–92; JoAnn DellaNeva, "Du Bellay: Reader of Scève, Reader of Petrarch," *Romanic Review* 79 (1988): pp. 402-03.

91. *Oeuvres poétiques, II: Recueils de Sonnets*, ed. Henri Chamard (rept. Paris: Marcel Didier, 1970), pp. 240–41.

92. Du Bellay, *Deffence;* text and translation cited from Margaret Ferguson, *Trials of Desire*, p. 42.

93. On this metaphor see Thomas M. Greene, "Petrarch and the Humanist Hermeneutic," in *Italian Literature, Roots and Branches: Essays in Honor of Thomas Goddard Bergin*, ed. G. Rimanelli and K. J. Atchity (New Haven: Yale University Press, 1976), pp. 215–17, and G. W. Pigman III, "Versions of Imitation in the Renaissance," *Renaissance Quarterly* 33 (1980): pp. 4–7.

94. Du Bellay does not insist on the model here, but it is repeated in the treatise: "Mais entende celuy qui voudra immiter, que ce n'est chose facile de bien suivre les vertuz d'un bon aucteur, & quasi comme se transformer en lui" [But he who wishes to imitate should understand that it is not an easy thing to follow well the virtues of a good author, and almost (as it were) transform oneself into him].

95. Thomas M. Greene, *The Light in Troy: Imitation and Discovery in Renaissance Lyric* (New Haven: Yale University Press, 1982), pp. 192, 194, 198–99.

96. Caldarini, *L'Olive*, notes the sonnet by G. Mozzarello published in Giolito I, p. 70.

97. Pasquier (*Le Monophile*, 1555) and Ronsard ("Response aux injures") are cited by Hermann Lindner, "Petrarkismus, Komödie, Stilistik: Normerfüllung und Normdekonstruktion in Ronsard's *Sonnets pour Hélène*," recalling the fundamental ontological difference between *Textproduzent* and *Textsprecher*, in *Der Petrarkistische Diskurs*, ed. Klaus W. Hempfer and Gerhard Regn (Stuttgart: Franz Steiner Verlag, 1993), pp. 392–93 (n. 24) and 398 (n. 50).

98. John O'Brien, "Foreword: Mercurian Exegesis," in *(Re)Interprétations: Etudes sur le seizième siècle*, ed. John O'Brien and Terence Cave (Ann Arbor: Department of Romance Languages, University of Michigan, 1995), p. 4.

Chapter 2. *Les Amours*, 1552–1553

1. Ronsard's opening with an adaptation of a "much imitated formula from one of Petrarch's sonnets" is noted by Grahame Castor, "Petrarchism and the Quest for Beauty in the *Amours* of Cassandre and the *Sonets pour Helene,*" in *Ronsard the Poet,* ed. Terence Cave (London: Methuen, 1973), pp. 81–82. On Marot's translation see JoAnn DellaNeva, "A propos de 'folle amour': Marot, Pétrarque et la Pléiade," in *Clément Marot, "Prince des poëtes françois" 1496–1996,* ed. Gérard Defaux and Michel Simonin (Paris: Champion, 1997), pp. 385–86, and for the use of the poem by Scève (*D* 278) and Du Bellay (*O* 62) see DellaNeva, *Song and Counter-Song: Scève's "Délie" and Petrarch's "Rime"* (Lexington, Ky.: French Forum, 1983), pp. 41–45, and "Illustrating the *Deffence:* Imitation and Poetic Perfection in Du Bellay's *Olive,*" *French Review* 61 (1987): pp. 41–48.

2. Gisèle Mathieu-Castellani, "La main dextre et l'autre, ou la rhétorique détournée," in *Sur des vers de Ronsard (1585–1985),* ed. Marcel Tetel (Paris: Aux Amateurs du Livre, 1990), p. 89.

3. William J. Kennedy argues that here Ronsard's poetry evokes norms that are not "the received Petrarchan ones"; see "Ronsard's Petrarchan Textuality," *Romanic Review* 77 (1986): pp. 88–89.

4. Bembo's sonnet "Se stata foste voi," which Ronsard may have recalled here, expresses a similar sentiment, while inscribing Petrarch into the chain: "Et se 'l mondo v'havea con quei, che feo / L'opra leggiadra, ond'Arno e Sorga crebbe, / Et egli a voi lo stil girato avrebbe / Ch'eterna vita dar altrui poteo. / Hor sete giunta tardo a le mie rime . . . ." See Charles Dédéyan, "Ronsard et Bembo," in *Ronsard e l'Italia/Ronsard in Italia* (Fasano di Puglia: Schena, 1988), p. 46. Kennedy identifies as subtext of this poem *R* 71, "Perché la vita è breve / e l'ingegno paventa a l'alta impresa" ("Ronsard's Petrarchan Textuality," pp. 90–91).

5. The opening sonnet of Pontus de Tyard's *Premier Livre des Erreurs amoureuses* is very similar: "Qui veut sçavoir . . . Qu'il vienne voir ma peine . . ." etc. Yet another parallel is found in a poem by Lodovico Dolce also known to Ronsard; see Grahame Castor, "The Theme of Illusion in Ronsard's *Sonets pour Helene* and in the Variants of the 1552 *Amours,*" *FMLS* 7 (1971): p. 361.

6. See Gisèle Mathieu-Castellani, *Les Thèmes Amoureux dans la Poésie Française, 1570–1600* (Paris: Klincksieck, 1975), esp. pp. 67–68.

7. See Francesco Erspamer, "Il canzoniere rinascimentale come testo o come macrotesto: Il sonetto proemiale," in *Italian Renaissance Studies in Arizona,* ed. Jean R. Brink and Pier R. Baldini, Rosary College Italian Studies 3 (River Forest, Ill.: Rosary College, 1989), pp. 17–26.

8. See the observations of Roberto Fedi, *La memoria della poesia: Canzonieri, lirici e libri di Rime nel Rinascimento* (Rome: Salerno, 1990), pp. 75–76.

9. See Yvonne Bellenger, "Pétrarquisme et contr'amours chez quelques poètes français du XVIe siècle," in *Der Petrarkistische Diskurs,* ed. Klaus W. Hempfer and Gerhard Regn (Stuttgart: Franz Steiner Verlag, 1993): they present "en leur centre, un personnage d'amant-poète dont l'histoire spirituelle constitue le sujet du

livre," if we take "spirituelle" to indicate the constant presence of "l'*acédie* d'un esprit tourmenté, hésitant, en proie aux pires conflits intérieurs" (pp. 356–57).

10. DellaNeva, "A propos de 'folle amour,'" pp. 381–82. She reminds us that Marot had translated *R* 248 as well as *R* 1, "faisant de son poème liminaire un amalgame complexe de ces deux sonnets," and we may well ask to what an extent the *contaminatio* practiced by Ronsard may have been suggested by these two translations (p. 388).

11. Marc Bensimon, ed., Ronsard, *Les Amours* (Paris: Garnier-Flammarion, 1981), p. 13.

12. Among the numerous critical observations of this response, see Fernand Desonay, *Ronsard poète de l'amour. Livre premier. Cassandre* (Brussels: Palais des Académies, 1952), p. 104: Ronsard is "pétrarquiste dans le sens où l'amoureux du *Canzoniere* apparaît comme le premier inquiet qui recherche la volupté des plaintes et le délicieux tourment des incertitudes."

13. From this opening sonnet, Michel Dassonville observes, "Ronsard ameutait le public d'une voix aussi tonitruante que celle qu'il avait employée pour annoncer les *Odes*"; "cet exhibitionnisme," he adds, "a au moins le mérite de promouvoir un art éminemment visuel et plastique." See *Ronsard: Etude historique et littéraire, III: Prince des Poètes ou Poète des Princes (1550–1556)* (Geneva: Droz, 1976), pp. 34, 35.

14. For a close examination of Ronsard's strategy in his "*contaminatio* of *R* 1 and *R* 248" see JoAnn DellaNeva, "Petrarch at the Portal: Opening Signals in *Les Amours de Ronsard,*" *Rivista di Letteratura Moderna e Comparate* 50 (1997): pp. 259–72; I am grateful to the author for making the article available to me in pre-publication form.

15. Robert Mélançon, "Sur la Structure des *Amours* (1552) de Ronsard," *Renaissance and Reformation* 13 (1977): p. 133.

16. See William J. Kennedy, *Rhetorical Norms in Renaissance Literature* (New Haven: Yale University Press, 1978), p. 49.

17. Among the surveys of these see especially Henri Weber, *La création poétique au XVIe siècle en France* (Paris: Nizet, 1956), Vol. 2, ch. 5, "La poésie amoureuse de la Pléiade (Etude de thèmes)."

18. For Muret's commentary, see Laumonier, V, xxi-xxx; Michel Simonin, "Muret à l'heure des Commentaires des *Amours,*" in *Commentaires au Premier Livre des Amours de Ronsard,* publ. by Jacques Chomarat et al. (Geneva: Droz, 1985), xxx–xxxvii. Ronsard's participation in the composition and revision of the commentaries to his poems is underlined by Isidore Silver in *Three Ronsard Studies* (Geneva: Droz, 1978), pp. 109–67.

19. M. M. Fon and François Lecercle, in *Commentaires au Premier Livre des Amours de Ronsard,* p. xxii.

20. François Rigolot, "Ronsard et Muret: Les pièces liminaires aux *Amours* de 1553," *Revue d'histoire littéraire de la France* 88 (1988): pp. 3–16; here p. 7. "En ce sens," he notes, "Muret est un parfait substitut du lecteur virtuel des *Amours.*"

21. Françoise Joukovsky, "La dynamique des Sonnets à Cassandre," *Revue de l'histoire littéraire de la France* 86 (1986): pp. 680–92; here p. 680. These *schémas* are here explored as "réseaux dynamiques" of forces perceptible in the structure of the *recueil*.

22. Muret's commentary is cited from *Les Commentaires au Premier Livre des Amours*, p. 49.

23. Ronsard will, in revising the poem, call the sincerity of her response into question, recalling her shedding a "larme d'argent . . . Lors que tu feins de me voir mal traité" [a silver tear . . . when you pretend to see me badly treated].

24. Castor, "Petrarchism and the Quest for Beauty," p. 82.

25. Examples of affirmations of this destiny by the two poets are cited by Mathieu-Castellani, *Les thèmes amoureux*, p. 54.

26. Alfred Glauser, *Le poème-symbole de Scève à Valéry* (Paris: Nizet, 1967), p. 51; Nathalie Dauvois, *Mnémosyne: Ronsard, une poétique de la mémoire* (Paris: Champion, 1992): around the figure of Cassandre is no longer crystallized only "l'antithèse de l'amour et de la mort . . . mais celle de l'image et de la parole . . . l'opposition du faux et du vrai . . . [et] du pouvoir et de l'impuissance de la parole" (p. 183).

27. See for example Jerome Schwartz, "The Ambiguous Augury in Ronsard's Sonnet 'Avant le temps . . . ' (*Amours*, I, 19)," *L'esprit créateur* 10 (1970): pp. 145–49, who cites earlier readings: "Our reading of the final tercet, the key to the poem, hinges upon the meaning to be attached to the 'dextre ésclair'" (p. 147).

28. François Rigolot, *Poétique et onomastique: L'exemple de la Renaissance* (Geneva: Droz, 1977), p. 207.

29. Compare the allegorical "barca" figuring the poet's passion: "anzi al mio dì mi trasportava al fine" (*R* 80, 14), and "fornito il mio tempo a mezzo gli anni" (*R* 254, 14); Ronsard's editors (Weber, Gendre) cite also *R* 237, 33—"questa ch'anzi vespro a me fa sera." Cf. the fear of an early death—"avant mes jours"—resulting from love's wounds in *A* 104.

30. Jean-Claude Moisan notes the relation between Cassandre's words in sonnet 19 and the opening poem in its 1584 version, remarking that with the latter the content is identified to the reader as the story of an amorous failure. See "L'organisation des *Amours de Cassandre*," *Etudes littéraires* 4 (1971): p. 177.

31. For discussion of this issue see *L* IV, 23; Donald Stone, *Ronsard's Sonnet Cycles: A Study in Tone and Vision* (New Haven: Yale University Press, 1966), p. 47; Schwartz, "Ambiguous Augury," pp. 148–49.

32. See, however, Jerry C. Nash's argument concerning the interpretation of the apparently ill-fated omen in "'Fantastiquant mille monstres bossus': Poetic Incongruities, Poetic Epiphanies, and the Writerly Semiosis of Pierre de Ronsard," *Romanic Review* 84 (1993): pp. 145–47.

33. For a recent exception see Jean Balsamo, *Les Rencontres des Muses: Italianisme et anti-italianisme dans les Lettres françaises de la fin du XVIe siècle* (Geneva: Slatkine, 1992), who observes that in the reference to Petrarch's "lamentables voix" Ronsard "ne se moquait pas de lui; il voulait montrer sa propre inexpérience dans l'expression du sentiment" (p. 228).

34. Dassonville, *Prince des Poètes*, p. 26. For Robert J. Clements, such pronouncements identify "the quasi-moral issue that underlay the Pléiade's objections" to Petrarchism; see "Anti-Petrarchism of the Pléiade," *Modern Philology* 39 (1941–42): pp. 15, 17.

35. On the significance of this and further revisions see Kennedy, "Ronsard's Petrarchan Textuality," p. 95.

36. Michel Dassonville, "Pétrarque juge de Ronsard," in *Der Petrarkistische Diskurs*, ed. Klaus W. Hempfer and Gerhard Regn (Stuttgart: Franz Steiner Verlag, 1993), p. 376.

37. For the procedure in this and other poems see Daniela Boccassini, "Figure de caccia nelle *Amours* de Ronsard," *Studi Francesi* 84 (1990): p. 193.

38. For the poems that set the chronology of "the evolving story of Petrarch's ideal autobiography" see Dennis Dutschke, "The Anniversary Poems in Petrarch's *Canzoniere*," *Italica* 58 (1981): pp. 83–101.

39. François Rigolot remarks that "si Laure entre dans la littérature le 6 avril 1327, il faut bien que Cassandre se trouve une date d'intronisation que dicteront les hasards du rythme et de la rime"; see *Poétique et onomastique*, p. 204.

40. A particularly provocative poem in this regard is *A* 156, "Ayant par mort mon cuoeur desalié." The mention of Love's renewed attack following the poet's loss of a beloved to death imitates *R* 271, and it is perfectly in keeping with the experience of Petrarch's poet—but not with that recorded in the *Amours*. Muret provides a straightforward biographical reading that, as Gendre observes in his edition, does not lessen its startling effect in the collection: "qu'en est-il de cette maîtresse défunte (s'il faut bien prendre au sens propre la 'mort' du v. 1) et de ce nouvel amour qui paraît inaugurer, dans le recueil, un second cycle, qu'aucun autre indice précis ne signal par ailleurs? Peut-être bien s'agit-il d'une simple fiction pétrarquiste, pour être fidèle au modèle jusqu'au bout!" (p. 489).

41. Desonay, *Ronsard poète de l'amour. Livre premier. Cassandre*, p. 100. Rigolot comments briefly but suggestively on the relocation of the beloved from Vaucluse to the Vendôme, "entre Loyr et Loyre, au pays des *Amours;*" see *Poétique et onomastique*, pp. 207, 209.

42. Dassonville, *Prince des Poètes*, p. 53.

43. On Vaucluse see Sara Sturm-Maddox, *Petrarch's Laurels* (University Park: Pennsylvania State University Press, 1992), ch. 2 ("Landscapes") and Epilogue, "Writing in the Shade of the Laurel." For Ronsard's continuing interest in the importance of place in the Petrarchan "story" see the "Elegie ou Amour Oyseau" of 1569 discussed in the Conclusion.

44. Take for example "Ciel, air et vent" (*A* 57), a poem that brings together all the elements of the décor of the story that evoke beyond question the region of Vendôme (Dassonville, *Prince des Poètes*, pp. 52–53). The poem contains readily identifiable Petrarchan echoes. Yvonne Bellenger cites Petrarch's "lieti fiori e felici" and Bevilacqua's "Herbe felici e prato avventurosa"; see "Le paysage sentimental des *Amours* de Ronsard," *Revue des Amis de Ronsard* 1 (1988): pp. 97–113; here p. 100.

45. For discussion of Bellerophon and other probable sources, see Luzius Keller,

"'Solo e pensoso,' 'Seul et pensif,' 'Solitaire et pensif,' mélancolie pétrarquienne et mélancolie petrarquiste," *Studi francesi* 49 (1973): pp. 4–5.

46. Ibid.; see esp. pp. 8–10. Keller observes that these poems informed by the Petrarchan presence form a minor cycle within the major cycle of the *Amours de Cassandre* (pp. 9–10).

47. On Ronsard's echoes of Petrarch's "mythe de l'ombre accueillante, du silence complice" see Desonay, *Ronsard. Livre premier. Cassandre,* pp. 102–3.

48. For differences between the two see Castor, "Petrarchism and the Quest for Beauty," pp. 87–88.

49. See Sara Sturm-Maddox, "Petrarch's Siren: *Dolce parlar* and *dolce canto* in the *Rime sparse,*" *Italian Quarterly* 27 (1986): pp. 5–19. The combination of "doux parler" and song occurs, for example, in *A* 137.

50. See Weber, *La Création poétique,* 1: p. 325; Desonay, *Ronsard. Livre premier. Cassandre,* pp. 100–101.

51. The sonnet amplifies a familiar Petrarchan motif; see Gregory de Rocher, "Dépliage cosmique dans un sonnet de Ronsard: Echos amplifiés du *dolce riso* pétrarquien," *Revue belge de philologie et d'histoire* 58 (1980): pp. 588–94. For the "extases surveillés" resulting from the contemplation of extraordinary beauty see Josiane Rieu, "La 'beauté qui tue' dans les *Amours* de Ronsard," *RHLF* 86 (1986): p. 699; the verses from *A* 3, cited as illustration, are closely copied from Petrarch.

52. Thomas M. Greene, *The Light in Troy: Imitation and Discovery in Renaissance Poetry* (New Haven: Yale University Press, 1982), pp. 202–3.

53. Du Bellay, *Olive* 67, "Que n'as-tu las (mon désir) de tant suivre." Verse 4 of Ronsard's poem, "Et ma douleur feroit aller à rive," echoes Petrarch's "e perchè il mio martir non giunga a riva" (*R* 164).

54. For Laura as "fera," see Fredi Chiappelli, "An Analysis of Structuration in Petrarch's Poetry," in *Francis Petrarch, Six Centuries Later,* ed. Aldo Scaglione (Chapel Hill and Chicago: NCSRLL and the Newberry Library, 1975), pp. 106–8.

55. Boccassini, "Figure di caccia," p. 195.

56. One of these was presented by Octavien de Saint Gelais in 1509; see Castor, "Petrarchism and the Quest for Beauty," p. 83, n. 1. Muret's commentary works out the allegory for the reader by adding a detail not included in the poem: "ses chiens voïans que la Fere ne veut aucunement fuir devant eus: Ains leur fait teste . . . de dépit se ruent contre leur maître, et le devorent." See Daniela Boccassini, "Petrarchismo e arte venatoria nelle *Amours de Cassandre:* 'Franc de raison, esclave de fureur,'" in *Ronsard e l'Italia/Ronsard in Italia* (Fasano di Puglia: Schena, 1988), pp. 113–25, who notes also contemporary interest in the hunt as sport.

57. André Gendre, *Ronsard, poète de la Conquète amoureuse* (Neuchâtel: Editions de la Baconnière, 1970), pp. 137–38.

58. See the comments of Castor, "Petrarchism and the Quest for Beauty," pp. 83–84.

59. I. D. McFarlane, "Mythology and Structure in Ronsard's *Les Amours* (1552–53)," in *Myth and Legend in French Literature: Essays in Honour of A. J. Steele,* ed. Keith Aspley, David Bellos, and Peter Sharratt (London: MHRA, 1982), pp. 60–61.

60. Helmut Hatzfeld, "The Role of Mythology in Poetry During the French Renaissance," *Modern Language Quarterly* 13 (1952): p. 403.

61. Guy Demerson, *La mythologie classique dans l'oeuvre lyrique de la Pléiade* (Geneva: Droz, 1972), p. 56.

62. Dassonville, *Prince des Poètes*, p. 61; Pierre Léonard, "Lectures de la mythologie chez Ronsard," *Studi Francesi* 17 (1973): p. 471. In Ann Moss's *Poetry and Fable: Studies in Mythological Narrative in Sixteenth-Century France* (Cambridge, England: Cambridge University Press, 1984), the name of Petrarch occurs twice in the index, in both cases to indicate not the direct imitation of the *Rime sparse* but in reference to "the Petrarchan heritage" and to "commonplaces and conceits peculiar to Petrarchism" (pp. 133, 157).

63. See Kathleen Anne Perry, *Metamorphosis and the Imagination in the Poetry of Ovid, Petrarch, and Ronsard* (New York: Lang, 1989), who further observes that the word *métamorphoses* itself "is used almost exclusively in the plural, as if to describe the simultaneous existence of multiple states of being within the same person" (pp. 145, 147).

64. Dassonville, *Prince des Poètes*, p. 57.

65. Ann Moss, "New Myths for Old," in *Ronsard in Cambridge: Proceedings of the Cambridge Ronsard Colloquium*, ed. Philip Ford et al. (Cambridge, England: Cambridge French Colloquia, 1986), pp. 55–56.

66. On a number of the various functions of the Apollo model in the *Amours* of 1552–53, see McFarlane, "Mythology and Structure," pp. 64–66.

67. See Dédéyan, "Ronsard et Bembo," p. 47; and Du Bellay's "ma doulce guerriere" of *Olive* 70, 2.

68. Weber, ed., citing Tibullus, IV, 5–6, as well as Petrarchan echoes, calls attention also to Marot's poem "Sur la maladie de s'amie" (p. 583).

69. The directness of Ronsard's Petrarchan inspiration is in this case highlighted by comparison with Du Bellay's development of the same theme in *Olive* 103 and 104.

70. On Petrarch, like Apollo, as an *exclusus amator* see Oscar Büdel, "Illusion Disabused: A Novel Mode in Petrarch's *Canzoniere*," in *Francis Petrarch, Six Centuries Later*, ed. Aldo Scaglione (Chapel Hill and Chicago: UNCSRLL and the Newberry Library, 1975), p. 144.

71. Moisan, "L'Organisation des *Amours de Cassandre*," p. 177.

72. Dassonville, *Prince des Poètes*, p. 39.

73. JoAnn DellaNeva, "Ravishing Beauties in the *Amours* of Ronsard: Rape, Mythology and the Petrarchist Tradition," *Neophilologus* 73 (1989): pp. 24–25. "That the poet must resort to violence to achieve his goal seems to signal a certain failure on the part of traditional petrarchist rhetoric" (p. 31).

74. See Dassonville, *Prince des Poètes*, pp. 42–43.

75. See François Rigolot, "Rhétorique de la métamorphose chez Ronsard," in *Textes et Intertextes: Etudes sur le XVIe siècle pour Alfred Glauser*, ed. F. Gray and M. Tetel (Paris: Nizet, 1979), p. 150, and for the lapidary metamorphosis, pp. 153–57.

76. John Brenkman, "Writing, Desire, Dialectic in Petrarch's *Rime 23*," *Pacific*

Coast Philology 9 (1974): p. 17; see Norbert Jonard, "I miti dell'Eros nel *Canzoniere del Petrarca*," *Lettere Italiane* 34 (1982): p. 465.

77. See for example *A* 31, "Aillez Démons qui tenez de la terre . . ." ending with "Ou bien en pierre ell' le transformera / D'un seul regard ainsi qu'une Meduse" [Or else she will transform him into stone with a single glance, as a Medusa does]; other poems in this and other collections are noted by Weber, ed., p. 509.

78. See Nancy J. Vickers, "Les Métamorphoses de la Méduse: Pétrarquisme et pétrification chez Ronsard," in *Sur des vers de Ronsard, 1585–1985*, ed. Marcel Tetel (Paris: Aux Amateurs du Livre, 1990), pp. 159–70. In *A* 8, she points out, Petrarch as poetic model "n'est pas 'impetrato' bien qu'au vers trois Pierre de Ronsard soit de manière redondante 'empierré'" (pp. 168–69).

79. Terence Cave, "Ronsard as Apollo: Myth, Poetry and Experience in a Renaissance Sonnet Cycle," *Yale French Studies* 47 (1972): p. 86.

80. See the reading of André Gendre, "Aspects du feu dans l'imaginaire de Ronsard amoureux," in *Ronsard et les éléments*, ed. André Gendre (Geneva: Droz, 1992), pp. 185–87.

81. Yvonne Bellenger relates this solution of metamorphosis of the self to one yet more radical, as in *A* 146, "Que tout par tout dorenavant se mue": "Effets ravageurs de l'amour incompris, par lesquels la métamorphose se mue en malédiction." See *Lisez la Cassandre de Ronsard. Etude sur "Les Amours" (1553)* (Paris: Champion, 1997), pp. 147–48.

82. Bellenger points out that each of the five explicit mentions of the word "metamorphoses" in the collection is preceded by a numeral expressing abundance—"cent," "mille"—and "se rapporte exclusivement à la transformation intérieure de l'amant quand son trouble lui fait perdre la notion de son identité et le dépouille de son ancien moi" (*Lisez la Cassandre de Ronsard*, pp. 143–44).

83. Weber notes that the desire of transformation into a flea is a theme of "pétrarquisme précieux," cultivated by the neo-Latin poets (ed., p. 523).

84. The phrase is that of Paul Laumonier, *Ronsard poète lyrique* (Paris: Hachette, 1923), p. 477; see also Rosa Maria Frigo, "Pétrarque devant la tribunal de Ronsard," in *Ronsard e l'Italia / Ronsard in Italia* (Fasano di Puglia: Schena, 1988), p. 175; Robert Garapon, *Ronsard chantre de Marie et d'Hélène* (Paris: SEDES, 1981), p. 21.

85. Greene, *The Light in Troy*, p. 210; Castor, "Petrarchism and the Quest for Beauty," p. 91. See also the latter's "Ronsard's Variants: 'Je vouldroy bien richement jaunissant,'" *MLR* 59 (1964): p. 387.

86. Bortolo Martinelli, *Petrarca e il Ventoso* (Bergamo: Minerva Italica, 1977), p. 38; for a reading of Petrarch's eroticism see Jonard, "I miti dell'Eros."

87. See François Rigolot, *Le texte de la Renaissance: Des Rhétoriqueurs à Montaigne* (Geneva: Droz, 1982); in Ronsard's poem, as he comments, if metamorphosis is barely evoked, seduction is presented "avec une complaisance splendide" (pp. 208–9).

88. Gendre, *Ronsard poète de la conquête amoureuse*, p. 211, and "Origines latines et néo-latines du sonnet 'Or que Juppin' de Ronsard," *Museum Helveticum* 48

(1991): p. 329. See also K. R. W. Jones, *Pierre de Ronsard* (New York: Twayne, 1970), p. 53.

89. McFarlane, "Mythology and Structure," p. 68.

90. On the Ode, see Raymond Lebègue, "Un volume de vers italiens annotés par Ronsard," *Bulletin du Bibliophile et du Bibliothécaire* (1951): p. 277. Muret tells the story of Philomena to explain the allusions of vv. 7 and 8 of the sonnet, citing Virgil and Horace as well.

91. See Terence Cave, "La contamination des intertextes: Le sonnet 'Or que Juppin,'" in *Ronsard: Colloque de Neuchatel*, ed. André Gendre (Geneva: Droz, 1987), pp. 66–67. Cave illustrates also the contrast to Du Bellay's hommage to Petrarch in "Ores qu'en l'air le grand Dieu du tonnerre" (pp. 71–72).

92. For a detailed assessment of Petrarch's depiction of Jove see Sara Sturm-Maddox, "*La pianta più gradita in cielo:* Petrarch's Laurel and Jove," in *Dante, Petrarch, Boccaccio: Studies in the Italian Trecento in Honor of Charles S. Singleton*, ed. A. S. Bernardo and A. L. Pellegrini (Binghamton, N.Y.: Medieval and Renaissance Texts and Studies, 1983), pp. 255–71.

93. Ronsard here echoes in part a sonnet by Bembo, "Se in me, Quirina, da lodar in carte," as noted by Weber, ed., p. 537, and Dédéyan, "Ronsard and Bembo," pp. 40–41; but Bembo's sonnet, which itself contains numerous Petrarchan echoes, makes no mention of flight or of the lady's elevation by the poet-lover.

94. Dassonville, *Prince des Poètes*, pp. 26–27.

95. Rigolot, *Poétique et onomastique*, pp. 203, 205. Binet writes that "Il se delibera de la chanter, comme Petrarque avoit faict sa Laure, amoureux seulement de ce beau nom, comme luy mesmes m'a dit maintefois."

96. Du Bellay devoted an entire dramatic sonnet to the comparison: *Honneste Amour* VIII. See Henri Weber, "Platonisme et sensualité dans la poésie amoureuse de la Pléiade," in *Lumières de la Pléiade* (Paris: Vrin, 1966): "ce qui séduit Du Bellay comme Ronsard . . . c'est la peinture du délire de la passion physique dont sont à la fois victime la Pythie et le poète" (p. 171).

97. See for example Gendre, ed., p. 473: "La tradition pétrarquiste imposait le choix d'une femme blonde. Mais Cassandre était brune."

98. On this return to the Petrarchan *contrari affetti* see Klaus W. Hempfer, "Die Pluralisierung des erotischen Diskurses in der europäischen Lyrik des 16. und 17. Jahrhunderts (Ariost, Ronsard, Shakespeare, Opitz)," *Germanish-Romanische Monatsschrift* N.S. 38 (1988): pp. 256–57.

Chapter 3. The *Sonets pour Helene*

1. The poem's original title was "A une Dame," appearing in his *Recueil de poésie;* the revision appeared in 1558 in the *Divers Jeux rustiques.* See Bernard Weinberg, "Du Bellay's 'Contre les Pétrarquistes,'" *L'Esprit créateur* 12 (1972): pp. 159–77, and for the charges of insincerity and mendacity leveled against the Petrarchan posture see Robert J. Clements, "Anti-Petrarchism of the Pléiade," *Modern Philology* 39 (1941–42): pp. 15–21.

2. Weber in the notes to the two collections indicates the combination of these

elements with other, frequently Petrarchan, echoes. For these collections and those of the *Continuation* and *Nouvelle Continuation des amours* (1555, 1556) see also James Hutton, *The Greek Anthology in France and in the Latin Writers of the Netherlands to the Year 1800* (Ithaca: Cornell University Press, 1946), pp. 350–53.

3. See William J. Kennedy, "Ronsard's Petrarchan Textuality," *Romanic Review* 77 (1986): p. 96, and note.

4. On the unification of the two *Continuations* into a second book of *Amours* symmetrical with the first, see Louis Terreaux, "Sur l'organisation du *Second Livre des Amours*," in *Ronsard in Cambridge*, ed. Philip Ford et al. (Cambridge, England: Cambridge French Colloquia, 1986), pp. 81–84.

5. See Louis Terreaux, "Le style 'bas' des *Continuations des Amours*," in *Lumières de la Pléiade* (Paris: Vrin, 1966), pp. 313–42; and the discussion of Philippe Walter, "Marie et les reflets du nom," *BHR* 46 (1984): p. 44.

6. A single example: ". . . la paysanne du Port Guyet eût été incapable de comprendre et de goûter une poésie érudite et subtile" (Micha, ed., p. xxii).

7. For examples among contemporary love sequences, see Richard Griffiths, "Humor and Complicity in Ronsard's 'Continuation des Amours,'" in *The Equilibrium of Wit: Essays for Odette de Mourges*, ed. Peter Bayley and Dorothy Gabe Coleman (Lexington, Ky.: French Forum, 1982), pp. 41–56.

8. André Gendre, ed., *Les Amours et Les Folastries (1552–1560)* (Paris: Le Livre de Poche, 1993), p. 51.

9. Michel Dassonville, *Ronsard: Etude historique et littéraire, III: Prince des poètes ou poète des princes (1550–1556)* (Geneva: Droz, 1976), p. 165. Hoyt Rogers and Roy Rosenstein affirm that the thematic of inconstancy has its origin in Ronsard; see "De l'inconstance thématique à une poétique de l'inconstance," *Neophilologus* 72 (1988), pp. 180–90; here pp. 181–82.

10. For Ronsard's treatment of the theme in his non-amorous poetry see Daniel Ménager, *Ronsard: Le Roi, le poète et les hommes* (Geneva: Droz, 1979), pp. 88–91.

11. See the observations of Marie-Luce Demonet-Launey, *XVIe Siècle: 1460–1610* (Paris: Bordas, 1988), pp. 70–71.

12. Yvonne Bellenger, "Pétrarquisme et contr'amours chez quelques poètes français du XVIe siècle," in *Der Petrarkistische Diskurs*, ed. Klaus W. Hempfer and Gerhard Regn (Stuttgart: Franz Steiner Verlag, 1993), pp. 360–61.

13. See Giovanni Parenti, "L'Infedeltà di Penelope et il Petrarchismo di Ronsard," *BHR* 49 (1987): p. 562. For Parenti, this "authorization to inconstancy" suggests the connection of the collections dedicated to Cassandre and to Marie along the lines of the example of Tibullus, whose elegies had been divided between Delia and Nemesi (p. 568).

14. Jacques Ferrand, *De la maladie d'Amour ou Mélancholie érotique* (Paris: Moreau, 1623), p. 34, cited in Jean Balsamo, *Les Rencontres des Muses: Italianisme et anti-italianisme dans les Lettres françaises de la fin du XVIe siècle* (Geneva: Slatkine, 1992), p. 227.

15. Parenti, "L'Infedeltà di Penelope," p. 561. See also the review of Petrarchan commentaries in Donald L. Guss, "Petrarchism and the End of the Renaissance,"

in *Francis Petrarch, Six Centuries Later: A Symposium*, ed. Aldo Scaglione (Chapel Hill and Chicago: University of North Carolina and the Newberry Library, 1975), pp. 385–88.

16. Roberto Fedi, *La memoria della poesia: Canzonieri, lirici e libri di rime nel Rinascimento* (Rome: Salerno, 1990), p. 73, who cites the passage from Bembo's response to Niccolò Astemio.

17. Parenti adds that Ronsard may have read it through the reductive filter of one of Petrarch's commentators, the "piatto buon senso di Gesualdo" ("L'Infedeltà di Penelope," p. 561).

18. Already in 1542, in *La Parfaicte Amye*, Antoine Héroët had targeted the issue of insincerity in Petrarchan protestations of suffering in love; see Dario Cecchetti, *Il Petrarchismo in Francia* (Turin: G. Giappichelli, 1970), pp. 49–50.

19. Parenti suggests that the passage reflects a minor tradition in the reading of the myth that was very probably well known to Ronsard ("L'Infedeltà di Penelope," pp. 547–55).

20. For a different reading of this response to Petrarch in terms of "life" and "literature" see Michel Dassonville, "Pétrarque juge de Ronsard," in *Der Petrarkistische Diskurs*, ed. Klaus W. Hempfer and Gerhard Regn (Stuttgart: Franz Steiner Verlag, 1993), pp. 380–81. Dassonville finds here an authentic "méprise" of Petrarch's attitude, one suggestive of the French poet's general "préjugé de lecture" that ignores the spiritual conflict fundamental to the *Rime*.

21. Richard L. Regosin, "Poétique et rhétorique de l'amour: Le propre et l'impropre de la lecture de Ronsard," in *Sur des vers de Ronsard, 1585–1985*, ed. Marcel Tetel (Paris: Aux Amateurs de Livres, 1990), p. 121.

22. "Tout est en jeu," comments Regosin, "le succès, la gloire, l'immortalité—face à une lecture erronée, et à la médisance" ("Poétique et rhétorique de l'amour," p. 118).

23. Ibid., p. 124.

24. For the text see *L* XII, pp. 256–77.

25. For the Genèvre "episode" see Yvonne Bellenger, "Le temps de l'amour dans les poèmes adressés à Genèvre," *Revue des Amis de Ronsard* 10 (1997): pp. 87–113. The last of the three poems that compose this small series, she points out, opens with "Le temps se passe et se passant, Madame, / Il faict passer mon amoureuse flame" (*L* XV, p. 326), and goes on to recount the end of the affair with Ronsard's acceptance of "l'inconstance aimable" (pp. 99–100).

26. See Claude Faisant, "Les relations de Ronsard et de Desportes," *BHR* 28 (1966): p. 337.

27. Gisèle Mathieu-Castellani, *Les thèmes amoureux dans la poésie française (1570–1600)* (Paris: Klincksieck, 1975), p. 213. For a survey of the phenomenon in its social and poetic evolution see pp. 212–19.

28. Fernand Desonay considers all of this collection within the context of patronage and incidental poetry. "C'est le moment de recourir à Pétrarque, de démarquer sans vergogne cette anthologie galante que lui offre le *Canzoniere*. Les cinq sonnets 'pétrarquisants' ne manquent pas de grâce; comme les précédents, ils

on dû être composés à la demande du Prince ou de l'ami"; see *Ronsard poète de l'amour*, III: *Du poète de cour au chantre d'Hélène* (Brussels: Duculot, 1959), pp. 126–27.

29. For a review of Ronsard's poetry for ladies at court see Marcel Françon, "Ronsard panégyriste de la cour," *Convivium* 22 (1954): pp. 556–64, and for *Les Amours d'Eurymédon et Callirée* see Dassonville, *Ronsard: Etude historique et littéraire*, V, pp. 123–34. On Ronsard's intense activity as "poète courtisan" during the 1560s and early 1570s see Desonay, *Ronsard poète de l'amour*, III: *Du poète de cour au chantre d'Hélène*.

30. See J. Vianey, *Le Pétrarquisme en France au XVIe siècle* (Geneva: Slatkine Reprints, 1969), 3ᵉ partie.

31. The verses of Jean de Montereul are recorded in Philippe Desportes, *Diverses amours et autres oeuvres meslees*, ed. V. E. Graham, p. 227; cited, with other testimony to Desportes's popularity, by Malcolm Smith, ed., *Sonnets pour Hélène* (Geneva: Droz, 1970), pp. 12–13.

32. Of the opening poem of Book I of the *Sonets*, Faisant suggests a possible precise allusion to Desportes in the mention of "un plus jeune écrivain" ("Les relations de Ronsard et de Desportes," p. 343).

33. See the comments of Desonay, *Ronsard poète de l'amour, III: Du poète de cour au chantre d'Hélène*, p. 347.

34. Henri Chamard, *Histoire de la Pléiade* (Paris: Didier, 1939), 3: p. 352; for a summary of Ronsard's involvement with the court during the reign of Charles IX and early in that of Henri III, see p. 373. Mary Morrison argues convincingly for Ronsard's challenge in terms of difference rather than of similarity; see "Ronsard and Desportes," *BHR* 28 (1966): pp. 294–322. For successive critical responses see Michel Dassonville, "Avatars des *Sonnets pour Hélène*," in *Le poète et ses lecteurs: Le cas Ronsard, Oeuvres & critiques* 6 (1981–82): pp. 95–99.

35. Among the poems in the *Rime* cited by editors and commentators are, for I, 10: 338; 339; 267; and 127; and for I, 40: 35; 155; 288; 193 (all noted in Weber).

36. *Les Amours*, Introduction, p. xxxiii.

37. For a concise survey of some of these see Dassonville, "Avatars des *Sonnets pour Hélène*," pp. 97–98.

38. Grahame Castor, "Petrarchism and the Quest for Beauty in the *Amours* of Cassandre and the *Sonets pour Helene*," in *Ronsard the Poet*, ed. Terence Cave (London: Methuen, 1973), pp. 99–100. See also Castor's "The Theme of Illusion in Ronsard's *Sonets pour Helene* and in the Variants of the 1552 *Amours*," *FMLS* 7 (1971) identifying as a marked feature of the *Sonets* "the expression of 'antipetrarchan' attitudes within a basically petrarchan framework" (p. 366, n. 16).

39. See Yvonne Bellenger, "Un personnage poétique nouveau: Hélène dans les *Amours* de Ronsard," *Quaderni dell'Istituto di lingue e letterature neo-latine* 2 (1982): pp. 7–26; here p. 20.

40. See Mathieu-Castellani, *Les thèmes amoureux*, p. 219.

41. Smith observes that the *Sonets* are "le reflet—parfois satirique—de ce milieu" (ed., *Sonnets pour Hélène*, p. 16).

42. Donald Stone, "L'évolution du sonnet amoureux chez Ronsard," in *Lumières de la Pléiade* (Paris: Vrin, 1966), pp. 343–62; here p. 345; see also *Ronsard's Sonnet Cycles: A Study in Tone and Vision* (New Haven: Yale University Press, 1966).

43. See Robert Garapon, "Le portrait de Ronsard par lui-même dans les *Sonnets pour Hélène,*" *Revue d'histoire littéraire de la France* 86 (1986): pp. 643–49; here p. 643.

44. Henri Weber comments that these are sufficient to form "une trame presque romanesque"; see "La circonstance et le symbole dans les Sonnets pour Hélène," in *Sur des vers de Ronsard, 1585–1985,* ed. M. Tetel (Paris: Aux Amateurs du Livre, 1990), pp. 171–80; here p. 171.

45. For the history of the suggestion see Dassonville, "Avatars des *Sonnets pour Hélène,*" p. 96. See also Smith, ed., on Ronsard's role as the king's accredited poet in relation to his return to love poetry (p. 9).

46. Françon, "Ronsard panégyriste," finds in the *Sonets* "des manoeuvres d'un courtesan" (p. 564). "Les *Sonnets pour Hélène . . . dediez à elle mesme* complètent la série des poésies qui sont offertes à des dames et demoiselles d'honneur à la cour" (p. 560).

47. Morrison, "Ronsard and Desportes," p. 297; the poem by Desportes is "Par vos graces, Madame, et par le dur martyre" (*Diane* I, xxxv). See also Faisant, "Les relations de Ronsard et de Desportes," p. 343.

48. Castor, "Petrarchism and the Quest for Beauty," p. 101. Hermann Lindner argues that many of its elements, from the May setting through the nature imagery and the mythological allusions, are in fact parodic with regard to the Petrarchan paradigm; see "Petrarkismus, Komödie, Stilistik. Normerfüllung und Norm-dekonstruktion in Ronsard's *Sonnets pour Hélène,*" in *Der Petrarkistische Diskurs,* ed. Klaus W. Hempfer and Gerhard Regn (Stuttgart: Franz Steiner Verlag, 1993), pp. 393–97; here p. 395.

49. *Les Amours diverses* XVII, added to the *Sonets* in 1584.

50. The poem first appeared in the *Amours diverses,* 14, in which this closing line was less aggressive: "Tu m'as tres-mal payé pour avoir bien servy."

51. They motivate too the bitter observation about current amatory fashion: "Et vrayment c'est aimer comme on fait à la Court, / Où le feu contrefait ne rend qu'une fumee" (I, 53, 13–14).

52. The judgment is that of Bellenger, "Un personnage poétique nouveau," p. 14.

53. See Sara Sturm-Maddox, *Petrarch's Metamorphoses: Text and Subtext in the Rime sparse* (Columbia: University of Missouri Press, 1985), ch. 2: "Apollo and Daphne: The Ovidian Subtext."

54. Kennedy, "Ronsard's Petrarchan Textuality," pp. 93–94.

55. Weber, ed., cites for the "trahison du coeur" indicted in this poem also *Rime* 274, 7–8.

56. These differences are examined in terms of Greimasian actantial analysis in Evelyn Birge Vitz, "Ronsard's *Sonnets pour Hélène:* Narrative Structures and Poetic Language," *Romanic Review* 67 (1976): pp. 249–67; for the lover as *Sujet* and as *Objet* see esp. p. 265.

57. Margaret Pelan, seeking "trustworthy internal evidence in the Sonnets" for the "real" nature of Ronsard's relation to Hélène, outlines as successive phases, first, confidence in reason, deliberate choice; then, motivated by Hélène's withdrawal, complaint of Reason's weakness, proclaiming himself vanquished by destiny. See "Ronsard's 'Amour d'Automne,'" *French Studies* 7 (1953): pp. 14–22.

58. *Les Amours*, p. 737. The same instantaneous *innamoramento* as the effect of Hélène's eyes is found in other poems, e.g. I, 13: "Si tost que je la vy, je fus mis en servage / De ses yeux."

59. Marco Santagata, "Per una storia della lirica italiana del Quattrocento," in *Der Petrarkistische Diskurs*, ed. Klaus W. Hempfer and Gerhard Regn (Stuttgart: Franz Steiner Verlag, 1993), p. 27.

60. Prominent among these was the salon of the Maréchal de Retz, of which Hélène was a prominent member; see the comments of Desonay in *Ronsard poète de l'amour*, III: pp. 204–19.

61. "Responce de P. de Ronsard, gentilhomme Vandomois, aux injures & calomnies de je ne scay quels Predicans & Ministres de Geneve," in *L* XI, pp. 116–76, here p. 167. Here, as Jean Starobinski observes, "Ronsard trouve la formule juste pour évoquer sa poésie amoureuse: il marque avec netteté l'antécédence de l'élan chaleureux dicté par la Muse, par rapport aux choix d'une 'maîtresse.'" See "Les journées plurielles de Pierre de Ronsard," in *Die Pluralität der Welten: Aspekte der Renaissance in der Romania*, ed. Wolf-Dieter Stempel and Karlheinz Stierle (Munich: Wilhelm Fink Verlag, 1987), p. 378.

62. "Elegie au Seigneur l'Huillier" (*L* X, p. 292). This "poësie en la jeune saison / Bouillonne dans nos coeurs, peu subjecte à raison, / serve de l'appetit." As André Gendre observes, here "poésie et amour sont consubstantiels et le phénomène de leur union ... ne saurait porter un autre nom que celui de libido"; see *Ronsard poète de la conquête amoureuse*, p. 454.

63. Nathalie Dauvois, *Mnémosyne: Ronsard, une poétique de la mémoire* (Paris: Champion, 1992), p. 203.

64. See ibid., pp. 203–5. "Maintenant je suis pris, & si je prens à gloire / D'avoir perdu le camp, frustré de la victoire: / Ton oeil vaut un combat de dix ans d'Ilion," writes Ronsard (I, 31); and "... Amour, pour te flatter, / Comme tu feis à Troye, au coeur me vient jetter / Ton feu, qui de mes oz se paist insatiable" (II, 9).

65. François Rigolot, *Poétique et onomastique: L'exemple de la Renaissance* (Geneva: Droz, 1977), pp. 221–22: Hélène "est l'*Haleine* par excellence, et se distingue de ses consoeurs par la conformité cratylique de la forme au contenu par décision naturelle."

66. Such an exhortation could have no counterpart in the *Rime sparse*. As Weber notes, this closing proverb is no doubt not original with Ronsard; a possible source is Ménander: "On peut tout atteindre par le soin et l'effort."

67. Vitz, "Ronsard's *Sonnets pour Helene*," p. 261.

68. See the discussion of Jean M. Fallon, *Voice and Vision in Ronsard's Les Sonnets pour Helene* (New York: Peter Lang, 1994), pp. 73–79.

69. Weber cites here *Rime* 71, "Non perch'io non m'aveggia / Quanto mia laude è ingiuriosa a voi," 87, and 186, "Se Virgilio et Omero avessin visto."

70. As Laurence Mall observes, Petrarch is evoked here "de façon contournée ... Ronsard commence par une hypothétique victoire d'Hélène sur Laure pour lui opposer aussitôt démenti, ce qui alors déplace le centre d'intérêt des femmes à leur poète." See "Nom et renom dans les *Sonets pour Helene* de Ronsard," *Australian Journal of French Studies* 15 (1988): pp. 115–31; here p. 119.

71. Garapon, "Le portrait de Ronsard par lui-même," p. 648.

72. Morrison, "Ronsard and Desportes," p. 302; see also Bellenger, "Un personnage poétique nouveau," esp. pp. 19–22.

73. Morrison, "Ronsard and Desportes," p. 305.

74. K. R. Jones, *Pierre de Ronsard* (New York: Twayne, 1970), p. 136. For a subtle exploration of the focus of Ronsard's poem in relation to "Di pensier in pensier" and the Petrarchan commentary tradition see Kennedy, "Ronsard's Petrarchan Textuality," pp. 98–102.

75. The Weber edition notes this opening in relation to the Petrarchan echoes in *SH* I, 19.

76. Kennedy, "Ronsard's Petrarchan Textuality," p. 99.

77. Castor, "Theme of Illusion," p. 362. Malcolm Quainton argues that the treatment of illusion and deception in the collection, particularly evident in the *songe amoureux*, reflects a "template of concerns" that links the *Sonnets pour Hélène* to the myth in which a phantom Helen occasioned the siege of Troy while the real Helen, virtuous and faithful wife, awaited her husband's return. See "Ronsard's *Sonnets pour Hélène* and the Alternative Helen Myth," in *(Re)Interprétations: Etudes sur le seizième siècle*, ed. John O'Brien and Terence Cave (Ann Arbor: Department of Romance Languages, University of Michigan, 1995), pp. 77–112; here p. 77.

78. *L* X, p. 290. Desonay points out, following Laumonier, that the advice to "contenter ses esprits" was a well-known philosophical formula among sixteenth-century poets; see *Ronsard poète de l'amour*, II: *De Marie à Genèvre* (Brussels: Duculot, 1951), pp. 180–81.

79. See Castor, "Theme of Illusion," p. 363.

80. Despite Henri Weber's remark that here "le désir de ne pas voir finir le songe ou le regret de le voir s'enfuir cèdent la place à une résignation mélancolique" acknowledged in the final verse; see "La circonstance et le symbole," p. 175.

81. See for example Weber's discussion in *La création poétique au XVIe siècle en France* (Paris: Nizet, 1956), 1: pp. 356–66.

82. See Castor, "Theme of Illusion," p. 366.

83. André Gendre, *Ronsard poète de la conquête amoureuse* (Neuchatel: La Baconnière, 1970), pp. 472–75; C. Chadwick, "The Composition of the *Sonnets pour Hélène*," *French Studies* 8 (1954): p. 331.

84. Mariann S. Regan, "The Evolution of the Poet in Ronsard's Sonnet Cycles," *Mosaic* 11 (1974): pp. 124–49; here p. 144.

85. Garapon, "Le portrait de Ronsard par lui-même," p. 647.

86. Bellenger, "Pétrarquisme et contr'amours," p. 365.

87. The cruel mockery of an *amie* who calls him "laid & vieillard"—"Quoy, dit-elle rêveur, tu a plus de cent ans / Et tu veus contrefaire encore le jeune homme"—

is met with the rejoinder that an old man should always be allowed to have his pleasures, all the more since his death is near (*L* VI, pp. 198–99).

88. In 1587 the last of these verses reads "L'autre partie est assez verte." This stanza, Laumonier points out, is not found in the anacreontic ode otherwise imitated in this poem, where an old man dancing is said to be white of hair but young in spirit. He notes that Ronsard's response to the reproach of aging was anticipated by Rabelais and by Hugues Salel in his *Chant amoureux d'un vieillard* of 1540 (*L* VI, p. 255, n. 3).

89. "... ta fin d'automne est supérieure encore au printemps d'une autre et ton hiver plus chaud que son été;" V, 258, cited by Weber, p. 754.

90. Lindner, "Petrarkismus, Komödie, Stilistik," pp. 397–402; here p. 399. He cites Montaigne's *Essais* III, 5: "[L]'amour ne me semble proprement et naturellement en sa saison qu'en l'aage voisin de l'enfance. . . . En la virilité, je le trouve desjà hors de son siege. Non qu'en la vieillesse." See also Madeleine Lazard, *La comédie humaniste au XVIe siècle et ses personnages* (Paris: Presses Universitaires de France, 1978), pp. 175–208: "Le vieillard amoureux."

91. Alfred Glauser, *Le poème-symbole de Scève à Valéry* (Paris: Nizet, 1967), p. 43.

92. Ibid., p. 43.

93. See Wido Hempel, "Liebe im Alter als literarisches Thema von Petrarca bis Michelangelo," in *Gestaltung-Umgestaltung: Beiträge zur Geschichte der romanischen Literaturen*, ed. Bernard König and Jutta Lietz (Tübingen: Gunter Narr Verlag, 1990), pp. 81–86.

94. For the moral and spiritual implications in the *Rime* see Sturm-Maddox, *Petrarch's Metamorphoses*, pp. 133–34.

95. For a survey of the philosophical vein in the love lyric see Isabelle Pantin, "Les *Amours* et leurs 'Noeuds de philosophie': Un aspect de l'attitude de Ronsard envers la tradition pétrarquiste," *Op. cit.* 9 (1997): pp. 49–56.

96. See the discussion of Hempel, "Liebe im Alter," p. 85.

97. See ibid., p. 84.

98. *Les Amours diverses*, 27, added to the *Sonets pour Helene* in 1584; Weber cites the verses from *Rime* 1 with regard to this opening. On this shame at having violated the order of nature see Bellenger, "Un personnage poétique nouveau," p. 23.

99. Castor, "Theme of Illusion," pp. 362, 361.

100. Kennedy, "Ronsard's Petrarchan Textuality," p. 87.

101. Castor, "Petrarchism and the Quest for Beauty," p. 112.

102. See Bellenger, "Un personnage poétique nouveau," p. 23.

103. See Henri Weber, "Autour du dernier sonnet de Ronsard: de la vieillesse à la mort, du cygne au signe," in *French Renaissance Studies in Honor of Isidore Silver*, ed. Frieda S. Brown (*Kentucky Romance Quarterly* 21, supplement 2 1974): p. 113.

104. See Odette de Mourgues, "Ronsard's Later Poetry," in *Ronsard the Poet*, ed. Terence Cave (London: Methuen, 1973), pp. 317–18.

105. Alan F. Nagel, "Literary and Historical Context in Ronsard's *Sonnets pour Hélène*," *PMLA* 94 (1979): 409; see also pp. 414–15.

106. See Desonay, III: p. 249; the aging Ronsard, "celui qui porte en lui l'échec et le dégôut de la *Franciade*, s'est proposé, dès l'instant qu'il a choisi de chanter Hélène, un dessein littéraire fort net."

107. See the conclusion of Gendre's examination of Ronsard's references to the possibility of transcending death in *Ronsard poète de la conquête amoureuse*, p. 457. Jean Fallon has recently argued that Ronsard's narrator-lover in the *Sonets* is sacrificed to the success of the poet-persona so that the triumph of poetry emerges even as the love story comes to a negative end. See *Voice and Vision*, esp. pp. 63–71.

Chapter 4. "Sur la mort de Marie"

1. Marc Bensimon, ed., *Les Amours (1552–1584)* (Paris: Garnier-Flammarion, 1981), p. 37. The death of Charles IX was followed in the same year (1574) by that of Marguerite de France; on this "année décidément funeste," see Michel Dassonville, *Ronsard: Etude historique et littéraire*, V: "*Un brasier sous la cendre (1565–1575)*" (Geneva: Droz, 1990), pp. 138–40.

2. See Roger Sorg, *Cassandre ou le secret de Ronsard* (Paris: Payot, 1925), Annexe XXI.

3. Fernand Desonay, *Ronsard poète de l'amour*. III: *Du poète de cour au chantre d'Hélène* (Brussels: Duculot, 1959), p. 164; on the contributions of other poets, see pp. 164–66.

4. See Bensimon, ed., *Les Amours*, p. 33.

5. See Alexandre Micha, ed., *Le Second Livre des Amours* (Geneva: Droz, 1951), p. xvii.

6. Robert Garapon, *Ronsard chantre de Marie et d'Hélène* (Paris: SEDES, 1981), p. 49; Micha, ed., *Second Livre des Amours*, p. xxvi.

7. Bensimon, ed., *Les Amours*, cites for "Un grand amour franchit jusqu'au fatal rivage" Propertius, Elegie XIX, "Ad Cynthiam."

8. Editors have identified in these verses echoes of at least three poems of the *Rime*: "Sua ventura ha ciascun dal dì che nasce" [Thus in the world each has his destiny from the day he is born] (*R* 303, 14); "Ma tu, ben nata, che dal ciel mi chiami" [But you, born in a happy hour, who call me from Heaven] (*R* 280, 12); "piè miei, vostra ragion là non si stende/ ov'è colei ch'esercitar vi sole" [my feet, your province does not extend to where she is who used to make you work] (*R* 275, 7–8). Its close model is instead *R* 358, 14, "E mia giornata ho co' suoi piè fornita" [I have completed my day with her steps], used again for the closing verse of *MM* 3: "Et me fit de ses pieds accomplir ma journée" [she made me conclude my day with her steps], a verse eventually to be revised in the 1584 collection to read, in place of "de ses pieds," "de son soir"; see Desonay, *Ronsard poète de l'amour*, III: *Du poète de cour au chantre d'Hélène*, pp. 171, 174–75, and notes.

9. Desonay, who finds the Petrarchan presence "invasive" in this collection, notes that these two alone "appear exempt" (ibid., p. 173).

10. The motif, while not prominent in the recognized Petrarchan imitation of the *Amours* of 1552, had been used by Ronsard to celebrate Marie *in vita*: "Lors que

fol je te vy, et depuis je n'ay peu / Rien voir apres tes yeux que tout ne m'ait despleu" [When, mad, I saw you, and since then I have been unable to see nothing, after your eyes, that has not displeased me] ("Le Voyage de Tours," 67–68).

11. Micha, ed., p. xxxvi.

12. Desonay, *Ronsard poète de l'amour*, III: *Du poète de cour au chantre d'Hélène*, p. 173.

13. Donald Stone, *Ronsard's Sonnet Cycles: A Study in Tone and Vision* (New Haven: Yale University Press, 1966), p. 155.

14. Here, Louis Terreaux observes, Ronsard did not even attempt to create the illusion of a lived experience; see "Sur l'organisation du *Second Livre des Amours*," in *Ronsard in Cambridge*, ed. Philip Ford et al. (Cambridge, England: Cambridge French Colloquia, 1986), p. 93.

15. For discussion of the 1578 alterations see Michel Dassonville, "Pour une interprétation nouvelle des *Amours* de Ronsard," *BHR* 28 (1966): pp. 259–65.

16. See Michel Dassonville, *Ronsard: Etude historique et littéraire*, III: *Prince des poètes ou poète des princes (1550–1556)* (Geneva: Droz, 1976), p. 169.

17. See Donald Stone, "French Petrarchism: Commitment or Compromise?" *Studi di letteratura francese* 4 (1975): pp. 127–28.

18. The presence of Petrarchan echoes, although not some of the most convincing of those identified in the pages that follow, is well documented in the Weber edition's notes to this collection.

19. Desonay, *Ronsard poète de l'amour*, III: *Du poète de cour au chantre d'Hélène*, p. 175.

20. For the specular relation between the two parts of Petrarch's collection see Sara Sturm-Maddox, *Petrarch's Laurels* (University Park: Pennsylvania State University Press, 1992), esp. ch. 6, "Cosmologies."

21. Micha, ed., *Le Second Livre des Amours*, p. 140. In the 1578–87 editions the "beau chemin" becomes "un droit chemin," a straight path, heightening the Petrarchan resonance of the lady as source of a joy "Ch'al ciel ti scorge per destro sentero" [that leads you to Heaven along a straight path] (*R* 13, 13, noted by Weber).

22. See *Amours* (1552), 2; in "Sur la mort de Marie" see "Stances," 64–66; "Elegie," 70.

23. "Tu vois l'estat auquel je suis, / Du ciel assise entre les anges" [You see my state, seated in heaven among the angels] ("Stances," 112–14); "nostro stato dal ciel vede, ode e sente [she sees, hears, and feels our state from Heaven] (*R* 295, 7; cp. 324, 345).

24. See Sturm-Maddox, *Petrarch's Laurels*, esp. pp. 197–98.

25. Françoise Joukovsky, "Ronsard et le mythe de la jeune morte," in *Ronsard en son IVe centenaire*. II: *L'art de la poésie* (Geneva: Droz, 1989), p. 188. In this otherwise perceptive study which discusses a number of the passages evoked here, only a single reference to Petrarch's poems appears, to the dream-vision of Laura "là-haut, parmi ceux que le troisième cercle enferme" (p. 184).

26. Ronsard had already, in the *Nouvelle Continuation*, closely imitated

Petrarch's development of the motif in relation to the theme of amorous solitude; see in particular sonnet 18, a dense set of allusions to several Petrarchan poems.

27. *Continuation des Amours (1555)*, 7. On the suggestiveness of Marie's name see François Rigolot, *Poétique et onomastique: L'exemple de la Renaissance* (Geneva: Droz, 1977), pp. 210–14; Philippe Walter, "Marie et les reflets du nom," *BHR* 46 (1984): pp. 37–47.

28. *Ronsard: Oeuvres complètes*, I, ed. Jean Céard, Daniel Ménager and Michel Simonin (Paris: Gallimard, 1993), p. 1329. This is the 1584–87 version, published earlier as ". . . Que d'un si petit champ tel poëte soit né" [that from so small a place such a poet was born]; the editors point out, as does Weber, the probable source in Ovid writing of Sulmona, whose echoes are present in other verses of the poem addressed to "mon livre."

29. Sorg, *Cassandre ou le Secret de Ronsard*, p. 249.

30. In the Weber edition these verses are related instead to another Petrarchan text, where Laura declares herself "in tutte l'altre cose assai beata, / in una sola a me stessa dispiacqui, / che'n troppo umil terren mi trovai nata" [in all other things well blessed, I was displeased with myself only in one, that I was born in too humble a place] (*Trionfo della Morte*, II: 163–65). Ronsard's verses are more conventional than the passage in the *Rime*, which is daring in its suggestion of an analogy between Laura and Christ; see Sturm-Maddox, *Petrarch's Laurels*, pp. 240–42.

31. Micha, ed., *Second Livre des Amours*, p. xvii.

32. On Scève's use of the epitaph see Gisèle Mathieu-Castellani, "Emblèmes de la mort," *Europa* nos. 691–92 (1986): p. 131. For Ronsard see the chapter "Relecture & réécriture" in Nathalie Dauvois, *Mnémosyne: Ronsard, une poétique de la mémoire* (Paris: Champion, 1992), pp. 39–78. As Louis Terreaux notes, "Epitaphes" constituted a sub-category of the *Poémes* until 1584, when they became autonomous; see "Ronsard et l'organisation de son oeuvre," in *Mélanges de philologie romane offerts à Charles Camproux* (Montpellier: C.E.O., 1978), II: p. 760.

33. See R. E. Hallowell, *Ronsard and the Conventional Roman Elegy* (Urbana: University of Illinois Press, 1954), who cites the examples of Propertius and Lygdamus (pp. 57–58).

34. For the function of such inscriptions see Olivia Rosenthal, "Les fictives épitaphes ou l'art de l'inscription dans les sonnets de vers amoureux du XVIe siècle," *Nouvelle Revue du Seizième Siècle* 12 (1994), 151–64, esp. pp. 152–53.

35. For the figure of the "Passant" prominent in these poems and in other epitaphs by Ronsard see Dauvois, *Mnémosyne*, pp. 50–55.

36. Thus his lament, with its combination of Christian and pagan colorations, is moving for reasons quite unlike that of Petrarch (ed., pp. xxxvii–viii).

37. Weber, citing the final verse of this passage, notes that the image of the labyrinth is frequent in Petrarch.

38. On Marie as the "incarnation authentique de l'amour de mai" and her association with the rose see Walter, "Marie et les reflets du nom," pp. 39–44; see also Gillian Jondorf, "Marie and the Rose," in *Ronsard in Cambridge: Proceedings of the Cambridge Ronsard Colloquium*, ed. Philip Ford et al. (Cambridge, England: Cambridge

French Colloquia, 1986), pp. 136–38. Among the poems of this sequence, "rose" occurs elsewhere only to describe Marie's "mains de roses" ("Chanson," 87); the "Elegie" avoids precision, recording that she died "aux mois de son printemps" (59).

39. On this mutual participation of life and death see Joukovsky, "Ronsard et le mythe de la jeune morte," pp. 186, 190.

40. "Sur le Livre des amours de Pierre de Ronsard" in *Les Trophées*, cited by Robert T. Denommé, *The French Parnassian Poets* (Carbondale: Southern Illinois University Press, 1972), p. 121.

41. On these returns see for example Kenelm Foster, *Petrarch, Poet and Humanist* (Edinburgh: Edinburgh University Press, 1984), pp. 44–45.

42. *Les Amours* (1552–53), 58, 12–14. This conception of an after-life as the continuation of pleasure is discussed in André Gendre, *Ronsard poète de la conquête amoureuse* (Neuchatel: La Baconnière, 1970), pp. 460–66.

43. See Hélène Moreau, "La morte et le passant. A propos d'Artuse de Vernon, recherche sur la poétique de l'épitaphe," in *Ronsard en son IVe Centenaire*, II: *L'Art de la poésie* (Geneva: Droz, 1989), p. 195.

44. Petrarch's own poems in this vein tend to desacralize Dante's lexicon; see Sara Sturm-Maddox, *Petrarch's Metamorphoses: Text and Subtext in the Rime sparse* (Columbia: University of Missouri Press, 1985), ch. 3.

45. For discussion of Ronsard's attitude toward death in these poems see Marc Bensimon, "Ronsard et la mort," *MLR* 57 (1962): esp. pp. 184–86.

46. *L* V, p. 249.

47. *L* VIII, pp. 235–36. On this poem see Moreau, "La Morte et le Passant," pp. 193, 196–99.

48. *L* XII, p. 269, v. 325, cited by Gendre, *Ronsard poète de la conquête amoureuse*, pp. 441–42.

49. On the absence of a transformation from earthly love to spiritual quest see for example Bensimon, ed., *Les Amours*, pp. 20–21.

50. *Elegie* 24 of the *Oeuvres* of 1584 (*L* XVIII, p. 146, v. 61), cited in Gendre, pp. 443–44.

Afterword. Rewriting and Reconstruction

1. *L* XV, pp. 206–11. The poem is addressed to the "capitaine Le Gast de Daufiné."

2. See Fernand Desonay, *Ronsard poète de l'amour*, III: *Du poète de cour au chantre d'Hélène* (Brussels: Duculot, 1959), p. 123 and n. 58. It indeed seems, he adds, that in this *Elegie* Ronsard is recounting a personal adventure.

3. "Certes le ciel te debvoit à la France, / Quand le Thuscan, & Sorgue, & sa Florence / Et son Laurier engrava dans les cieux" (*A* 170, 9–11).

4. Terence Cave, *The Cornucopian Text: Problems of Writing in the French Renaissance* (Oxford: Clarendon, 1979), pp. 225–26.

5. Ronsard's preoccupation with the organization and preservation of his poetic legacy is emphasized in Du Perron's *Oraison funebre* for the poet. See *Oeuvres*

complètes, ed. Jean Céard, Daniel Ménager and Michel Simonin (Paris: Gallimard [Bibliothèque de la Pléiade], 1993, pp. ix–x: "ce que Du Perron confirme . . . c'est le prix qu'attachait le poète à l'édition de ses 'escripts,' au point d'avoir forgé, avec le temps, mais avec plus de prudence que l'on ne l'a cru, une authentique et inouïe *poétique de l'édition.*"

6. Michel Dassonville, "Pour une interprétation nouvelle des *Amours* de Ronsard," *BHR* 28 (1966): p. 242. Fernand Desonay provides a detailed stylistic analysis of Ronsard's *rifacimenti* in *Ronsard poète de l'amour. Livre premier. Cassandre* (Brussels: Palais des Académies, 1952), ch. 5: "Le Premier Livre des *Amours.*"

7. See Isidore Silver, ed., *Les Oeuvres de Pierre de Ronsard: Texte de 1587,* Vol. 5 (Chicago: University of Chicago Press; Paris: Didier, 1968), pp. 11–12, and his introduction to *L* volume XVIII.

8. See *Ronsard: Etude historique et littéraire,* III: *Prince des poètes ou poète des princes (1550–1556)* (Geneva: Droz, 1976), p. 68.

9. Desonay calls attention to the number of poems intensifying the presence of "le leit-motiv pétrarquien de l'amour souffrance mortelle et doux plaisir, de l'amour qui nous prostre et, du même coup, nous allège" (*Ronsard poète de l'amour, Livre premier. Cassandre,* p. 163). For a detailed analysis of the 1553 collection see Dassonville, "Pour une interprétation nouvelle," pp. 243–51.

10. During this relatively brief span of years Ronsard had also published *Le Bocage* and two volumes of *Meslanges,* many of whose poems, along with two odes from the series that he continued to augment, were added to either the *Premier Livre* or the *Second Livre* of the *Amours* in 1560.

11. "Le Septiesme Livre des Poèmes de Pierre de Ronsard Gentil-Homme Vandosmois," I. The poem, Ann Moss observes, extends Cassandre's "story in time . . . , through recapitulation and repetition of the past to an ending in stasis, a metamorphosis into an icon that is the poem itself in which time past is preserved for ever"; see "New Myths for Old?" in *Ronsard in Cambridge,* ed. Philip Ford et al. (Cambridge, England: Cambridge French Colloquia, 1986), p. 65.

12. See Gisèle Mathieu-Castellani, *Les thèmes amoureux dans la poésie française (1570–1600)* (Paris: Klincksieck, 1975), pp. 55–56, where this difference is attributed to both changing conceptions of *amour* and an evolution in *moeurs.*

13. On Ronsard's "Distanznahme" in this poem see Klaus W. Hempfer, "Die Pluralisierung des erotischen Diskurses in der europäischen Lyrik des 16. und 17. Jahrhunderts (Ariost, Ronsard, Shakespeare, Opitz)," *Germanish-Romanische Monatsschrift* N.S. 38 (1988): p. 257.

14. Desonay, *Ronsard poète de l'amour, Livre premier. Cassandre,* p. 216. Desonay admits that this conclusion is "pétrarquienne, peut-être," but reluctantly: "Je ne rejette pas l'influence de Pétrarque. A condition qu'il s'agisse du sentiment plutôt que des mots, du coeur ému plutôt que des formules de style."

15. Weber, ed., p. 671.

16. On Ronsard's palinode resulting from the *Vergeblichkeit der Liebe* see Hempfer, "Die Pluralisierung des erotischen Diskurses," pp. 257–58.

17. Louis Terreaux, "Ronsard et l'organisation de ses oeuvres, ou la destinée

d'un livre de poèmes," in *Mélanges de philologie romane offerts à Charles Camproux* (Montpellier: C.E.O., 1978), II: pp. 753–66; here p. 757.

18. The progression of the variants of this verse is suggestive, as Desonay notes: from "Me vienne voir: il verra ma douleur" in the early version, to "Me vienne lire: il lira ma douleur," in 1578, and finally to "Me vienne lire, il voirra la douleur"; see *Ronsard poète de l'amour*, V: pp. 238–39.

19. François Rigolot, *Le Texte de la Renaissance: Des Rhétoriqueurs à Montaigne* (Geneva: Droz, 1982), p. 191, n. 10.

20. Ann Moss observes that it is only in the 1578 version, with the alteration of "me vienne voir" and the swan-image, that "the writing and readable subject executes its own death and resurrection in a song sung of itself unto itself." See "'Me vienne lire': Reading Ronsard," in *(Re)-Interprétations: Etudes sur le seizième siècle*, ed. John O'Brien and Terence Cave (Ann Arbor: Department of Romance Languages, University of Michigan, 1995), p. 114.

21. Silver, ed., *Les Oeuvres de Pierre de Ronsard, Texte de 1587*, p. 71.

22. Desonay, *Ronsard poète de l'amour, Livre premier. Cassandre*, pp. 249, 238–39.

23. Grahame Castor, "The Theme of Illusion in Ronsard's *Sonets pour Helene* and in the Variants of the 1552 *Amours*," *FMLS* 7 (1971): pp. 372–73. "The poet's anguish is conveyed now not only by the actual meaning of the words, but also by the awkward, yet strangely moving *enjambment* from line 13 to 14, and the resultant ending, out-of-step almost, on the ironical 'un enfant pour son maistre.'"

24. Ibid., esp. pp. 370–73.

25. Brian J. Mallett, "Some Uses of *Sententiae* in Ronsard's Love-Sonnets," *French Studies* 27 (1973): pp. 135–37.

26. See Nathalie Dauvois, *Mnémosyne: Ronsard, une poétique de la mémoire* (Paris: Champion, 1992), pp. 60–63, 68.

27. Micha, ed., notes that this passage develops vv. 32–35 of Idyll X of Theocritus (p. 141) and finds classical sources for the later passage *in morte* as well; for the temple consecrated to Marie's memory he notes the temple consecrated to Caesar at the beginning of Virgil's *Georgics* III (p. 170).

28. See Micha, ed., p. xvii: "Les vers où le poète se console en évoquant le beau passé disparu, sorte d'émouvant poème du *Souvenir*, rendent un tout autre son que ceux où il rappelle avec complaisance sa gloire littéraire et où, à coups de souvenirs classiques, il élève un temple et consacre des jeux à la mémoire de la jeune morte."

29. For example: "Occhi miei, oscurato è 'l nostro sole, / anzi è salito al Cielo et ivi splende" [My eyes, darkened is our sun, rather it has risen to Heaven and there shines] (*R* 275, 1–2); "et non mi posson ritener l'inganni / del mondo, chi i' 'l conosco" [and the deceits of the world cannot hold me back, for I know them] (*R* 357, 5–6).

Index

Sara Sturm-Maddox is professor of French and Italian at the University of Massachusetts, Amherst. Her previous books include *Petrach's Metamorphoses: Text and Subtext in the "Rime sparse"* (1985), *Petrarch's Laurels* (1992), and, with her husband, Donald Maddox, the edited volume *Froissart Across the Genres* (University Press of Florida, 1998).